# Jewish Messiahs in a Christian Empire

# Jewish Messiahs in a Christian Empire

## A History of the Book of Zerubbabel

*Martha Himmelfarb*

||| Harvard University Press

*Cambridge, Massachusetts & London, England* | *2017*

Second printing

*Library of Congress Cataloging-in-Publication Data*
Names: Himmelfarb, Martha, 1952– author.
Title: Jewish messiahs in a Christian empire : a history of the Book of Zerubbabel /
  Martha Himmelfarb.
Description: Cambridge, Massachusetts : Harvard University Press, 2017. | Includes
  bibliographical references and index.
Identifiers: LCCN 2016043277 | ISBN 9780674057623
Subjects: LCSH: Messiah—Judaism. | Sefer Zerubbabel. | Apocalyptic
  literature—History and criticism. | Eschatology, Jewish. | Christianity—Influence. |
  Apocryphal books (Old Testament)—Criticism and interpretation. | Judaism—
  Byzantine Empire—History—Medieval and early modern period, 425–1789—Sources.
Classification: LCC BM615 .H56 2017 | DDC 296.3/36—dc23
LC record available at https://lccn.loc.gov/2016043277

*For Asher and Shira, Margaret and Ben-Aviv,*
*Ruth and Phil, Abigail and Sam*

# CONTENTS

Jewish Messiahs in a Christian Empire

# Introduction

THE BOOK OF ZERUBBABEL, which I shall henceforth refer to by the Hebrew equivalent, *Sefer Zerubbabel*, is a short Hebrew work reporting an angelic revelation about the events that will inaugurate the messianic era, restore the people of Israel to its land, and bring the Third Temple down from heaven. It was composed during a period of struggle between the Persian and Byzantine empires in the early seventh century of the Christian era, which it understands as signaling the imminent arrival of the eschaton, the end of the world as we know it, and the beginning of the age of redemption. It takes its name from its first-person narrator, the recipient of the revelation; the name is intended to identify him as the Jewish governor of Judea appointed by the Persians in the late sixth century BCE. The first Persian Empire brought an end to the Babylonian Empire that had destroyed the First Temple in 586 BCE. The Persians then permitted the exiled Judeans and their descendants to return to their homeland and build a new temple, which was completed in 515 BCE, during Zerubbabel's term in office. It is presumably his association with this great moment of restoration that made Zerubbabel seem an appropriate recipient of revelation in a work concerning the final restoration of the temple and the Jewish people; the attribution has the additional advantage of conferring the authority of antiquity on prophecy.

To the best of my knowledge, this is the first book-length treatment of *Sefer Zerubbabel*. It is certainly deserving of one. The messianic drama worked out in its pages serves to illumine earlier rabbinic messianic traditions by suggesting the existence of common sources, and it gives us insight into the ongoing impact of Christianity on Jews, showing us both the appeal of the Christian messianic narrative and the anxieties it produced. What is more, it had a major influence on later Jewish messianism into the early modern period. Indeed, as we shall see, it was invoked in the seventeenth century in the course of the debate about the messianic claims of Shabbetai Zvi, the most important Jewish messianic claimant after Jesus.

*Sefer Zerubbabel* opens with its hero in prayer, brooding over the lost temple.[1] In the narrative setting of *Sefer Zerubbabel*, the temple in question is the First Temple, but seventh-century CE readers of the work could presumably share Zerubbabel's distress since the Second Temple, built under Zerubbabel, had been destroyed by the Romans in 70 CE and never rebuilt. Zerubbabel's prayer leads to a conversation with God, and soon God carries Zerubbabel to Rome, which a seventh-century reader in the Byzantine Empire would have understood to mean the new Rome, that is, Constantinople. There Zerubbabel encounters Menahem b. (son of) Ammiel, the messiah descended from David, the great king of Israel and traditional ancestor of the messiah according to most post-biblical Jewish sources. The messiah is imprisoned, suffering and despised, and because of his humble appearance, Zerubbabel at first does not recognize him for who he is. The messiah, briefly enraged at Zerubbabel's failure, then transforms himself into a handsome young man. Now apparently persuaded of the messiah's identity, Zerubbabel asks when he will come to bring salvation. But before the messiah responds, an angel, sometimes referred to as Michael and sometimes as Metatron, arrives to answer Zerubbabel's questions. He tells Zerubbabel that the eschatological drama will begin with the appearance of Hephzibah, the mother of Menahem, who, armed with a miraculous staff, will defeat two kings who threaten

Israel. Her triumphs will be followed by the appearance of Nehemiah b. Hushiel, the messiah descended from Joseph, who will gather the people to Jerusalem, where they will live for forty years, restore sacrifice, and register Israel by families. Shiroi, king of Persia, will attack, but Hephzibah will defeat him with the help of her staff.

Then the angel takes Zerubbabel to a "house of disgrace and scorn," that is, a church, where he sees a beautiful stone statue of a virgin. The angel explains that after lying with Satan, the statue will give birth to Armilos, the eschatological opponent of the Jews, who will kill Nehemiah b. Hushiel. Only then will Menahem b. Ammiel arrive, accompanied by Elijah the prophet. At first the elders and sages will fail to recognize Menahem as the messiah because of his humble appearance, again enraging him. But when he and Elijah bring Nehemiah back to life, all Israel will believe that he is the messiah. Then Menahem, Nehemiah, and Elijah will preside over the resurrection of all the dead of Israel, Menahem will kill Armilos, and God himself will descend to fight the eschatological enemies, Gog and Magog and the forces of Armilos, while Nehemiah, Elijah, and Zerubbabel defeat the remnants of the enemy. The Jews will again offer sacrifices, and in response to their sweet smell, an enormous temple made in heaven will descend to earth.

But *Sefer Zerubbabel* does not end with this suitably climactic event. It goes on to offer a brief recapitulation of the deeds of Nehemiah, Hephzibah, and Menahem, arranged according to weeks of years (seven-year units) and single years, with a list of ten kings who will rule the nations during the last seven years. Shiroi, king of Persia, is the ninth king. The tenth is Armilos. The text notes his establishment of various idolatrous cults, including the worship of the statue that is his mother. There follows a list of Armilos's bizarre physical features, which belongs to a genre of descriptions of the antichrist found in both Jewish and Christian texts. Again Menahem slays Armilos, and the second account comes to an end, and with it, *Sefer Zerubbabel*.

By the time *Sefer Zerubbabel* was composed, there was a significant body of writing by Jews about the messiah and the eschatological drama.[2] In general, the biblical prophets imagined God himself managing the events of the end without a human assistant, but several prophetic passages, most notably Isaiah 11, looked forward to an ideal Davidic king who would rule justly in the end of days; it is not clear whether Isaiah 11 dates to before or after the Babylonian conquest and the end of the Davidic dynasty in 586 BCE. Later in the Second Temple period, close to the turn of the era, some Jewish texts imagine an eschatological high priest alongside a royal messiah, while others envision a messiah more divine than human, though of course the Davidic king of Isaiah 11 is more than merely human in his ability to slay the wicked with the breath of his mouth. It is in the context of such expectations that the early Christian movement emerges. Other texts, we should note, continue to make God the true hero of the eschatological drama, either without a messianic assistant at all or with one who plays only a very limited role.

In 66 CE, not long after the career of Jesus, the Jews of Palestine rebelled against their Roman rulers. In 70 CE, the Romans took back Jerusalem and burned the temple. This time, it would not be restored. Some Jews responded to the destruction of the Second Temple with intense eschatological hope, as the apocalypses 2 Baruch and 4 Ezra demonstrate. But the literature of the tannaim, the rabbis of 70–220 CE, shows rather little interest in eschatology and messianism, perhaps because the catastrophic failure of a second revolt, the Bar Kokhba revolt of 132–135 CE, persuaded them of the danger of such expectations. There is significantly more messianic material in later rabbinic texts, most prominently the Bavli (Babylonian Talmud), likely completed in the sixth or seventh century in Persia, and also the Yerushalmi (Palestinian or Jerusalem Talmud) and Pesiqta of Rav Kahana, both compiled in fifth-century Palestine.[3] These texts, and others contemporary with them, contain a range of messianic traditions including many about the Davidic messiah, the dominant messianic figure for the rabbis. In addition, both the fifth-century Palestinian midrash Genesis Rabbah and the Bavli refer to a warrior messiah descended from the patriarch Joseph, and the Bavli alludes to the death of this messiah. Apart from messianic traditions as such, rabbinic literature also contains eschatological timetables and applications of the four-kingdoms schema of the book of Daniel, which emphasize that the end has been predetermined; a messiah sometimes plays a role in these scenarios.[4] But no rabbinic work provides anything like a coherent narrative of the life of the messiah, nor does combining the traditions scattered through them add up to one.

Against the background of Jewish messianic expectations just sketched, a number of aspects of *Sefer Zerubbabel*'s eschatological drama stand out. First, as we have seen, *Sefer Zerubbabel* gives a significant role to the mother of the Davidic messiah; the only place in earlier Jewish literature a mother of the messiah appears is a single story preserved in several versions in rabbinic literature. *Sefer Zerubbabel*'s mother is not, however, very motherly; rather, she is a warrior. It is also noteworthy that the Davidic messiah of *Sefer Zerubbabel*, though ultimately triumphant, is described in language drawn from Isaiah 53's suffering servant. As for the messiah son of Joseph, *Sefer Zerubbabel* is the first text to offer an account of his life and death rather than simply to allude to them and the first to mention his resurrection at the hands of the Davidic messiah and Elijah. Finally, in addition to its heroes, *Sefer Zerubbabel* offers a villain who appears nowhere in classical rabbinic literature: Armilos, the great eschatological enemy, born of the union of Satan and a beautiful statue of a virgin.

The goal of this book is to understand *Sefer Zerubbabel* by placing it in its appropriate cultural contexts: contemporary Byzantine culture and Christian messianism on the one hand, and Jewish culture and particularly Jewish messianism on the other. In addition, I hope to show how study of *Sefer Zerubbabel* serves to illumine Jewish messianism of the era between the rise of Christianity and the rise of Islam, and more specifically, to suggest a new way of understanding the significance of the scattered and often enigmatic messianic traditions in rabbinic literature.

I begin with the Byzantine and Christian context. As I have already suggested, I read *Sefer Zerubabbel* as evidence for heightened Jewish eschatological expectations in the wake of the Persian conquest of Jerusalem in 614, which meant that for the first time in three centuries Jerusalem was not under Christian rule. In treating *Sefer Zerubbabel* as a product of the first part of the seventh century, I follow the scholarly consensus of the twentieth century, which sees the wars between the Byzantine and Persian empires as an appropriate background for the work; the absence of any reference to Arabs or Muslims indicates a date before the Muslim conquest, which put a definitive end to those wars.

Some years ago, David Biale offered *Sefer Zerubbabel* as an example of "counter-history," the polemical inversion of themes and motifs of another culture for use against that culture.[5] Thus, for example, *Sefer Zerubbabel*'s depiction of Armilos uses Christian traditions about the antichrist to imply that Christian Rome is itself the antichrist. In a recent book entitled *Judaism and Imperial Ideology in Late Antiquity*, Alexei M. Sivertsev objects that the label "counter-history" fails to give enough weight to the ways in which Byzantine Jewish texts including *Sefer Zerubbabel* embraced aspects of Byzantine culture even as they rejected many of its central assumptions: "Byzantine Jewish literature participated in the symbolic universe of Byzantine imperial culture by partly appropriating and partly subverting the mainstream meaning of the latter's cultural codes."[6]

Later, I discuss several aspects of Sivertsev's reading of *Sefer Zerubbabel*. I share Sivertsev's view that *Sefer Zerubbabel* needs to be understood in relation to the Christian empire in which it was composed.[7] Thus, for example, while the figure of the mother of the messiah is not entirely unprecedented in Jewish literature, there is no Jewish precedent for Hephzibah's role as a warrior in *Sefer Zerubbabel*. But in contemporary Byzantine culture the Virgin Mary appears in a similar role. I also share Sivertsev's view that *Sefer Zerubbabel*'s relationship to Byzantine culture runs deeper than Biale suggests when he characterizes *Sefer Zerubbabel* as "systematically invert[ing]" Christian themes and motifs.[8] But while I agree that at some points the imperial ideology on which Sivertsev focuses has a significant impact on *Sefer Zerubbabel*, as in the depiction of Hephzibah as warrior just noted, my argument focuses on a different aspect of Byzantine culture: Christianity itself. I argue, for example, that the story of the birth of Armilos from a beautiful statute of a virgin impregnated by Satan is intended as a parody of the story of the virgin birth rather than, as Sivertsev suggests, a play on Byzantine anxieties about pagan statues.

The other crucial context for understanding *Sefer Zerubbabel* is, of course, Jewish texts and traditions. Earlier I discussed briefly messianic expectations in biblical prophecy, texts of the Second Temple period, and the rabbinic literature from the centuries before *Sefer Zerubbabel,* noting that later rabbinic texts display more interest in the messiah than do earlier texts. The most developed account of the late emergence of rabbinic messianism that I know is that of Philip Alexander, who attempts to place rabbinic ideas in the context of popular messianic expectations.[9] To elicit these popular expectations, Alexander turns to works that stand outside the rabbinic corpus proper: the Amidah, the central prayer of the Jewish liturgy; the Aramaic translations of the Bible known as targumim; piyyutim, the Hebrew and Aramaic liturgical poems composed for synagogue use starting in perhaps the fifth century; the hekhalot literature, texts combining the adjuration of angels and ascent to the divine throne pseudepigraphically attributed to great rabbis of the second century; and late antique Hebrew apocalyptic works, especially *Sefer Zerubbabel.*[10] In Alexander's view, rabbinic literature up to the late fifth century demonstrates active avoidance of messianism, an avoidance he understands as a response to both the disastrous rebellions against Rome and the rise of Christianity.[11] The nonrabbinic genres, on the other hand, reflect the ongoing existence of a popular messianism with roots in the Second Temple period. Then, sometime around the late fifth century, the rabbis joined their fellow Jews in embracing ideas that they had until then held in suspicion.[12] Alexander is cautious about offering an explanation for this "complete U-turn," but he is inclined to see it as part of a larger apocalyptic revival in which Christians, Zoroastrians, and eventually Muslims participated as well.[13]

I believe that Alexander is correct about the importance of messianic traditions for many Jews during the first four or five centuries of this era even as these traditions are largely ignored by the rabbis, but the picture he sketches is not without problems. To begin with, the claim of a "complete U-turn" is an overstatement. Even if much of classical rabbinic literature is reticent about the messiah or not very interested in him, that does not mean that his eventual appearance was not taken for granted, as the occasional mentions in the texts suggest. Also, as Alexander himself would admit, of the texts he looks to for evidence for popular messianic traditions, only the Amidah can confidently be placed in the first few centuries of this era. It is not clear that any of the others predate the sixth or seventh century. The targumim of most interest for Alexander's purposes are the later ones, which, at least in their final form, postdate the rabbinic "U-turn"; the early targumim, as Alexander forthrightly acknowledges, are far less interested in messianism.[14] As for the piyyutim, Alexander notes that messianic themes appear in the work of three of the earliest poets known by name: Yose b. Yose, Yannai, and Qillir. But of the three only Yose b. Yose is likely to have lived before the sixth century.[15] Nor are any of the hekhalot texts plausibly dated before the sixth century.[16] Most scholars date the earliest of the Hebrew apocalyptic works, *Sefer Zerubbabel* and *Sefer Eliyyahu*, to the beginning of the seventh century, and even Hillel Newman's critique of the consensus, to be discussed in Chapter 1, places *Sefer Zerubbabel* no earlier than the sixth century. In other words, the nonrabbinic works may well preserve messianic traditions from the early centuries of this era, but the texts themselves took shape after messianism becomes more prominent in rabbinic literature, which complicates the process of extracting those putatively earlier traditions.

Furthermore, I shall argue here that an examination of the rabbinic parallels to elements of *Sefer Zerubbabel*'s messianic drama demonstrates that there is another place to look for popular messianic traditions: the rabbinic corpus itself. When I first began to study *Sefer Zerubbabel* almost thirty years ago, I understood its parallels to rabbinic literature as evidence for its knowledge of rabbinic tradition. But I have come to believe, as I argue later, that the parallels reflect not *Sefer Zerubbabel*'s dependence on the rabbis but rather the common debt of *Sefer Zerubbabel* and the rabbis to a larger body of messianic traditions.

As we shall see, the rabbis sometimes allude to a tradition about the messiah without offering much detail, as if they expect their audience to recognize it. Thus, for example, as will be discussed in Chapter 5, two passages in rabbinic literature mention the death of the messiah son of Joseph without explaining how it came about, and they also fail to explain his role in relation to the Davidic messiah. In other cases, the rabbinic use of a messianic tradition seems designed to undercut it. This, I shall argue, is the best explanation for the story of the birth of a messiah descended from David who disappears not long after his birth, to be discussed in Chapter 2. What is significant for our purposes is that in each case *Sefer Zerubbabel* embraces the tradition with great enthusiasm even as it adapts it for its own purposes, while the rabbinic texts reflect a more cautious and ambivalent attitude.

If I am correct, *Sefer Zerubbabel* provides a lens that allows us to see the evidence that rabbinic literature provides for the messianic hopes and eschatological expectations of Jews outside the circles of the rabbinic elite during the centuries in which the rabbis kept their distance from those hopes. Thus, one contribution of this book is to shed new light on the nature and development of rabbinic messianism by providing a glimpse of nonrabbinic Jewish attitudes on this fraught subject. The rabbis' discomfort with these more popular traditions, I suggest, derives at least in part from the way the traditions show the impact of Christianity. It is true that the rabbis sometimes respond to Christian claims by adapting Christian narratives and motifs in an attempt to trump those claims. In Genesis Rabbah, for example, Abraham is several times depicted in terms that recall Christian claims for Jesus. The suffering Abraham endures in obeying God's commands to undergo circumcision and to sacrifice his beloved son Isaac is said to guarantee the redemption of his descendants, and, even more remarkable, through a play on words, Abraham is made to participate in the creation of the world.[17] But I suspect that Genesis Rabbah is willing to depict Abraham in these terms precisely because he is not the messiah; that is, it defuses the anxiety produced by borrowing elements of the Christian depiction of Jesus by applying those elements not to the messiah but to a figure of the past. There could be no similar approach to defusing anxiety about the borrowings from Christians in the popular Jewish stories about the messiahs that I believe the rabbis knew. For that reason, the rabbis kept at arms' length traditions that *Sefer Zerubbabel* embraced even as it developed them for its own purposes.

The plan of the book is as follows: The first chapter treats questions related to *Sefer Zerubbabel* as a text and sketches the historical context in which it was composed. I begin by considering the witnesses to the text of *Sefer Zerubbabel*, of which the two most important are the fourteenth-century autograph manuscript of *Sefer Hazikhronot*, the Book of Remembrances, which is the basis for the summary of *Sefer Zerubbabel* above, and the first printed edition of 1519; there are important differences between the two witnesses, and most of the other manuscript evidence aligns with one or the other. Next I turn to formal features of *Sefer Zerubbabel*: genre and language. Although scholars often refer to *Sefer Zerubbabel* as an apocalypse, I argue that the author of *Sefer Zerubbabel* was unaware of such a genre and modeled his work on biblical prophecy, particularly the book of Ezekiel; the author's impressive effort to write a biblical Hebrew rather than the rabbinic Hebrew used by contemporary texts is perhaps related to the desire to imitate biblical prophecy. Finally, I discuss the date of *Sefer Zerubbabel* and its implications for understanding the work.

Chapters 2 through 5 treat the heroes of *Sefer Zerubbabel*'s eschatological scenario. Chapter 2 focuses on the figure of Hephzibah. It begins by attempting to make sense of her role as warrior by considering the role of the Virgin Mary in contemporary Byzantine culture. It then turns to the remarkable story that first appears in the Yerushalmi about the mother of a messiah named Menahem who disappears as an infant. I argue that this story, with its problematic mother, hints at the existence of a popular Jewish story in which the mother is more motherly and the baby's disappearance is only temporary, and I suggest that *Sefer Zerubbabel* knew the more positive version of the story. The chapter also discusses the names *Sefer Zerubbabel* gives to the messiah and his parents in relation to rabbinic traditions about the name of the messiah. Finally, it considers the significance of *Sefer Zerubbabel*'s depiction of the beautiful statue of a virgin and her son Armilos, whose father is Satan, and the cultural background against which they are best understood.

Chapters 3 and 4 discuss Menahem b. Ammiel, the Davidic messiah, with a focus on his depiction in terms drawn from the suffering servant of Isaiah 53. Chapter 3 treats the very limited evidence for messianic interpretation of the suffering servant in Jewish texts of the Second Temple period in relation to Christian identification of the suffering servant with Christ. It compares the depiction of Menahem in *Sefer Zerubbabel* to that of the suffering messiah encountered by R. Joshua b. Levi in a story in the Bavli. Although the story in the Bavli probably dates from the third century and thus might have been available to *Sefer Zerubbabel*, I argue that *Sefer Zerubbabel* draws not on the story itself but on traditions that the story also used.

Chapter 4 considers the appeal of the idea of a suffering messiah in two Jewish texts composed in the first part of the seventh century, roughly contemporary with *Sefer Zerubbabel*: the piyyut "'Az mi-lifnei vereishit," "Then, Before 'In the Beginning,'" and a set of interrelated homilies in Pesiqta Rabbati, a collection of rabbinic homilies for special Sabbaths and other occasions. Both works claim that the messiah's suffering gains redemption for Israel just as the servant's does in Isaiah 53 and, of course, Jesus's does as well. But if *Sefer Zerubbabel* lacks this more sophisticated theological position, it shares with Pesiqta Rabbati a critical attitude toward the rabbinic elite. Pesiqta Rabbati makes its attitude explicit while *Sefer Zerubbabel* only implies it in its picture of the failure of the sages to recognize the Davidic messiah when he first manifests himself. The chapter concludes with a consideration of the significance of Targum Jonathan's somewhat earlier interpretive translation of Isaiah 53, which turns the suffering servant into a triumphant messiah who does not suffer.

Chapter 5 treats *Sefer Zerubbabel*'s second messiah, the messiah descended from Joseph. Against the opinion of some scholars, I find no evidence for such a figure in the Second Temple period, and I reject the view that his death is a later development in the story of an originally triumphant warrior messiah son of Joseph. *Sefer Zerubbabel* is the first work to offer a coherent story of his career, but the traces of the story in rabbinic literature make it clear that it is not an invention of *Sefer Zerubbabel*. Furthermore, *Sefer*

*Zerubbabel* has clearly adapted the story it inherited, turning the messiah son of Joseph from the war messiah into a civic leader, likely as a result of its incorporation of the figure of Hephzibah.

Chapter 6 considers the afterlife of *Sefer Zerubbabel* and its significant impact on later Jewish messianism, which is perhaps somewhat surprising. After all, the decades of struggle between the Byzantine and Persian empires reflected in its eschatological scenario turned out to be of little lasting significance. From 638, only a few years after the Emperor Heraclius's triumphant return, Jerusalem was ruled neither by Christians nor Persians but by Arabs, a new power on the world scene. Yet despite its failure to anticipate the rise of Islam, many Jewish works written under Muslim rule are significantly indebted to *Sefer Zerubbabel*, and the manuscript evidence indicates that it was well known in western Europe as well. I consider how later readers understood its claims to authority, and I attempt to explain why some elements of its narrative proved more influential than others.

# CHAPTER ONE

# Text and Context

THIS CHAPTER is concerned with introductory matters that are nonetheless of great importance for understanding *Sefer Zerubbabel* or any other work: text, genre and language, and date. I begin by considering the challenges involved in studying a work to which the witnesses display so many differences, some of major importance. The witnesses consist of four manuscripts, a printed edition earlier than at least two of the manuscripts, a nineteenth-century edition based on two manuscripts of which the current location is unknown, four fragments from the Cairo Genizah, and a fragment copied as part of a larger manuscript. They fall into two distinct groups, with some significant variation within each group, and, as yet, no edition takes account of all of them. I focus on the form of *Sefer Zerubbabel* found in the manuscript of a medieval anthology, *Sefer Hazikhronot*, the Book of Remembrances. It is the longest text of *Sefer Zerubbabel* to have come down to us; it includes most of the elements known from the other witnesses.

Next I discuss the generic features of *Sefer Zerubbabel*. Scholars often label *Sefer Zerubbabel* an apocalypse because it claims to present a revelation about the end of history; revelations about the end of history are a characteristic subject of apocalypses from the Second Temple and early Christian eras, such as the books of Daniel and Revelation. But I see no evidence that the author of *Sefer Zerubbabel* was aware of the existence of the apocalypse as a genre. Rather, I believe that the most important model for *Sefer Zerubbabel* is the book of Ezekiel and that its author made some effort to represent *Sefer Zerubbabel* as a work of prophecy. This is the background against which I understand another noteworthy feature of *Sefer Zerubbabel*, the author's effort to compose his work in biblical Hebrew in an era in which other Jews wrote in rabbinic Hebrew.

Finally, I turn to the question of the date of *Sefer Zerubbabel*. For the last century, the scholarly consensus has understood the allusions to a war involving the king of Persia as placing *Sefer Zerubbabel*'s composition in the early decades of the seventh century, during the wars between Persia and the Byzantine empire but before the Muslim conquest, of which *Sefer Zerubbabel* is entirely unaware. But such a dating does not fit *Sefer Zerubbabel*'s explicit eschatological chronology. Hillel Newman has recently used that chronology to argue for a date in the early or middle sixth century. While Newman's discussion raises important questions, I shall argue in favor of the consensus dating on grounds not only of the role of the king of Persia but also of the particular aspects of Byzantine and Jewish culture that had an impact on *Sefer Zerubbabel*.

### The Witnesses to *Sefer Zerubbabel*

As I have just indicated, *Sefer Zerubbabel* comes down to us in several manuscripts, fragments, and an early first edition.[1] The eclectic text produced by Yehudah Even Shmuel was described by Salo Baron as "more readable than authentic," a judgment Hillel Newman has recently described as diplomatic;[2] it cannot be used for serious discussion of the work. There is to date no critical edition, and there are major difficulties, practical and theoretical, in the way of such an edition, as I shall discuss shortly.[3]

*Sefer Hazikhronot*, the anthology containing *Sefer Zerubbabel*, is the work of a certain Eleazar b. Asher Halevi, who lived in the fourteenth century, probably in the Rhineland. It is a compilation of Hebrew texts, both rabbinic and nonrabbinic, and a few Aramaic ones arranged to trace the course of history from the creation of the world to the end of days; not surprisingly, *Sefer Zerubbabel* appears in the section devoted to the eschaton. *Sefer Hazikhronot* survives in a single manuscript in Eleazar's own hand, now found in the Bodleian Library of Oxford University, MS Heb. d. 11.[4] It is the earliest witness to a complete text of *Sefer Zerubbabel*. The form of *Sefer Zerubbabel* it contains includes virtually all of the elements found in other forms of the work as well as material unique to it. For that reason—the inclusiveness of its text, not the early date of the manuscript—I have chosen to make it the basis of my discussion. I summarize it in the introduction and translate it in the Appendix, and any reference to *Sefer Zerubbabel* not otherwise qualified is to it.[5] But I am attentive throughout the book to the differences between this form of the work and a second form best represented by the first edition, and I consider other witnesses whenever their readings are of interest. For the text of *Sefer Zerubbabel*, I use the edition published by Israël Lévi in 1914, which follows the manuscript of *Sefer Hazikhronot* but provides an apparatus with readings from other witnesses as well.[6] I have also consulted silver prints of the relevant folios of the *Sefer Hazikhronot* manuscript, and at one important point I have corrected a mistake in Lévi's edition.[7]

Four other witnesses reflect a form of *Sefer Zerubbabel* close to that found in the *Sefer Hazikhronot* manuscript. Two of them are also manuscripts from the Bodleian Library. Oxford MS Opp. 236a, an Ashkenazic manuscript of the seventeenth century, was known to Lévi and appears in his apparatus; its text is very close to that of the *Sefer Hazikhronot* manuscript.[8] Lévi did not know of Oxford MS Opp. 603, an Ashkenazic manuscript dated 1568–71. It is considerably abbreviated compared to *Sefer Zerubbabel* from the *Sefer Hazikhronot* manuscript, lacking the passage about Armilos in the list of the ten kings and other elements. There are also occasional differences in wording between it and the *Sefer Hazikhronot* manuscript, which, however, have little significance for meaning.[9]

The third of these witnesses, which Lévi does cite in his apparatus, is the 1853 publication of *Sefer Zerubbabel* by Adolph Jellinek, based on two Leipzig manuscripts of which I do not know the current whereabouts.[10] It is shorter than *Sefer Zerubbabel* according to the *Sefer Hazikhronot* manuscript, lacking, among other things, the passage about Armilos in the list of ten kings. Finally, a fragment of *Sefer Zerubbabel* from the Cairo genizah, T-S A45.5, contains elements of the eschatological scenario that appear in this group of witnesses but not in the other group.[11]

The most important representative of the other form of *Sefer Zerubbabel* is the first printed edition, published in Constantinople in 1519.[12] It differs from the *Sefer Hazikhronot* manuscript and the witnesses associated with it in several ways. It is generally shorter, sometimes because it lacks doublets that appear in the *Sefer Hazikhronot* manuscript and at other times because it has lost material integral to the narrative, yet it contains some elements lacking in *Sefer Zerubbabel* according to *Sefer Hazikhronot*. The most important difference between the first edition and the witnesses associated with the *Sefer Hazikhronot* manuscript is their disagreement over who is responsible for the death of the messiah descended from Joseph. For the *Sefer Hazikhronot* manuscript group, it is Armilos;[13] this is the narrative I followed in the introduction. For the first edition, it is Shiroi king of Persia;[14] in its narrative, Armilos does not enter the fray until the climax of the eschatological drama, after Menahem has already manifested himself as messiah. And while both the *Sefer Hazikhronot* manuscript and the first edition make the king of Persia the ninth king in the list of ten kings, the first edition delegates to him some of the activities attributed to Armilos, the tenth king, in the *Sefer Hazikhronot* manuscript.[15]

Hillel Newman has recently identified another witness to the form of *Sefer Zerubbabel* found in the first edition: MS JTS 2325/20, a fifteenth-century Byzantine manuscript.[16] It too attributes the death of the messiah descended from Joseph to the king of Persia and thus lacks an account of Armilos's attack on Jerusalem (193). It does not, however, call the king of Persia Shiroi but rather *'rs*, perhaps to be vocalized *Aras*; in the list of ten kings at the end of the work, the king of Persia, unlike the other kings, is not given a name (194).

Overall, the text of this manuscript is significantly abbreviated even compared to the first edition, although occasionally it is more expansive or clearer than the first edition. At a number of points its wording differs from that of the first edition without much difference in meaning. Newman also notes that the passage from *Sefer Zerubbabel* in Oxford MS Heb. f. 27 (42r–v), a manuscript that contains a number of short passages from longer works, reflects a form of *Sefer Zerubbabel* close to that of the first edition, with the death of the messiah son of Joseph attributed to Shiroi (42r).[17] Finally, the remaining genizah fragments of *Sefer Zerubbabel*, T-S A45.7, T-S A45.19, and T-S A45.22, also appear to reflect the form of *Sefer Zerubbabel* found in the first edition.[18] Like the first edition, all three fragments attribute only a single list of achievements to the revealing angel, and it is the same list that appears in the first edition; I shall return to the implications of these lists shortly. It is interesting, but likely coincidental, that fragments including this passage survive from three different manuscripts. The manuscript to which T-S A45.7 belonged contained only a portion of *Sefer Zerubbabel*, which came to an end with the report of the stars swerving from their paths at Hephzibah's arrival; the passage is followed by a title that apparently indicates Saadya's *Book of Beliefs and Opinions*.[19] As just noted, MS Heb. f. 27 also contains an excerpt from *Sefer Zerubbabel* rather than the full text. In Chapter 6, I will have more to say about the quantity, dates, and geographical distribution of the witnesses to *Sefer Zerubbabel*.

## The Text of *Sefer Zerubbabel*

I hope that the summary of *Sefer Zerubbabel* in the introduction succeeds in conveying its content, but it certainly does not adequately convey its texture. A significant portion of *Sefer Zerubbabel* is assembled from self-contained units, such as the description of the antichrist and the list of ten kings, that likely existed prior to their inclusion there, and there has been little effort to smooth transitions and eliminate repetition. Readers of my summary of *Sefer Zerubbabel* would not know that in the *Sefer Hazikhronot* manuscript the revealing angel introduces himself to Zerubbabel not once but twice, each time with a different list of achievements.[20] Even more jarring, the angel is given two different names, Michael and Metatron; despite significant differences in their deployment, both names appear in all of the witnesses. The name Michael goes back to the Second Temple period as the name of the angelic prince of Israel in the book of Daniel (10:21, 12:1). The name Metatron emerges only in later rabbinic times and is prominent in the hekhalot literature as the name of the chief angel in the angelic hierarchy; Peter Schäfer has recently stressed that the name appears first in Babylonian sources and only later, after it is well established there, in sources from the Byzantine world.[21] It is not hard to understand the slippage between Michael and Metatron since both are names for the angel at the head of the angelic hierarchy, but it is nonetheless troubling to find the angel called by both names in a single text. At one point in the *Sefer Hazikhronot* manuscript, an editor or copyist attempted to solve the problem by identifying the angel as "Michael, who is Metatron."[22] At another point, the editorial effort, if that is what it is, simply does not make sense: "Michael answered Metatron."[23] Once, the variant traditions are allowed to stand side by side: "Zerubbabel answered Metatron and Michael."[24] The other witnesses associated with the *Sefer Hazikhronot* manuscript also contain two names for the angel and two introductory speeches; the names do not always appear in the introductory speeches, however, and their use does not always match that of the *Sefer Hazikhronot* manuscript.[25]

Perhaps even more disconcerting than the angel's two introductions and two names are the doublets of events in the eschatological scenario according to the *Sefer Hazikhronot* manuscript. The Mount of Olives splits twice in response to two different instances of God's descent upon it,[26] and after the descent of the temple from heaven and its establishment on five mountaintops, the apparent climax of the scenario, there follows a summary of the events described previously that contradicts the earlier narrative by placing Nehemiah's arrival before Hephzibah's.[27] Jellinek's edition offers a shorter and more straightforward conclusion that contains only a single instance of the splitting of the Mount of Olives and lacks the reordering of events, while Oxford MS Opp. 603 includes neither the splitting of the Mount of Olives nor the summary that reorders the events of the narrative.[28]

When we turn to the other group of witnesses, many of the doublets and inconsistencies of the *Sefer Hazikhronot* manuscript are gone. In these texts, as already indicated in relation to three of the genizah fragments, the revealing angel offers only one list of achievements, and the texts attempt to resolve the problem of the angel's two names when the angel introduces himself: "I am Metatron, the Prince of the Presence, and Michael is my name," "I am Metatron Michael Metatron, the Prince of the Lord's host," or "I am Metatron, Michael, the Prince of the Lord's host."[29] After the angel's introduction, neither the first edition nor MS JTS2325/20 uses the name Michael again; the fragmentary character of the genizah texts means that the absence of one of the names cannot be decisive.[30] The first edition and MS JTS 2325/20 also offer a smoother climax to the eschatological scenario, with only a single instance of the splitting of the Mount of Olives, although both texts include the reordering of events after the description of the enormous eschatological temple;[31] again, the fragmentary character of the genizah texts excludes them from consideration here.

It is possible that the shorter and sometimes smoother text of the first edition and associated witnesses reflects an earlier form of *Sefer Zerubbabel,* while the *Sefer Hazikhronot* manuscript, MS Opp. 236a, and, to a lesser extent, Jellinek's edition and MS Opp. 603 reflect a later form that has accumulated alternate versions of some passages. This is Newman's position, although his view is based largely on a different consideration, his understanding of the 990-year messianic chronology of the first edition; I shall return to his argument later in the chapter.[32] But while Newman is surely correct that the *Sefer Hazikhronot* manuscript reflects additions to *Sefer Zerubbabel* in the course of transmission, I am inclined to read the smoother text of the first edition not as evidence for a more pristine form of *Sefer Zerubbabel* but rather as an effort to correct and improve a form that already contained some of the problematic elements of the *Sefer Hazikhronot* manuscript. It is difficult, for example, to understand the ways the revealing angel introduces himself in the witnesses associated with the first edition as anything

other than attempts at harmonization provoked by a text that referred
to the angel by two different names. Indeed, it seems clear that both
groups of witnesses are struggling with this problem. In that case,
since the existence of the two separate lists of angelic achievements is
likely linked to the two different angelic names, the absence of a
second list in the first edition and the witnesses associated with it
could well reflect editorial activity aimed at producing a smoother
text rather than the absence of a second list in the source text.

It is also noteworthy that the narrative of the first edition is less
coherent at some points than that of the longer text of the *Sefer
Hazikhronot* manuscript. The place of Armilos in the narrative is
perhaps the most striking example. According to the *Sefer
Hazikhronot* manuscript, the Davidic messiah arrives after Armilos
has attacked Jerusalem and killed the messiah descended from
Joseph.[33] The first edition introduces Armilos at the same point in
the narrative as does the *Sefer Hazikhronot* manuscript through a
similar account of Zerubbabel's trip to the church where Armilos's
mother, the beautiful stone statue, is found.[34] Yet perhaps because
it ascribes the death of the messiah descended from Joseph to the
king of Persia, it does not include Armilos's attack on Jerusalem in
its narrative, and only at the conclusion of the work, in the list of ten
kings, does it provide a brief account of Armilos's activity without,
however, any mention of an attack on Jerusalem.[35] Nonetheless, it
places the arrival of the Davidic messiah "in the days of Armilos,"
a phrase that does not appear in the *Sefer Hazikhronot* manuscript
and is perhaps an attempt to make up for the absence of Armilos's
attack on Jerusalem, and at the end of the text, Menahem slays
Armilos.[36] In this case the missing material surely indicates not the
preservation of an earlier and more pristine form of *Sefer Zerubbabel,*
but rather a not entirely successful revision that gives the king of
Persia a more significant role in the eschatological drama without
fully resolving the implications for the role of Armilos.

There are points, to be sure, where comparison of the different
witnesses to *Sefer Zerubbabel* helps us to correct one witness on the
basis of others. But, as we can see from the use of preexisting traditions and even literary units, attested in all of the forms of the work
that have come down to us, *Sefer Zerubbabel* is not an authored

work in the usual sense. Furthermore, the manuscripts show that at least some of the copyists felt free to abbreviate and change the wording as they saw fit. In my view, the textual situation just sketched makes *Sefer Zerubbabel* a poor candidate for a critical edition, a scholarly genre developed by classicists as a means of recovering the original text of authored works. It is a much better fit for a synoptic edition of the kind pioneered by Peter Schäfer for the roughly contemporary hekhalot texts, the literature of early Jewish mysticism.[37] Even more than *Sefer Zerubbabel*, the hekhalot texts are composed of separable units, such as hymns, adjurations, spells, and ascent accounts, and the content of any given work can vary significantly from manuscript to manuscript. A synoptic edition lines up the manuscripts so that the parallel passages can be compared without attempting to determine the best or most original text. Although an authorial hand is more in evidence in *Sefer Zerubbabel* than in the hekhalot texts, I believe that *Sefer Zerubbabel* too would be better served by a synoptic edition, which would help to clarify the ways in which the text developed and changed over time.

### *Sefer Zerubbabel* and the Genre Apocalypse

For more than a century, scholars have referred to *Sefer Zerubbabel* as an apocalypse.[38] Its subject, the coming of the two messiahs and the inauguration of the new era, is certainly apocalyptic in the sense that it envisions a dramatic end to the world as we know it. Yet scholars of apocalyptic literature of the Second Temple period distinguish between the literary genre apocalypse, characterized by a constellation of formal features that typically include a revealing angel and either symbolic visions or revelatory journeys, on the one hand, and apocalyptic content, predictions or description of the eschatological drama that appear in texts in a variety of genres, on the other. *Sefer Zerubbabel*'s content is undeniably apocalyptic, and it also shares several formal features with the apocalypses of the Second Temple period: a hero drawn from the biblical past, a revealing angel, a journey with the angelic interlocutor, eschatological timetables, and phrases drawn from the books of the prophets.[39] But the only apocalypse we can be certain *Sefer Zerubbabel* knew is the book of Daniel. Daniel clearly had a major impact on *Sefer Zerubbabel*, and since it appears as part of the third section of the Hebrew canon, Writings, the author of *Sefer Zerubabbel* would not have understood it as prophecy. Yet Daniel never announces itself as an apocalypse, and there was nothing to make the author of *Sefer Zerubbabel* aware of the existence of such a genre. The other apocalypses of the Second Temple period and the decades immediately following were largely abandoned by Jews well before the seventh century, and there is no indication that *Sefer Zerubbabel* had any knowledge of them as transmitted by Christians. I have argued elsewhere that the visions at the end of *Sefer Eliyyahu*, the Book of Elijah, another Hebrew apocalyptic work composed during the early decades of the seventh century, respond to the book of Revelation, which calls itself an "apocalypse" (Rev 1:1), but there is nothing in *Sefer Zerubbabel* to suggest that it knew the New Testament work.[40] In Chapter 3, I discuss the importance for *Sefer Zerubbabel* of Menahem's participation in the resurrection of Nehemiah and suggest a parallel in a late seventh-century Christian apocalyptic work. But there is no indication that *Sefer Zerubbabel* knew apocalyptic works by Byzantine Christians, and even if it did, these texts typically lack many of the distinctive formal features of apocalypses from the turn of the era.

Altogether, then, the author of *Sefer Zerubbabel* could hardly have set out to write an apocalypse because he would have been unaware of the existence of such a literary genre. And while *Sefer Zerubbabel* is deeply indebted to the book of Daniel at several points, its most important model in my opinion is the book of Ezekiel. The debt to Ezekiel is evident from the very opening of *Sefer Zerubbabel*:

> The word that came to Zerubbabel ben Shealtiel, governor of Judah, on the twenty-fourth day of the seventh month. The Lord showed me this vision there. I was prostrate in prayer before the Lord my God during the apparition of the vision I saw on the Chebar [River].[41]

The term I have translated "vision," *mar'eh*, appears in the opening verse in Ezekiel, in the plural, "visions of God," and many times later in the book in the singular.[42] The term translated "apparition," *ḥazon*, also appears in Ezekiel, though less frequently,[43] and it is more closely associated with the book of Isaiah, which begins with it. But the location of the vision, the Chebar canal, was known to any reader of *Sefer Zerubbabel* as the location of the opening vision of the book of Ezekiel, the famous chariot vision.

As the narrative of *Sefer Zerubbabel* unfolds, "a spirit lift[s Zerubbabel] between heaven and earth"[44] to take him to Rome, a clear echo of the mode of transportation by which the prophet Ezekiel travels from Babylonia to Jerusalem (Ezek 8:3). Zerubbabel's walking tour of Rome recalls the tour of the eschatological temple and its surroundings at the end of the book of Ezekiel (40–48). The similarity is particularly significant since the eschatological temple is the very subject about which Zerubbabel is brooding when the revelation begins: "What will be the form of the eternal house?"[45] Nor does *Sefer Zerubbabel* lose sight of the question. One of the climactic elements of the eschatological scenario is the descent of a new temple from heaven.[46]

The elements of content and form of the book of Ezekiel on which *Sefer Zerubbabel* draws are, to be sure, elements that might be termed proto-apocalyptic. They clearly provide the models for Enoch's ascent to the heavenly temple (1 Enoch 14) and his tour to the ends of the earth (1 Enoch 17–36) in the Book of the Watchers (1 Enoch 1–36), the earliest ascent apocalypse.[47] But for the author of *Sefer Zerubbabel,* these elements belong to prophecy. Even the use of a pseudepigraphic recipient of revelation, a practice typical of apocalyptic literature of the Second Temple period, is best understood as part of *Sefer Zerubbabel*'s effort to present itself as prophecy—thus the choice of a figure from the Persian era, when prophecy was still possible.

## Rabbinic Style and the Language of *Sefer Zerubbabel*

The language and style of *Sefer Zerubbabel* reflect the importance it places on modeling itself on biblical prophecy. Comparison to *Sefer Eliyyahu*, the contemporary Hebrew apocalyptic work just mentioned, makes *Sefer Zerubbabel*'s distinctive features clear. *Sefer Eliyyahu* presents its version of the eschatological drama—the defeat of Rome, the coming of the messiah, the descent of the heavenly Jerusalem—by assembling a series of units in different genres that reflect the influence of a range of sources. These units include a brief account of a revelatory journey very close to a passage in the Book of the Watchers (1 Enoch 17–19), a sometimes confusing messianic timetable, and the series of visions already mentioned that respond to the New Testament book of Revelation. The dominant influence on the form and style of *Sefer Eliyyahu*, however, is undoubtedly rabbinic literature. *Sefer Eliyyahu* mimics the rabbinic practice of providing proof texts to support its claims, and it contains twenty-four of them, a large number for such a short work; most are introduced with a standard rabbinic formula for citing proof texts: "as it is said." In one remarkable passage, *Sefer Eliyyahu* presents a variety of opinions about the name of the last king in the style of rabbinic halakhic debate. Another echo of rabbinic literature, this one perhaps unconscious, is *Sefer Eliyyahu*'s mixture of Hebrew and Aramaic, common in Palestinian midrashim compiled in the fourth and fifth centuries.[48] Given *Sefer Eliyyahu*'s composition in the seventh century, a time when rabbinic culture was well on the way to becoming dominant, the impact of rabbinic literary practices is not surprising.

Although it too was composed in the seventh century, *Sefer Zerubbabel* shows much less evidence of the impact of rabbinic literary practices than does *Sefer Eliyyahu*. *Sefer Zerubbabel* is considerably longer than *Sefer Eliyahhu*, but the text of *Sefer Zerubbabel* in the *Sefer Hazikhronot* manuscript contains only three proof texts.[49] Even more striking, *Sefer Zerubbabel* is written in a type of Hebrew very different from that of *Sefer Eliyyahu* and other contemporary works, one that attempts to avoid features characteristic of rabbinic Hebrew and instead to make use of features characteristic of biblical Hebrew.[50] This unusual language, which must have required considerable effort to achieve, is presumably inspired by the desire to present *Sefer Zerubbabel* as a prophetic work.[51] Unless otherwise indicated, the examples and figures are drawn from the *Sefer Hazikhronot* manuscript, but it should be emphasized that despite some differences among the witnesses, all of them reflect an effort at distinctively biblical language.

Perhaps the most pervasive of the characteristically biblical elements in *Sefer Zerubbabel* is the *vav* consecutive. The *vav* consecutive with both imperfect and perfect verbs is a standard feature of biblical narrative, but it virtually disappears in post-biblical Hebrew.[52] Yet the *vav* consecutive with an imperfect verb is the dominant way of expressing the past in the portions of *Sefer Zerubabbel* in which Zerubbabel describes his experience receiving the revelation, and the verb form appears elsewhere in *Sefer Zerubbabel* as well. *Sefer Eliyyahu* does not make use of the *vav* consecutive, nor do the hekhalot texts, even in the narrative portions.

For masculine plural nouns, adjectives, and participles, *Sefer Eliyyahu* makes use of both the *–im* ending of biblical Hebrew and the *–in* ending that appears alongside it in rabbinic Hebrew as a result of the influence of Aramaic;[53] sometimes one ending appears next to the other. *Sefer Zerubbabel* consistently uses the *–im* ending found in biblical Hebrew. Indeed, in the one instance in which it incorporates an Aramaic passage from Daniel (Dan 7:18), the *Sefer Hazikhronot* manuscript replaces the proper Aramaic masculine plural ending *–in* of Daniel's *'elyonin*, "exalted," with *–im*.[54] Not all of the witnesses are as consistent as the *Sefer Hazikhronot* manuscript, however. The list of Armilos's features in the text in Jellinek's edition, for example, refers to his two heads, *qoqodin*, and MS JTS 2325/20 refers to the nations bringing, *mevi'in*, Israel into the wilderness.[55]

*Sefer Zerubbabel* also makes use of forms of the infinitive that appear frequently in biblical Hebrew but that fell out of use in post-biblical Hebrew. Zerubbabel's first-person descriptions of his reception of communication from the divine sphere contain six instances of the infinitive with *b-* or *k-*,[56] and the angelic revealer once makes use of an infinitive without a preposition introducing it.[57] In rabbinic Hebrew, in contrast, infinitives are virtually always introduced with *l-*.[58] Five infinitives have a suffix serving as their subject, a biblical usage that has disappeared in post-biblical Hebrew.[59] *Sefer Zerubbabel* also contains an infinitive absolute used to emphasize a

finite verb of the same root, another biblical usage that disappears
in later Hebrew.[60] In addition, it makes occasional use of other verb
forms that appear with some frequency in the Bible but disappear in
rabbinic Hebrew: the cohortative form, though, as is often the case
in later biblical Hebrew, without a cohortative meaning;[61] the
lengthened form of the imperative;[62] and the distinctive feminine
form of the third-person plural of the imperfect.[63]

Another aspect of the attempt to mimic biblical style in *Sefer
Zerubbabel* is its frequent use of the relative pronoun *'asher*, which
is no longer in use in rabbinic Hebrew. To be sure, the dominant
relative pronoun in *Sefer Zerubbabel* is *she-*, which first appears in
late biblical books and replaces *'asher* in later Hebrew.[64] By my
count, there are twenty-five occurrences of *'asher* in the *Sefer
Hazikhronot* manuscript compared to thirty-five of *she-*.[65] For purposes of comparison, *'asher* appears in *Sefer Eliyyahu* only in biblical quotations. The two relative pronouns can appear in close
proximity to each other in *Sefer Zerubbabel*, including once in the
same sentence,[66] and there is no consistent pattern to the use of one
or the other that I can discern other than the repeated use of *she-* in
the two angelic self-introductions.[67]

*Sefer Zerubbabel* also attempts to restrict itself to biblical vocab-
ulary. It contains only a few words with roots that are not attested
in the Bible.[68] Comparison to *Sefer Eliyyahu* is again illuminating.
The much shorter *Sefer Eliyyahu* uses significantly more words that
do not appear in the Bible and more verbal roots attested in the
Bible in conjugations in which they do not appear in the Bible.[69]

Not only does *Sefer Zerubbabel* avoid nonbiblical language, but it
is also replete with phrases borrowed from biblical books, particularly the books of Isaiah, Ezekiel, Zechariah, and Daniel.[70] So too the
biblical idiom "answered and said" appears nine times in the account
of the conversations between its protagonist and the revealing angel;
eight of the instances consist of the imperfect with *vav* consecutive.[71]
The meaning of the passages would not be changed by use of a more
straightforward single verb; the idiom is clearly intended to produce
what the author understood as biblical diction. In contrast, *Sefer
Eliyyahu*, despite the many proof texts or perhaps because of them,
uses only a few biblical phrases in its own narrative.

It is true that no reader would mistake its language for biblical Hebrew, but the understanding of biblical language *Sefer Zerubbabel* demonstrates is nonetheless impressive. The fairly consistent avoidance of certain nonbiblical features suggests an awareness of what differentiates biblical language from post-biblical that goes beyond the effort to imitate particular biblical passages. The author of *Sefer Zerubbabel* must have been quite learned. On the other hand, he kept his distance from rabbinic culture. In contrast to *Sefer Eliyyahu*, the impact of rabbinic literary practice on *Sefer Zerubbabel* is limited. Nor, apparently, did our author identify with the learned elite of his own day, for he depicts "the elders and sages" as failing to recognize the Davidic messiah when he first appears, indeed, as despising him.[72] Now, to be sure, the messiah's unprepossessing appearance, described in language drawn from Isaiah 53, makes their mistake easier to understand; in fact, Zerubbabel himself makes the same mistake when he first meets the messiah.[73] Furthermore, the contemptuous response of the elders and sages fulfills Isaiah's prophecy (Isa 53:3). Still, *Sefer Zerubbabel* can hardly be said to reflect admiration for these members of the elite. We shall see that Pesiqta Rabbati expresses real hostility toward the "righteous of the generation," who hold the "mourners of Zion" in contempt. Given the distance between *Sefer Zerubbabel* and Pesqita Rabbati in other respects, their shared picture of a division between the rabbinic elite and more messianically inclined Jews, who clearly were themselves members of some kind of elite, is striking. I shall discuss the relevant passages in more detail in Chapter 4, but unfortunately, given the state of our knowledge of Jewish society in the first part of the seventh century, it is very difficult to draw concrete historical conclusions.

## The Historical Context of *Sefer Zerubbabel*

For rabbinic literature, Rome is the "evil empire" and the great eschatological enemy. It is not surprising that Jews living under the rule of the empire that destroyed the Second Temple or the rule of the Byzantine Empire, its eastern heir, would harbor such feelings.

Thus it is not surprising to find that *Sefer Zerubbabel* treats Rome, embodied in Armilos, as the greatest of the eschatological enemies. But the role of Persia in the eschatological drama is more revealing about the circumstances under which *Sefer Zerubbabel* was composed. According to the *Sefer Hazikhronot* manuscript, the king of Persia, Shiroi, attacks Nehemiah and the people of Israel and dies just before the arrival of Armilos; so too the list of ten kings at the end of the work lists the king of Persia as the ninth king, with Armilos as the tenth. As already noted, the king of Persia plays an even more important role in the first edition, where it is he rather than Armilos who kills Nehemiah.[74]

It is Persia's place in *Sefer Zerubbabel*'s eschatological scenario and the name of its Persian king that led Israël Lévi to place the composition of *Sefer Zerubbabel* in the seventh century.[75] Because *Sefer Zerubbabel* sets 990 years from the destruction of Jerusalem by the Romans as the time of the messiah's arrival, most nineteenth-century scholars who discussed the question dated it to the mid-eleventh century, shortly before the completion of 990 years from the destruction of the Second Temple in 70.[76] Lévi argued for the seventh-century date on the basis of the role of the Persian king in the eschatological scenario and identified Shiroi as Kavadh II, Siroes in Greek and Latin sources. Shiroi ruled Persia only briefly (628–29) after deposing and murdering his father Khosrau (Chosroes) II; Khosrau had ruled Persia from 590, presiding over decades of conflict with the Byzantine Empire. According to Lévi, the designation of a historical figure, the Persian king, as the enemy of a mythic one, the messiah son of Joseph, could have taken place only after the death of the historical figure; thus *Sefer Zerubbabel* could not have been composed before 629, and since it knows nothing of the Muslim conquest, it must have been composed before 636.[77] The dating of the eschaton to 990 years after the destruction of Jerusalem by the Romans was to be understood as the contribution of a copyist troubled that events had not unfolded as predicted; its presence in all versions of *Sefer Zerubbabel* indicates that all derive from a manuscript that contained the improvement.[78]

The general framework of Lévi's dating has been widely accepted although questions can be raised about both ends of the period he delimits. The ground on which he insists that *Sefer Zerubbabel* could have been written only after Shiroi's death is certainly open to question, but Shiroi's reign was so brief that even if the work was written as soon as Shiroi became king, this adjustment adds only a year to Lévi's window. On the other end of the window, the year 636 is rather late for *Sefer Zerubbabel*'s ignorance of the Muslim invasion of the eastern provinces of the Byzantine Empire; a more likely date for awareness of the invasion is probably a few years earlier.[79]

It is not surprising that the wars between Byzantium and Persia in the early seventh century would have seemed deeply significant to a Jewish observer. By the beginning of the seventh century, Jerusalem had been a Christian city for almost 300 years. When the Persians conquered it in 614, Christians were shocked by the loss, which they saw as threatening the Christian identity of the city. The Church of the Holy Sepulcher, the most important church in the city, was damaged by fire in the course of the fighting, and the Persians removed its most revered relic, the Holy Cross, and carried it off to Persia.[80] But if Christians mourned, Jews, at least according to Christian accounts, were delighted. They allied themselves with the Persians and took advantage of the opportunity to take bloody revenge on the Christians. While the veracity of the Christian accounts with their strongly anti-Jewish tone is by no means certain, especially since most were written much later than the events they describe, it would not be surprising if many Jews preferred the Persian conquerors to the evil empire, which had taken Jerusalem away from the Jews and remade it as a Christian holy city.[81]

Yet for *Sefer Zerubbabel* the Persians too are enemies even if second to the Romans. Some scholars have read *Sefer Zerubbabel*'s account of Nehemiah's reign in Jerusalem and the resumption of sacrifices as evidence for the activity of a Jewish leader authorized by the Persians.[82] The end of this leader's rule would have come when the Persians reconsidered their support for the Jews, perhaps in an effort to make their presence more acceptable to their Christian subjects. The first edition's account of Nehemiah's death at the hands of Shiroi is understood to suggest that the Persians put an end to this experiment by putting the Jewish ruler to death.[83] Proponents of this view find further evidence for a brief period of Jewish rule and the death of a Jewish leader at the hands of the Persians in a piyyut entitled *"Ha'et lig'or,"* "The Time to Rebuke."[84] The piyyut predicts the arrival of the Persians ("Assyria") and the restoration of sacrifices,[85] but after three months of rule the "anointed of war" is killed by Armilos according to one manuscript or by another leader, presumably a Persian, according to the other.[86]

But Persia's triumph was short-lived. In 628, the Byzantine emperor Heraclius took Jerusalem back from the Persians, and in 630, he arranged a dramatic restoration of the Holy Cross to the Church of the Holy Sepulcher.[87] In the course of the restoration or shortly thereafter he issued an edict ordering the baptism of all the Jews in his realm; the edict appears to have been preceded by some local incidents of forced baptism.[88] The call for baptism may reflect anger at the Jews for betraying their Christian rulers and siding with the Persians, but it has also been understood as one aspect of a larger effort by Heraclius to unify his realm in order to prevent a repetition of the Persians' exploitation of divisions within the Byzantine Empire, including not only divisions between Christians and Jews but also divisions among Christians with differing theological positions and ecclesiastical allegiances as well.[89] Of course, Jews living in the Byzantine Empire would hardly have been likely to take such a broad view of Heraclius's goals.

The years Lévi suggests for the composition of *Sefer Zerubbabel* are the years in which Christian rule was being restored to Jerusalem and Palestine more generally. They would have been years of disappointment for Jews who had welcomed the Persian conquest, although if *Sefer Zerubbabel* and *"Ha'et lig'or"* preserve the memory of a brief period of Jewish political power after the Persian conquest which the Persians brought to a swift end, the disappointment would have begun even earlier. But I am inclined to caution, both about what really happened and what we can know about what really happened, and I am not persuaded that it is possible to offer a coherent argument for marking off part of *Sefer Zerubbabel* as *vaticinium ex eventu*, prophecy after the fact.[90] In the spirit of caution, I will treat the entire work as an expression of apocalyptic hopes for which the immediate inspiration was the disappointment of the expectations raised by the temporary end of Christian rule in Jerusalem.

## A Challenge to the Consensus

The consensus in favor of an early seventh-century date for *Sefer Zerubbabel* has recently been challenged by Newman, who argues that the work should be dated to the early or mid-sixth century.[91] While I do not accept Newman's conclusions, some of his criticism of arguments for the seventh-century date is well-taken. The argument, as I have already noted, is related to Newman's preference for the first edition. It runs as follows: the first edition and witnesses associated with it predict the 990-year period from the destruction of the temple to the messianic age without identifying the destruction as that inflicted by the Romans. In the context of a revelation to Zerubbabel, a hero of the return from the Babylonian exile, we should assume that the destruction in question is the destruction of the First Temple by the Babylonians in 586 BCE.[92] Furthermore, even in the *Sefer Hazikhronot* manuscript and associated witnesses used by Lévi, only the first mention of the 990 years explicitly identifies the destruction as that perpetrated by the Romans; the other two mentions leave the perpetrators unnamed. On this basis, we can conclude against Lévi that the 990-year schema is original to *Sefer Zerubbabel,* but in its original form it took as it starting point the first destruction, the destruction relevant to the career of the historical Zerubbabel. Counting seventy years from the destruction of the First Temple in 586 to the building of the Second Temple, dedicated in 515, and adding 420 years for the Second Temple period as traditionally reckoned in Jewish sources including *Sefer Zerubbabel,* a 990-year period points to 570 as the date for the eschaton.[93] The name Shiroi, which can hardly predate the 620s, is best understood as an addition to the text, introduced only after the original eschatological date had passed; indeed, it is altogether absent from MS JTS 2325/20.[94]

Lévi resolves the conflict between the implications of the name Shiroi and the period of 990 years from the destruction in favor of Shiroi; the 990-year period is understood as a later addition to the work. For Newman, the 990-year period is retained, though its starting point is understood differently, and the name Shiroi is taken to be a later addition to the work. In a sense, then, Newman's argument is the mirror image of Lévi's.

Newman also argues that the 990-year period from destruction to messiah is not simply an ad hoc response to the failure of the work's original eschatological schema as Lévi contended, citing another instance of a 990-year time-table in a passage in Pirqe Rabbi Eliezer, a work composed in the eighth or ninth century, long after the eschatological date the tradition predicts. But if, as Newman plausibly suggests, Pirqe Rabbi Eliezer "takes over an existing apocalyptic topos from an earlier age in which it was not yet in need of interpretive apologetics," why could *Sefer Zerubbabel* not have done the same?[95]

A more important difficulty for Newman's position is that Persia plays a significant role in all of the versions of *Sefer Zerubbabel*, with the king of Persia an eschatological enemy second only to Armilos. Indeed, as already noted, by attributing the death of the messiah son of Joseph to the king of Persia, the first edition and the witnesses associated with it, which Newman sees as preserving a more original form of the work, place greater emphasis on Persia's role in the eschatological drama than do the *Sefer Hazikhronot* manuscript and the witnesses associated with it. The text of the first edition is somewhat confused in its account of the death of the messiah son of Joseph, reporting the mourning for the messiah before it reports his death, but the name it gives the messiah's killer, *Shido*, must be a corruption of Shiroi.[96] In MS JTS 2325/20 the Persian king bears a different name, but it is undoubtedly he who slays the messiah (193). The passage preserved in Oxford MS Heb. f. 27 is also clear on this point: it is Shiroi king of Persia who kills the messiah (42r). Furthermore, the first edition and MS JTS 2325/20 agree with the *Sefer Hazikhronot* manuscript in identifying the ninth of the ten kings who will arise in the end of days as the king of Persia, and they give a more elaborate account of his activities than does the *Sefer Hazikhronot* manuscript. Here the first edition, like the *Sefer Hazikhronot* manuscript, calls the king Shiroi; MS JTS 2325/20 does not name him. In addition, as I pointed out earlier, both the first edition and MS JTS 2325/20 omit altogether the account of Armilos's attack on Jerusalem, drastically diminishing Armilos's role.

Thus, even if we accept his view that the name Shiroi is a later addition to *Sefer Zerubbabel*, Newman still needs to explain why a work composed in the early or middle part of the sixth century would give such a prominent role to the king of Persia in its eschatological scenario. It is true that even at the best of times there was a certain amount of tension between the Byzantine Empire and its great neighbor, and it is not impossible to imagine a Jewish writer granting the role of penultimate enemy in the eschatological drama to Persia during the decades before 570, as Newman's argument would require. On the other hand, the Persian invasion of Palestine in the early seventh century provides a more obvious context for the introduction of the king of Persia into an inherited eschatological scenario focused on Rome.

It is worth noting that despite their differences both forms of the narrative show some difficulty in integrating this penultimate eschatological enemy. Just as the *Sefer Hazikhronot* manuscript reports without explanation the death of the king of Persia after he has attacked Jerusalem and brought an end to the restoration overseen by the messiah son of Joseph but before Armilos has appeared, the first edition fails to account for the disappearance of the king of Persia after he has killed the messiah son of Joseph but before the Davidic messiah arrives. I am not suggesting the existence of an early version of *Sefer Zerubbabel* in which the king of Persia was altogether absent. Rather, it seems likely that the eschatological schema *Sefer Zerubbabel* adapted did not originally make room for Persia. If so, the differences between the two groups of witnesses on the role of the king of Persia may reflect differing approaches to smoothing the introduction of a penultimate eschatological enemy into a scenario that did not originally have one.

Newman also appeals to the larger Byzantine context to make the case for *Sefer Zerubbabel* as an early sixth-century work, noting that the sixth century was a time of heightened eschatological expectations among Christians. "Jews did not need ambient Christian chiliasm in order to cultivate their own messianism," he writes, "but it is not farfetched to imagine Jewish messianic expectations being amplified by the pervasive influence of their surroundings."[97] This is a sentiment I would thoroughly endorse. Indeed, I believe that the safest way to date *Sefer Zerubbabel* is by attempting to determine the historical context for its larger themes and motifs. I have just argued that the role given to Persia in *Sefer Zerubbabel* fits better in the early decades of the seventh century than in the first half of the sixth century. Let me offer two further examples of elements of *Sefer Zerubbabel* that fit more comfortably in the seventh century shortly before the Muslim conquest rather than in the early or mid-sixth century. One is the figure of Hephzibah, the mother of the Davidic messiah. In Chapter 2, I argue that the depiction of Hephzibah as a warrior and her role as defender of Jerusalem echo the Byzantine picture of the Virgin Mary as the patron and guardian of Constantinople. Elements of this picture predate the seventh century, but the closest Byzantine analogy to *Sefer Zerubbabel*'s depiction of Hephzibah's military prowess in defense of Jerusalem is the use of icons of the Virgin in the defense of Constantinople during the Avar siege in 626. Another, which I have already mentioned but will discuss in more detail in Chapter 4, is the surprisingly critical attitude to the learned that *Sefer Zerubbabel* shares with Pesiqta Rabbati, which is usually dated to the early seventh century.

To be sure, if Newman's earlier date could somehow be definitively shown to be correct, the precise background to the depiction of Hephzibah in *Sefer Zerubbabel* would need to be reconsidered, as would the relationship between the attitudes to the learned of *Sefer Zerubbabel* and Pesiqta Rabbati. I am convinced that the larger points I argue about the relationship between *Sefer Zerubbabel* and Christianity on the one the hand and *Sefer Zerubbabel* and rabbinic tradition on the other would nonetheless stand. Furthermore, given the complexities of the textual evidence and the gaps in our knowledge of the history of the sixth and seventh centuries, it seems to me that attempting to find the right context for the content of *Sefer Zerubbabel* is a more effective approach to dating it than relying on the chronology of its eschatological scenario or the name of the Persian king.

# CHAPTER TWO

# The Mother of the Messiah

MANY ELEMENTS of *Sefer Zerubbabel* have precedents in rabbinic messianic traditions: the centrality of Rome, the fact of two messiahs, the suffering of the Davidic messiah, the death of the messiah son of Joseph. But there is little in rabbinic literature to prepare a reader for Hephzibah, *Sefer Zerubbabel*'s warrior mother of the Davidic messiah. The depiction of a woman, especially a mother, as a warrior certainly demands explanation, but even without regard to her activity, attention to the mother of the messiah is most unusual in a Jewish text. For Christians, interest in the mother of the messiah goes back at least as far as the gospels of Matthew and Luke. Yet while the earliest Christian writings are so often indebted to ancient Jewish traditions, none of the messiahs of surviving Second Temple literature is equipped with a mother. Perhaps traditions about the messiah's mother once existed but were not transmitted because Christian adoption of the figure rendered her unacceptable, but there is little to encourage such a reconstruction. As we shall see, rabbinic literature does contain a story about the mother of the messiah, but it took shape after Christianity was on its way to becoming the dominant religion of the Roman Empire.

Thus we need to consider the likelihood that the rabbinic story, like *Sefer Zerubbabel*, reflects the impact of the figure of the Virgin Mary on ancient Jews.

Much of this chapter is concerned with that impact. I begin by considering Hephzibah's career in *Sefer Zerubbabel* and, in particular, her military exploits, in relation to the role of the Virgin as patron and protector of Constantinople for seventh-century Byzantine Christians. Later in the chapter, I discuss a piyyut that draws on *Sefer Zerubbabel* for the figure of Hephzibah but depicts her in light of the Byzantine identification of the Virgin with the rod of Aaron (Num 17:23 [17:8]), with the blossoming of the rod prefiguring the virgin birth. From *Sefer Zerubbabel*, I turn to the earliest version of the rabbinic story about the mother of the messiah, a passage in the Yerushalmi about a less-than-doting mother of a baby messiah who vanishes soon after his birth. I argue that the Yerushalmi story is best understood as a sarcastic rabbinic response to a popular Jewish story that depicted the mother in a more favorable light. Finally, I consider Hephzibah's evil counterpart: the beautiful stone statue that becomes pregnant by Satan and gives birth to Armilos, *Sefer Zerubbabel*'s antichrist.

## The Mother of the Messiah in *Sefer Zerubbabel*

Hephzibah's appearance marks the beginning of the eschatological drama of *Sefer Zerubbabel*. Cosmic wonders announce her arrival to do battle against the kings of Yemen and Antioch: a great star shines before her, and the stars swerve from their paths. She comes bearing a staff of salvation that had been hidden away in the city of Rakkat in Naphtali. This staff had been given by God to Adam and passed on to Moses and Aaron; it is the staff that blossomed to denote Aaron's right to priesthood after the rebellion of Korah (Num 17:23).[1]

If the figure of a female warrior was something new in a Jewish text, the staff and at least one of the cosmic wonders might have seemed more familiar to *Sefer Zerubbabel*'s earliest audience. I know no parallel in ancient Jewish literature to the great star shining before Hephzibah, and perhaps its background should be sought in Byzantine Christian sources. But the stars swerving from their paths may be intended to recall the stars fighting from their paths in the Song of Deborah (Jud 5:20). As for the staff, several passages in later rabbinic texts describe the transmission of a miraculous staff from one biblical hero to another, including a passage in Numbers Rabbah (18:23) that claims that after having been passed from king to king of Judah, it was hidden away for the messiah.[2] None of the passages about such a staff, including the one in Numbers Rabbah, is likely to be earlier than *Sefer Zerubbabel*, but the traditions they record could have been in circulation at the time *Sefer Zerubbabel* was written. Furthermore, the blossoming staff came to be identified with the Virgin in Byzantine homilies and hymns. I see no evidence for knowledge of this identification in *Sefer Zerubbabel*, but "'*Oto hayom*," "That Very Day," a piyyut that reworks the eschatological scenario of *Sefer Zerubbabel*, plays on it, as Alexei Sivertsev has shown.[3] I discuss the piyyut's depiction of Hephzibah later in this chapter.

My discussion of subsequent episodes in Hephzibah's career relies on the *Sefer Hazikhronot* manuscript; as discussed in Chapter 1, the first edition lacks an account of Armilos's attack on Jerusalem, which is of particular importance for understanding the figure of Hephzibah. The rest of Hephzibah's story according to the *Sefer Hazikhronot* manuscript runs as follows: five years after her appearance, Nehemiah b. Hushiel, the messiah descended from Joseph, arrives on the scene. He gathers all Israel to Jerusalem, and sacrifices are restored. But after forty years, Shiroi king of Persia attacks, and it is Hephzibah rather than Nehemiah who goes out to meet him. Shiroi then dies—as mentioned in Chapter 1, the text does not explain how—but he is followed by Armilos, the greatest of the eschatological enemies, who kills the messiah son of Joseph. During the assault by Armilos's forces, Hephzibah guards the east gate of Jerusalem to prevent him from entering the city.[4] Yet when her son makes his appearance, Hephzibah turns her staff over to him and disappears from *Sefer Zerubbabel*'s narrative. She is mentioned again only in a summary of the eschatological wars near the end of the book.[5] She does not participate in her son's triumph.

The role of warrior and protector of Jerusalem that *Sefer Zerubbabel* attributes to the mother of the messiah becomes less surprising once it is placed in the context of contemporary Byzantine developments.[6] By the time *Sefer Zerubbabel* was composed, the Virgin Mary had more than once played a role in Byzantine warfare in a concrete sense. During his naval campaign against the reigning emperor Phocas in 610, Heraclius took icons of the Virgin into battle with him. During the Avar siege in 626, very close to the likely date of *Sefer Zerubbabel*'s composition, the patriarch Sergius sought to protect Constantinople by painting images of the Virgin and Christ child on the gates of the west side of the city, where the Avars were assembled.[7] The Avars eventually lifted the siege without entering the city, and the poet George of Pisidia gives the Virgin a central role in his poem on the war against the Avars.[8]

The Virgin's role in the siege of Constantinople is only one aspect of her close association with the city. The *tykhe* that had once served as the personification and guardian of Constantinople came to seem unsuitable to Christians, modeled as she was on pagan goddesses, and by the beginning of the seventh century, the Virgin had taken over the *tykhe*'s role as Constantinople's patron and protector.[9] Sivertsev suggests that *Sefer Zerubbabel* represents Hephzibah as playing the same role for Jerusalem, the capital city of the future messianic empire, that the Virgin plays for Constantinople. The name Hephzibah, which means "My delight is in her," appears in Isaiah as an epithet for Jerusalem (Isa 62:4), making its bearer almost an embodiment of Jerusalem; her defense of the city against Armilos shows her as the guardian of the city.[10]

But one difference between the Virgin as protector of Constantinople and Hephzibah as guardian of Jerusalem is particularly important for understanding *Sefer Zerubbabel*. The Virgin tends to operate together with her son. In his effort to defend Constantinople, the patriarch Sergius, as just noted, had images of the Christ child painted alongside those of his mother, and in his poem on the defeat of the Avars, George of Pisidia depicts the Virgin beseeching her son on behalf of the city, emphasizing her ability, both motherly and feminine, to play on his sympathy.[11] In *Sefer Zerubbabel*, in contrast, Hephzibah operates independently of her son. She appears at the beginning of the unfolding of the events of the eschaton, well before her son, to wage war against the two kings of Yemen and Antioch. Indeed, she is associated more closely with the messiah descended from Joseph than with her own son, the messiah descended from David. When Shiroi attacks, it is she who fights against him, and it is she who protects Jerusalem after the messiah son of Joseph is slain. She is never depicted engaged in characteristically maternal behavior, nor even in characteristically feminine activities. Finally, despite her importance early in the scenario, once her own son appears, she turns over the staff and disappears. I will attempt to make sense of Hephzibah's career and the tensions it embodies in the course of this chapter.

## The Mother of the Messiah in the Yerushalmi

I turn now to the first place a mother of the messiah appears in a Jewish text: a remarkable story in the Yerushalmi about the disappearance of a baby messiah soon after his birth. Like Hephzibah, the mother in the story does not behave in typical motherly fashion, but otherwise her character and behavior have nothing in common with those of Hephzibah. She is certainly not a warrior. Yet the baby messiah in the story bears the name Menahem just as the Davidic messiah of *Sefer Zerubbabel* does, though their patronyms are different, and I shall argue that a careful reading of the story illumines a number of aspects of *Sefer Zerubbabel* and vice versa. I should also note that, as far as I know, a mother of the messiah appears nowhere in classical Jewish literature apart from the Yerushalmi story and texts dependent on it and *Sefer Zerubbabel* and texts that draw on it.

The story in the Yerushalmi (y. Ber. 2.4/12-14) comes during a discussion of the name of the messiah inspired by the mention of David in the fourteenth blessing of the Amidah, the central prayer of the Jewish liturgy, which concludes, "who rebuilds Jerusalem" (y. Ber. 2.4/11).[12] The story is told by R. Yudan in the name of R. Aibo to support the opinion that the messiah's name will be Menahem.[13] Both R. Yudan and R. Aibo were fourth-generation Palestinian

amoraim, active in the first half of the fourth century. A slightly
revised version of the Yerushalmi story appears in Lamentations
Rabbah (1:51, to Lam 1:16); the revision is clearly aimed at eliminating some of the most troubling aspects of the earlier form of the
story. The most important differences will be noted in my
discussion.

The Yerushalmi story, composed in Aramaic, runs as follows:[14]

It happened that a certain Jew was plowing when his cow lowed. A
certain Arab passed by and heard its sound. "Jew, Jew," he said,
"Unharness your ox[15] and disengage your plow, for the temple has
been destroyed." It lowed a second time. "Jew, Jew," he said,
"Harness your oxen and engage your plows,[16] for the king messiah
has been born." The Jew said, "What is his name?" He said,
"Menahem." He said, "And what is his father's name?" He said,
"Hezekiah." He said, "Where is he from?" He said, "From the royal
city, Bethlehem of Judah."

The Jew went and sold the oxen[17] and plows and became a peddler of swaddling clothes for babies. He went from city to city until
he came to that city. All the women made purchases except the
mother of Menahem. He heard the voices of the women saying,
"Mother of Menahem, mother of Menahem, come, make a purchase
for your son." She said, "I would like to strangle him, the enemies of
Israel, for on the day he was born, the temple was destroyed."

He said, "We trust that as it was destroyed in his wake, in his
wake it will be rebuilt." She said, "I have no money."[18]

He said, "What does that matter to him?[19] Come and make a
purchase for him, and if you don't have any money today, I'll come
back after a while and collect it."

After a while he came to that city and said to her, "How is the
baby doing?" She said, "After you saw me, winds and whirlwinds
came and snatched him out of my hands."

R. Bun said, "Why do we need to learn from this Arab? Isn't there
a complete scriptural passage to this effect: 'Lebanon will fall by a
majestic one' (Isa 10:34)?[20] And what is written after that? 'A shoot
shall come forth from the stump of Jesse'" (Isa 11:1).

The story begins with the lowing of a cow announcing bad news
followed immediately by good news: the temple has been destroyed,

but at the very moment of its destruction, the messiah is born. The cow's message is interpreted for its Jewish owner by a passing Arab; Arabs were known in antiquity for their knowledge of the language of animals. Furthermore, while prophetic cows may be unusual in rabbinic literature, signs involving speaking cows and oxen are well attested in Roman literature.[21] With the report of the events come directions for the farmer, to stop plowing at news of the destruction and to resume plowing at news of the birth of the messiah. It is not clear whether the Arab understands the directions to be contained in the cow's lowing or whether he has added them himself. But the meaning of the directions is clear, and despite their source, they are in tune with the rabbinic view of the significance of the loss of the temple: while at first it might have appeared that life could no longer continue as it had before, the promise of the messiah's eventual appearance put life back on its previous course since the remedy for the loss had been provided.

Yet while the farmer follows the advice to unharness ox and plow, he ignores the advice to harness them once again in the wake of the birth of the messiah. Instead, he decides to become a peddler of swaddling clothes, an occupation that provides him with the opportunity to go off in search of the new-born messiah.[22] But as he does so he ignores the information the Arab has supplied about the baby's location, and instead of heading straight to Bethlehem, he makes his way from city to city before finally arriving in the right place.

Having arrived in Bethlehem equipped with the baby's name, the peddler soon finds the mother. But she is unwilling to buy anything from him, because, she tells him, "I would like to strangle him, the enemies of Israel, for on the day he was born, the temple was destroyed." Even with the rather awkward plural "the enemies of Israel" in apposition, the most obvious referent of the pronominal suffix "him" is the baby, and even with the appositive phrase, it is hard to avoid the conclusion that the mother is expressing the desire to strangle her own son rather than the person or persons responsible for the destruction of the temple.[23] The phrase is presumably a later addition to the story, intended to mitigate that shocking sentiment; the version of the story in Lamentations Rabbah softens the mother's sentiment by having her tell the peddler not that she wishes to strangle someone but rather that she "fears difficulties" for her son. This understanding of the text of the Yerushalmi story finds support in the euphemistic or apotropaic use of "enemies of Israel" as a substitute for "Israel" elsewhere in rabbinic literature.[24] The instance in the Yerushalmi passage is somewhat different, to be sure, since the true subject of the mother's words is not the people of Israel but a particular individual.

Eventually the peddler bestows swaddling clothes on the mother without payment, promising to return to collect from her sometime in the future. The promise to return seems aimed at checking up on the mother as much as at collecting what she owes for the merchandise. Indeed, upon his return to Bethlehem, the peddler learns that the cow's good news was short-lived. Before the baby messiah had a chance to grow up, he vanished, snatched away by the wind—if his mother is to be believed. The alternative that the story forces us to consider is even more troubling. Perhaps the mother is lying about the wind, which in the normal course of things is unlikely to cause a baby's disappearance. Perhaps the mother herself is responsible for the disappearance. After all, she explains her unwillingness to buy her son swaddling clothes by saying that she would like to strangle him. Yonah Frankel suggests that the winds should be understood as rescuing the baby from the mother's murderous intentions. He reads the phrasing of the mother's report—"snatched him *from my hands*"—as reflecting her guilt about her hostility toward the child.[25] By expressing her desire to kill the baby, the mother has perhaps forfeited her right to be believed about his fate. But while we may not be sure whether she is telling the truth about the winds, one thing of which we can be certain is that her wish to be rid of her baby has been fulfilled. I am inclined to read the story as depicting the mother caught in a sort of nightmare in which the disappearance of the baby is at once fulfillment of her desire to murder him and punishment for it.

Frankel also notes that ʿalʿulin, the word I have translated as "whirlwinds," is a rare term used by Targum Jonathan, an Aramaic translation of the prophets that originated in Palestine but became the semi-official targum of the synagogues of Babylonia, for the wind that carries Elijah to heaven (2 Kgs 2:1, 11).[26] The use of this particular word might therefore be intended to suggest that the winds have taken the baby to heaven just as the whirlwind took Elijah.[27] Many scholars have drawn the same conclusion.[28] In support of this view, the idea of a messiah already in existence awaiting the moment of his mission is attested as early as 4 Ezra (12:32, 13:25–26), a Jewish apocalypse from the late first century or early second century CE, and it appears also in the Bavli (b. San. 98b), *Sefer Zerubbabel*, and later works perhaps dependent on them; I shall have more to say about this idea later. But while both the biblical text and Targum Jonathan make the heavenly destination of the whirlwind explicit, there is nothing in the story in the Yerushalmi that requires us to conclude that the baby has been taken to heaven. Indeed, in a way, it does not really matter where the baby messiah has been taken. What matters is that he has disappeared and that there is no reason to expect his return anytime soon. A similar attitude is reflected in R. Bun's question at the conclusion of the story, which implies that not only the Arab but even the story itself is unnecessary since Scripture has already promised that the messiah will come. The passage R. Bun cites, however, provides no reason to expect that coming to be imminent. As Frankel and Newman point out, the farmer turned peddler had it wrong. The proper response to the destruction of the temple and the birth of the messiah—as the cow or her Arab interpreter indicates—is to carry on as before.[29]

## The Baby Messiah, the Christian Messiah, and the Story behind the Yerushalmi's Story

In a study of the version of the story of the disappearing baby messiah found in Lamentations Rabbah, Galit Hasan-Rokem has argued that the story is virtually a Jewish version of the nativity stories of the gospels of Matthew and Luke.[30] Hasan-Rokem's reading of the rabbinic story would be more difficult to sustain for the story as it appears in the Yerushalmi with its murderous mother and the child's uncertain fate. But in Lamentations Rabbah, the mother's anger toward her son has become anxiety about his future, and perhaps even more important, this version of the story does not end with the baby's disappearance but with the peddler's interpretation of the disappearance: "Didn't I tell you that as it was destroyed in his wake, it will be rebuilt in his wake?" If the baby's disappearance in the Yerushalmi story appears to call into question the cow's prophecy, the peddler's comment in Lamentations Rabbah is a statement of confidence that, despite appearances, God's plan for the baby remains in force. Hasan-Rokem also makes much of Frankel's observation about the relationship of the term for whirlwinds to the story of Elijah.

Hasan-Rokem notes a number of parallels between the story as told in Lamentations Rabbah and the stories in the gospels.[31] The shared claim to Bethlehem as the birth place of the messiah presumably reflects the prophecy of Micah 5:1 and thus might have arisen independently in both traditions,[32] but the other parallels are not dependent on Jewish Scripture. The Arab of the rabbinic story, Hasan-Rokem suggests, is the counterpart of the magi of the gospel of Matthew (2:1–12), while the Arab's interpretation of the cow's message to the farmer as he plows in the field parallels the annunciation to the shepherds in the field in the gospel of Luke (2:8–14). Like the magi in Matthew, the farmer turned peddler of the Jewish story travels to Bethlehem to encounter the baby messiah. Both traditions include a sign from nature: the star the magi follow in the Christian nativity story (Matt 2:2, 9–10) and the lowing of the cow in the Jewish story of the birth of the messiah. The peddler's insistence that the mother take the clothing for the baby even without payment makes the clothing an equivalent to the gift of the magi (Matt 2:11). Both infants face danger. In the Christian story, the danger comes from Herod (Matt 2:7–16), while in the story in Lamentations Rabbah, the mother fears danger from an unspecified source. Baby Jesus is saved from Herod on the advice of an angel (Matt 2:13),[33] and the peddler attempts unsuccessfully to save the baby messiah by returning to visit him. In keeping with her understanding of a reservoir of shared folk traditions in Roman Palestine, Hasan-Rokem understands the similarities between the Jewish and Christian stories to reflect not a Jewish response to Christian legends of the nativity but rather traditions on which both Jews and Christians drew; she emphasizes that the adoption of these traditions by the gospel writers did not lead Jews to abandon them.[34]

While I agree with Hasan-Rokem that the Christian nativity story is crucial for understanding the story of the birth of the disappearing baby messiah, I have argued for a rather different understanding of the relationship. I am not persuaded that the pairs of motifs Hasan-Rokem points to constitute parallels. Rather, it seems to me, the element from the rabbinic story in each of the pairings is almost a parody of the element from the gospels.[35] In contrast to the magi, who are directed to baby Jesus by a star (Matthew), or the shepherds, to whom angels appear to announce the good news (Luke), the Jewish farmer learns of the birth of the messiah from a cow and its Arab interpreter. While the magi follow the star to Bethlehem to find the baby it announces, the peddler ignores the Arab's explicit indication that the baby is to be found in Bethlehem, a location the significance of which a Jew should certainly be expected to understand, and peddles his wares elsewhere before making his way to the city of David. The swaddling clothes that the peddler bestows on Menahem's mother without payment are a poor substitute for the gold, frankincense, and myrrh of the magi. But the most important difference is of course in the outcome of the babies' encounter with danger. An angel alerts Joseph to Herod's desire to kill baby Jesus, allowing the family to escape to Egypt so as to be able to return in safety at the death of Herod (Matt 2:13–15); this baby messiah will grow up before he faces the danger from which he cannot escape. Menahem, on the other hand, disappears before he has outgrown his swaddling clothes.

And if I am correct that the elements of the rabbinic story are not a positive Jewish adaption of the elements of the Christian nativity story but a parody of those elements, the most central element of the parody is undoubtedly the murderous mother, a profoundly troubling counterpart to the Virgin Mary as depicted in the nativity accounts of Matthew and Luke and later Christian tradition. The fact that Lamentations Rabbah eliminates the mother's most upsetting utterances to make her a more sympathetic character testifies to the transmitters' discomfort with the dark tone of the Yerushalmi story. Yet the true object of the parody in the Yerushalmi story can hardly be the Christian nativity story because it does not undercut Christian claims for Jesus to tell the story of the disappearance of a messiah with a different name, a messiah awaited by the Jews, before he could even begin to accomplish his mission.

Peter Schäfer has recently offered an intriguing reading of the Yerushalmi story that shares my view that the elements of the story in the Yerushalmi poke fun at the Christian nativity account but understands the story as a rabbinic effort to make sense of the fraught relationship between Judaism and the emerging Christian movement while turning Christian claims to Jewish advantage. He argues that the real reason the mother in the Yerushalmi story wishes her baby dead is not the coincidence of his birth and the destruction of the temple. Rather, the mother understands that Christians will use the baby's birth to claim that the covenant between God and the Jewish people has been superceded by a new covenant so that the temple is no longer part of God's plan. Against the Christian narrative, in which the messiah was killed at the hands of his own people, the storyteller insists that the mother did not murder the baby despite her desire to do so. For the baby is not a false messiah. That is, he is not only the Christian messiah; he is also the Jewish messiah. Given the complications his birth entails, however, there is no choice but to make the baby disappear. He has been born prematurely, and so he is taken to heaven to await the appropriate time for his coming. The story is thus a clever Jewish appropriation of the Christian idea of the second coming as well as a powerful reflection on the birth of Christianity and the role of Judaism in that birth.[36] Yet brilliant though it is, Schäfer's reading of the story in the Yerushalmi seems to me unlikely to be the ancient meaning of the story since it requires a willingness on the part of the rabbis to recognize at least some aspects of Christian messianic claims for Jesus.

In my view, the story in the Yerushalmi is best understood as a disapproving rabbinic response to a popular Jewish nativity story for a messiah named Menahem. In other words, the skepticism of the Yerushalmi story is directed toward *Jewish* messianic expectation.[37] Even if the messiah has been born, the story says, it makes no difference since his mission has not been accomplished. The proper response is to continue living life as before his birth—and before the destruction of the temple that made his birth seem so urgent. Presumably the story or stories at which the Yerushalmi story is aimed included a loving mother and perhaps other elements drawn from Christian stories about their baby messiah. They may have depicted the birth of the messiah as compensation for the destruction of the temple, thus offering an indirect response to Christian claims that the destruction was punishment for the crucifixion of Jesus.[38] They must have included the disappearance of the baby messiah. For these storytellers, the messiah had not yet arrived, and the stories would have made it clear that the winds had taken the baby to an appropriate hiding place where he could grow to adulthood as he awaited the call to begin his messianic mission.

Such a story, it seems to me, lies behind *Sefer Zerubbabel*'s unambiguously positive depiction of the mother of the messiah together with its picture of the messiah hidden away in Rome to await the moment of his mission. When I first wrote about the relationship between the Yerushalmi story and *Sefer Zerubbabel*, I understood *Sefer Zerubbabel*'s narrative as a reinterpretation of the Yerushalmi account in a more optimistic mode, along the lines of the version of the story in Lamentations Rabbah.[39] But there is nothing to suggest direct dependence of *Sefer Zerubbabel* on the rabbinic story as told in either Lamentations Rabbah or the Yerushalmi; it is notable that *Sefer Zerubbabel* does not suggest that Menahem was deposited in Rome by the whirlwinds that are the most striking detail in the rabbinic accounts of the baby's disappearance. And once I came to understand *Sefer Zerubbabel* as drawing for its picture of the suffering messiah son of David and the dying messiah son of Joseph not on rabbinic tradition but rather on the same popular stories hinted at in rabbinic texts, I realized that *Sefer Zerubbabel*'s picture of the messiah in Rome before the events of the eschaton unfold might well reflect the sort of popular story the Yerushalmi story criticizes, in which the baby messiah was carried off from Bethlehem to the heart of the evil empire to await the moment that his mission would begin.[40]

### The Names of the Messiah and His Parents

As we have already seen, in addition to the fact of a mother for the
messiah, one notable point of contact between the story in the
Yerushalmi and *Sefer Zerubbabel* is the messiah's name, Menahem.
But the texts differ on the names of Menahem's parents: in the
Yerushalmi story, an unnamed mother and Hezekiah as father; in
*Sefer Zerubbabel*, Hephzibah and Ammiel. Yet the only woman in
the Bible to bear the name Hephzibah was the wife of King Hezekiah
(2 Kgs 21:1), so the parental names too are clearly related.

Menahem appears among the names suggested for the messiah in
a discussion in the Yerushalmi that immediately precedes the story
of the baby messiah as well as in a similar discussion in the Bavli (b.
San. 98b), which is, however, independent of the one in the
Yerushalmi. The name can hardly be intended to call to mind the
only biblical figure to bear it, a wicked king of Israel (2 Kgs 15:13–
22). Rather, the meaning of the name, comforter, makes it appropriate for the messiah. The Bavli's citation of Lamentations 1:16 as
an argument in favor of the name serves to emphasize the meaning,
even as it insists on the messiah's absence: "For far from me is a
comforter (*menaḥem*) to revive my spirit."

The discussion in the Yerushalmi does not give a name for
Menahem's father, but the discussion in the Bavli refers to Menahem
as son of Hezekiah just as the story of the disappearing baby messiah in the Yerushalmi does. The biblical Hezekiah was one of the
very few kings of Judah to gain the approval of the book of Kings (2
Kgs 18:1–8); as a king of Judah, he was, of course, a descendant of
David. King Hezekiah himself figured in Jewish messianic speculation, although perhaps only to counter the Christian messianic
reading of the birth of a royal child prophesied by Isaiah of Jerusalem
(Isa 7:10–17, 9:5–6). In context, the prophecies point to the birth of
Hezekiah, whose father, Ahaz, was king at the time.[41] According to
a tradition in the Bavli that appears to go back to third-century
Palestine, God had intended to make Hezekiah the messiah but was
diverted from his plan by the Attribute of Justice's complaint that
Hezekiah had neglected to offer praise to God in thanksgiving for

the miracles wrought on his behalf (b. San. 94a).[42] An unattributed tradition on the same page of the Bavli applies the names of Isaiah 9:5 for the royal child ("Wonderful counselor . . .") to Hezekiah but defuses a messianic reading by making them an indicator of Hezekiah's role in the defeat of Sennacherib, thus placing their actualization in the era of the historical Hezekiah, by then long past.

The tradition about Hezekiah as potential messiah may help to explain the choice of Hezekiah rather than, for example, Josiah, an even more pious descendant of David according to the book of Kings (2 Kgs 23:25), for the messiah's father. For if Hezekiah had almost become the messiah himself, surely he would make an appropriate father for the actual messiah. It is also worth noting that Menahem shares the first two letters of his name with the name of the son who succeeded Hezekiah, judged by the book of Kings to be the worst king ever (2 Kgs 21:1–18, 23:26): Manasseh. Making Hezekiah the father of a messiah named Menahem might have seemed an appropriate way to compensate him for the wickedness of Manasseh.

As already noted, a further link between the messiah and Hezekiah appears in the name Sefer Zerubbabel gives to the mother of the messiah: Hephzibah. To be sure, Hephzibah, "my delight is in her," is a name rich in symbolism; as we have seen, the book of Isaiah applies it to Jerusalem (Isa 62:4), understood as the embodiment of Israel. But given the prominence in rabbinic tradition of the name Hezekiah for the father of a messiah named Menahem, it seems likely that the name Hephzibah for the messiah's mother is somehow connected to Hezekiah, even though Sefer Zerubbabel calls Menahem's father Ammiel.[43] Taken together, then, the discussions of the name of the messiah in the Yerushalmi and the Bavli, the Yerushalmi story about the disappearing baby messiah, and Sefer Zerubbabel attest a tradition that the name of the messiah was Menahem and the name of his father, Hezekiah. Furthermore, although the name Hephzibah for the messiah's mother appears only in Sefer Zerubbabel and in texts dependent on it, it is quite plausible that the tradition in question included that name. At the very least, it could be said to imply it. Since anyone with knowledge of the Bible and, for the name Menahem, an understanding of

Hebrew might have found these names particularly suitable for the messiah and his parents, the tradition need not have originated among the rabbis.

The name Ammiel for the messiah's father is, to my knowledge, nowhere attested in that role apart from *Sefer Zerubbabel* and works indebted to it. Its significance is by no means obvious. The Bible contains several minor figures named Ammiel: the spy from the tribe of Dan (Num 13:12), the father of one of David's followers (2 Sam 9:4–5, 17:27), and a Levite gatekeeper (1 Chr 26:5). The most promising for our purposes is Ammiel the father of Bathshua, a wife of David according to the book of Chronicles (1 Chr 3:5). Bathshua is clearly to be identified with Bathsheba of Samuel and Kings since she is listed in Chronicles as the mother of Solomon, Bathsheba's most important son; the name of Bathsheba's father is Eliam (2 Sam 11:3), of which Ammiel is an anagram. Yet despite his connection to David, Ammiel is not an ideal father for the messiah since he cannot provide him with Davidic descent.

To further complicate matters, while *Sefer Zerubbabel* repeatedly calls Menahem the son of Ammiel, it also refers to Hephzibah as the wife of Nathan. Most of the witnesses—in this case not only the *Sefer Hazikhronot* manuscript and the two other Bodleian manuscripts but also MS JTS 2325/20—identify the Nathan in question as Nathan the prophet, who plays a central role in the biblical narrative of David's life, bringing word of God's covenant to David (2 Sam 7), chastising him for his adultery with Bathsheba and murder of her husband (2 Sam 12), and, at the end of David's life, securing the succession for Bathsheba's son, Solomon (1 Kgs 1).[44] The first edition, on the other hand, refers to Hephzibah's husband as "Nathan son of David, the prophet" and simply "Nathan son of David."[45] This Nathan is known to us only from lists of David's sons (2 Sam 5:14, 1 Chr 3:5); he plays no role in the narrative.

It is of course quite possible for the father of a child to be a different person from the mother's husband, but the identification of Menahem's father as Ammiel and Hephzibah's husband as Nathan does seem to call for some explanation.[46] The failure of *Sefer Zerubbabel* to provide one may suggest that it understands the two pieces of information as somehow compatible, and the list in

Chronicles in which Nathan son of David makes one of his two appearances in the Hebrew Bible may provide a clue to its thinking. While the list in Samuel is silent on the name of Nathan's mother, the list in Chronicles designates him a son of Bathshua b. Ammiel. If David's son Nathan were his father, Menahem would be the grandson of Ammiel.[47]

But this solution suffers from the fact that only the first edition of *Sefer Zerubbabel* refers to Hephzibah's husband as Nathan the son of David. Still, even the first edition identifies Nathan the son of David with his much better known contemporary the prophet in one of its two references to him, and it is possible that the *Sefer Hazikhronot* manuscript and other witnesses assume that the two Nathans are one and the same although the role of Nathan in the biblical narrative makes such an identification chronologically impossible. There is some evidence that David's son Nathan was the object of more attention in the later Second Temple period than one might have predicted on the basis of the biblical references since the gospel of Luke traces Jesus's descent from David by way of Nathan rather than of Solomon (Luke 3:31); it is also worth noting that Luke's genealogy includes Zerubbabel (Lk 3:27).[48]

Descent from David via Nathan has the advantage of bypassing the disappointing royal line that passes through Solomon, the line to which Hezekiah belonged, in favor of a different path to Davidic descent.[49] Of course, the same avoidance of the royal line could be achieved by taking another son of David as father or ancestor. But Nathan son of David might have been a particularly appealing choice either because he was already identified with the prophet or because the coincidence of names made it relatively easy to provide this obscure son of David with prophetic credentials. *Sefer Zerubbabel* is the first Jewish text to explicitly identify the two Nathans, but the identification appears earlier in discussions of Jesus's genealogy in Julius Africanus's *Letter to Aristides* from the third century and Eusebius's *Gospel Problems and Solutions* in the fourth century, where it is part of a discussion of Jewish views of the ancestry of the messiah.[50] Thus it is possible that *Sefer Zerubbabel* is drawing on earlier Jewish tradition when it calls Hephzibah's husband "Nathan son of David, the prophet."

But even if we are satisfied that *Sefer Zerubbabel* knew traditions that made the messiah a descendant of Nathan the son of David and identified this Nathan with Nathan the prophet, we still have to explain why it consistently refers to the Davidic messiah as son of Ammiel. Richard Bauckham suggests that it is precisely the obscurity of the name Ammiel that makes it attractive to *Sefer Zerubbabel*, which depicts its messiah living incognito in Rome.[51] I would offer a different suggestion as a partial solution to the problem, although I would emphasize that it does not fully resolve it. Ammiel means something like "people of God." *Sefer Zerubbabel* thus provides both parents of the Davidic messiah with names that embody the people of Israel. Furthermore, Menahem son of Ammiel, Comforter son of People-of-God, is surely an appropriate name for the messiah, just as is the name *Sefer Zerubbabel* gives the messiah descended from Joseph, Nehemiah son of Hushiel, God-comforts son of God-hastens.

### Hephzibah in "'*Oto Hayom*"

The only ancient Jewish work I know other than *Sefer Zerubbabel* in which Hephzibah makes an appearance is the piyyut "'*Oto hayom*," "That Very Day."[52] The piyyut consists of two sections with significant differences in locale and cast of characters. The first section describes a series of wars, including one between Edomites and Ishmaelites in the land of Israel (line 22), and culminates in the coming of the Davidic messiah and the judgment of the wicked (lines 28–31); the picture of the wars between Edom and Ishmael as a prelude to the coming of the messiah suggests a date shortly after the rise of Islam, a date compatible with the style of the piyyut.[53] The second section begins with what appears to be an allusion to *Sefer Zerubbabel*: "And the vision (*ḥizzayon*) of the son of Shealtiel shall come to pass" (line 32). In both the Bible and *Sefer Zerubbabel*, Zerubbabel is the son of Shealtiel. The term for vision, *ḥizzayon*, is biblical, a less common variant of *ḥazon*, the term that introduces the prophecies of Isaiah, Obadiah, and Nahum in the books that bear their names. It is difficult to know how much weight to put on a single word, but the use of "vision" to refer to *Sefer Zerubbabel* fits well with *Sefer Zerubbabel*'s effort to present itself as prophecy.

The piyyut then turns back to the time just before the triumph of the Davidic messiah and offers a more detailed account of that period than it does in the first section, an account that appears to be modeled on the eschatological scenario of *Sefer Zerubbabel*. In "*'Oto hayom*," as in *Sefer Zerubbabel*, Hephzibah is the first of the eschatological heroes to arrive. As in *Sefer Zerubbabel*, her mission is associated with a staff of salvation that belonged to a series of patriarchs and is preserved in a city of Naphtali in the Galilee (lines 34–35, 39–43),[54] and, as in *Sefer Zerubbabel*, she slays two enemy kings (line 36).[55] But, as Sivertsev has shown, "*'Oto hayom*" also introduces an idea unknown in *Sefer Zerubbabel*, the idea that Hephzibah herself is the staff of salvation:

> And He will give the staff of Israel's salvation,
> In the city of Naphtali in Kadesh in Galilee, He gives the staff of God.
> And Hephzibah will come before God,
> And she will kill two kings with the word of God,
> In order to awaken in her Menahem son of Ammiel.
> God gave from of old
> To Adam, Methuselah, with whom God made peace,
> Noah, Abraham, Isaac, Israel,
> Judah, Moses, Aaron, the holy one of God.
> And she [is the one] who blossomed by the word of God.[56]
>     (lines 34–43)

*Maṭṭeh*, staff, is masculine in Hebrew; the feminine verb for the blossoming and the feminine pronoun for its subject make the identification with Hephzibah unavoidable. Sivertsev argues that the passage just quoted should be read against the background of contemporary Byzantine identification of the Virgin with Aaron's blossoming staff (Num 17:23 [17:8]), in which the blossoming alludes to the virgin birth. This background justifies the translation "to awaken in her" rather than "to awaken by her," which the Hebrew would also permit and which might otherwise seem more appropriate.[57]

With the appearance of Menahem b. Ammiel, however, there emerges a major disagreement between the piyyut and *Sefer Zerubbabel*: according to "*'Oto hayom*," Menahem b. Ammiel is the messiah son of Joseph, not the Davidic messiah (lines 46–50). Yet the piyyut continues along lines familiar from *Sefer Zerubbabel*. The messiah son of Joseph leads all Israel to Jerusalem, offers sacrifices, and registers the people by family unit (lines 51–53); Harmilios, as the great eschatological enemy is called here, appears and kills him; and finally, the messiah son of David arrives and brings the messiah son of Joseph back to life, causing the people of Israel to believe in him (lines 54–56).[58]

Sivertsev notes that the identification of Menahem b. Ammiel as messiah son of Joseph is not unique to "*'Oto hayom*"—it is found also in the eighth- or ninth-century narrative midrash Pirqe Rabbi Eliezer (chap. 19), where, however, Hephzibah does not appear— and suggests the possibility that this form of the tradition is earlier than the one in *Sefer Zerubbabel* and that Hephzibah was originally understood as the mother of this messiah rather than the messiah descended from David.[59] If so, *Sefer Zerubbabel* might have chosen to transfer the name Menahem b. Ammiel to the Davidic messiah to bring its story closer to the rabbinic traditions that named the Davidic messiah Menahem. It would then have assigned the mother originally associated with the messiah descended from Joseph to the messiah son of David. In support of this possibility Sivertsev points out that *Sefer Zerubbabel* shows Hephzibah fighting alongside the messiah son of Joseph rather than her own son, perhaps a remnant of a tradition that originally identified her as the mother of the messiah son of Joseph.[60] Furthermore, Sivertsev argues that although "*'Oto hayom*" as a whole must postdate the rise of Islam, if the two sections of the piyyut were originally separate works, a date based on the content of the first section need not apply to the second section, making it possible that the second section is earlier than *Sefer Zerubbabel*; such a date would strengthen an argument for the priority of Meneahem b. Ammiel as messiah son of Joseph.[61] Sivertsev does not insist too hard on this understanding, preferring not to decide among the possibilities: two independent traditions about Menahem b. Ammiel or dependence of one text on the other, in either direction.[62]

In my opinion, the piyyut's allusion to the "vision of the son of Shealtiel" is a strong indication of a debt to *Sefer Zerubbabel*. Sivertsev never addresses the significance of the allusion directly, but he could argue that it refers not to *Sefer Zerubbabel* as we have it but to traditions associated with Zerubbabel, which could of course differ somewhat from those preserved in the text that has come down to us.[63] But taken together with the impressive parallels to *Sefer Zerubbabel*, the mention of the vision of the son of Shealtiel seems to me good reason for concluding that " *'Oto hayom*" drew on *Sefer Zerubbabel*.[64] The silence of the second section of the piyyut on the wars between Byzantium and the Arab armies might then reflect the contents of *Sefer Zerubbabel*, which was composed before the rise of Islam, rather than pre-Islamic provenance. Furthermore, as already discussed, the name Menahem b. Ammiel points to Davidic ancestry for the messiah who bears it as does the name Hephzibah for his mother. If so, it is " *'Oto hayom*"'s transformation of Menahem b. Ammiel into the messiah son of Joseph that requires explanation. I would view it as an effort to improve on *Sefer Zerubbabel*'s somewhat puzzling depiction of Hephzibah's association with the messiah son of Joseph as closer than that with her own son.[65] There is nothing in Pirqe Rabbi Eliezer that requires knowledge of *Sefer Zerubbabel*, but given *Sefer Zerubbabel*'s impact on apocalyptic speculation in the centuries following its composition (see Chapter 6), it is possible that Pirqe Rabbi Eliezer knew a tradition that attempted to improve on *Sefer Zerubbabel* just as " *'Oto hayom*" did. It is also worth noting that neither " *'Oto hayom*" nor Pirqe Rabbi Eliezer provides a name for the messiah descended from David.

Finally, I would also note that " *'Oto hayom*"'s identification of Hephzibah with the blossoming staff is a bit anticlimactic if she is the mother not of the ultimate messiah but only of his predecessor; such an identification seems more appropriate for the mother of the Davidic messiah. Perhaps here too " *'Oto hayom*" adapted a tradition originally focused on the mother of the Davidic messiah.

### The Beautiful Statue and Its Son

*Sefer Zerubbabel* contains another female figure in addition to Hephzibah: the marble statue of a virgin found in a "house of disgrace and merrymaking" in Rome, presumably a church.[66] While *Sefer Zerubbabel* never mentions Hephzibah's physical appearance, it emphasizes the beauty of the statue.[67] The statue is the wife of Satan, and it bears him a son named Armilos, whom we have already encountered as the last and greatest of Israel's enemies; as his ancestry and role indicate, he is at once the Christian messiah and the equivalent of the Christian antichrist. His name is probably derived from Romulus, the founder of Rome;[68] he is thus also the personification of the Roman Empire, the last oppressive empire, or so Jews hoped. The name does not appear to be *Sefer Zerubbabel*'s invention since variations on the name appear in the roughly contemporary *Sefer Eliyyahu*.[69]

In a previous publication, I suggested that the beautiful statue represents *Sefer Zerubbabel*'s response to the "sculptural environment" in which it was written.[70] But I have come to realize that this suggestion is mistaken. Byzantine church art depicted the Virgin, Christ, and the saints in mosaic and relief but not in sculpture in the round.[71] Sivertsev is thus correct to call attention to the anomalous character of *Sefer Zerubbabel*'s statue in a Byzantine context, but his claim that *Sefer Zerubbabel*'s depiction of the statue plays on contemporary Byzantine anxiety about statues from the pagan past that could still be seen in cities throughout the Byzantine Empire seems to me problematic.[72]

It may well be true that as actual pagan worship disappeared Christians came to see the surviving statues as endowed with dark powers. But if the difficulty these statues posed for Christians in the seventh century was their ambiguous status as decommissioned idols, there is nothing ambiguous about the status of the beautiful marble statue in *Sefer Zerubbabel*. It is an idol, plain and simple, as is quite clear from the fact that at one point Armilos makes all nations worship it.[73] The first edition makes the equation explicit. When Zerubbabel first sees the statue, the angel tells him: "It will be the chief (*rosh*) of all idolatry."[74] The depiction of the statue in *Sefer Zerubbabel*, then, is not a subtle manipulation of Byzantine anxieties about once-pagan statues but an assertion of the continuity of Christianity and idolatry, whether in ignorance of Byzantine church decoration or in defiance of it.

Nor am I persuaded by Sivertsev's reading of the story of the birth of Armilos as "the mystery of a beautiful ancient statue that gets bewitched by an evil spirit and spells out the doom of the empire as a result," a story "built around the standard *topoi* of contemporaneous Byzantine literature."[75] Sivertsev's only example of a Byzantine account of demonic possession of a statue comes from the early seventh-century historian Theophylact Simocatta, who reports that statues in Alexandria announced the assassination of the Emperor Phocas days before word of the murder reached the city (*History* 8.13.7–14).[76] *Sefer Zerubbabel*'s statue, on the other hand, never utters a word. Nor does *Sefer Zerubbabel* in any way suggest that the birth of Armilos involves bewitching or demonic possession. Indeed, it is quite explicit about how Armilos is conceived: Satan "lies with" the statue, a standard biblical term for sexual relations.[77]

Indeed, Sivertsev's attempt to place the story of the birth of Armilos in a distinctively Byzantine context seems to me to miss the point of the story, which is surely intended as a parody of the narrative of the virgin birth: the mother of the antichrist is a statue of the Virgin, but its child is conceived through sexual relations, and the father of the child is not God but Satan. Perhaps no further explanation for *Sefer Zerubbabel*'s story is necessary. But it may be significant that the Greeks and Romans told stories of men who engaged in sexual relations with statues. One such story was the tale of Pygmalion, who fell in love with a statue of his own making that later comes to life and bears him a son. Another, which lacks the happy ending, tells of a man so overcome by the beauty of the famous statue of Aphrodite in Knidos that he attempted to have sexual relations with it and then committed suicide. Both stories are attested as early as the first century of this era.[78] For Clement of Alexandria, these stories demonstrate the folly of idolatry.[79] But for Jews who understood Christians as idolaters, they might have made it easier to imagine Satan engaging in sexual relations with the beautiful statue. Altogether, it seems to me that they constitute a more compelling context for *Sefer Zerubbabel*'s narrative than Byzantine anxiety about ancient statues.

Sivertsev has made an important contribution to the study of *Sefer Zerubbabel* by improving our understanding of how the figure of Hephzibah responds to contemporary Byzantine ideas about the Virgin. But the sophisticated critique of Byzantine imperial ideology that he finds in *Sefer Zerubbabel*'s story of the statue and Armilos seems to me more his invention than *Sefer Zerubbabel*'s. We know from the story in the Yerushalmi that *Sefer Zerubbabel* inherited the figure of the mother of the messiah from earlier Jewish tradition, even if it dramatically reshaped the figure in response to contemporary culture. We have no evidence for the beautiful statue in Jewish texts that predate *Sefer Zerubbabel*. If Sivertsev's reading is correct, the statue might well be *Sefer Zerubbabel*'s own invention since it reflects ideas current among Christians in the seventh century; at the very least, it would have undergone a significant reworking in light of seventh-century concerns, just as the figure of Hephzibah has. It seems to me, however, that *Sefer Zerubbabel*'s depiction of the statue points in a different direction. I suspect that, as with the mother of the messiah, *Sefer Zerubbabel* inherited the statue from earlier Jewish tradition, but for the statue, in contrast to Hephzibah, I see little evidence of a seventh-century makeover.

Jews in the Byzantine Empire lived among Christians who revered the mother of their messiah. I have argued that some Jews told stories involving a mother of the messiah of their own because they found such a figure extremely attractive and that *Sefer Zerubbabel* was heir to the resulting traditions. These likely included the name Hephzibah, which fits well with traditions attested in rabbinic literature that give the name Hezekiah to the father of Menahem, but less well with *Sefer Zerubbabel*'s Ammiel, and the birth of the messiah in the distant past, as the names Hezekiah and Hephzibah imply, as well as the subsequent concealment of the messiah to await the moment at which his mission could be fulfilled.

But it is also clear that *Sefer Zerubbabel* developed the figure of the mother of the messiah in new ways. If I am correct that the

Yerushalmi's story of the disappearing baby messiah pokes fun at a popular story, the mother of the original story was surely a more tender-hearted maternal figure than Menahem's mother in the Yerushalmi. Yet while Hephzibah is presented in unambiguously positive terms in *Sefer Zerubbabel*, she is very far from maternal in her behavior. Rather, she is a successful warrior who defends the holy city from its enemies. This role for the mother of the messiah must be *Sefer Zerubbabel*'s own contribution to her image, a response to an understanding of the role of the Virgin that, as far as we can tell, does not emerge until the early seventh century.

I also argued that the attraction exercised by the figure of the mother of the messiah caused considerable anxiety among the rabbis, who poked fun at a popular story about the messiah's birth by turning it into a story about the messiah's disappearance.[80] But that anxiety can also be seen in *Sefer Zerubbabel*, which provides a negative mother figure alongside the positive one: the beautiful marble statue of a virgin is the mother of their greatest enemy. Hephzibah's disappearance from the scene before the conclusion of *Sefer Zerubbabel*'s eschatological scenario is perhaps further indication of a certain ambivalence toward the idea of a mother for the messiah.

As we shall see, the two-messiah schema of *Sefer Zerubbabel* has a profound impact on later Jewish messianism, and the figure of Armilos also plays an important role in later Jewish apocalyptic literature, often together with his mother the stone statue. But the figure of Hephzibah all but disappears from Jewish literature. In Chapter 6, I consider whether this disappearance is a reflection of the anxiety just noted or rather a loss of interest among Jews living under Muslim rule on whom the Virgin Mary no longer exercised so powerful an attraction.

# CHAPTER THREE

# The Messiah Son of David and the Suffering Servant

MENAHEM B. AMMIEL, the son of Hephzibah and descendant of David, is not *Sefer Zerubbabel*'s only messiah or eschatological hero, but he is clearly the dominant one. It is he who inaugurates the eschatological showdown with the forces of evil, and it is he who slays Armilos, the leader of the eschatological enemies. But while descent from David and military accomplishments are to be expected of a messiah, *Sefer Zerubbabel*'s picture of Menahem draws extensively on a perhaps more surprising source, the description of the suffering servant of the Lord in the book of Isaiah. Suffering is of course central to the Christian understanding of Jesus's career, and this chapter and the next show that the idea of a messiah modeled on the suffering servant was attractive to many ancient Jews as well. This chapter discusses *Sefer Zerubbabel*'s account of the career of Menahem with particular attention to the impact of the fourth servant poem, Isaiah 52:13–53:12 (henceforth, Isaiah 53). I begin by considering the limited evidence for a messianic interpretation of the servant of Isaiah 53 in texts of the Second Temple era in relation to the place of such an interpretation in early Christian literature. Next I turn to the story from the Bavli in which the third-century amora Joshua b. Levi meets the messiah sitting among the poor and diseased at the gates of Rome, binding and unbinding his wounds (b. San. 98a). Finally, I discuss *Sefer Zerubbabel*'s use of Isaiah 53 for its description of Menahem b. Ammiel and the relationship between *Sefer Zerubbabel*'s picture and the picture of the Bavli story. Chapter 4 places *Sefer Zerubbabel* in relation to two other Jewish texts that, like *Sefer Zerubbabel*, come from the seventh century and understand the messiah in terms drawn from the suffering servant, the midrashic collection Pesiqta Rabbati and "*'Az milifnei vereishit*," a piyyut for the Day of Atonement by the great payyetan Eleazar be-rabbi Qillir, and a third, somewhat earlier, text, the remarkable interpretive translation of Isaiah 53 in Targum Jonathan, which eliminates any mention of suffering.

## The Suffering Servant in Second Temple and Early Christian Texts

The suffering "servant of the Lord" is the subject of four poems scattered through 2 Isaiah (Isa 40–55), the portion of the book of Isaiah scholars attribute to an anonymous prophet active among the exiles in Babylonia on the eve of its conquest by Cyrus of Persia in 539 BCE.[1] Readers ancient and modern have debated whether the servant is to be understood as the people of Israel, who are called "servant of the Lord" elsewhere in 2 Isaiah, or as an individual. Nor is there any agreement among those who favor identification with an individual about who that individual is. And, to further complicate matters, it is possible that the poems do indeed understand the servant as an individual but that they do not all agree on who that individual is.[2] Joseph Blenkinsopp suggests, for example, that the servant of the first poem is Cyrus, but that the prophet was soon disappointed in Cyrus, and, in the second and third poems, has come to understand himself as taking on the role he had attributed to Cyrus; the fourth poem, which reflects on the servant's death, is the work of one of the prophet's disciples.[3] Fortunately, for our purposes here we need not resolve the question of the intentions of the poems' author or authors. What is important for us is how ancient readers, Jewish and Christian, read the poems.

The fourth servant poem has several distinctive themes. One is its claim for the redemptive value of the suffering, culminating in death, that the servant endures for Israel's sins. This passage stands virtually alone in the Hebrew Bible as an instance of vicarious suffering by a human being.[4] Another is the poem's expectation of some kind of post-mortem vindication for the servant. This vindication comes to be understood as resurrection or afterlife, but the poem was composed in the sixth century BCE, before the emergence of the beliefs about the afterlife characteristic of turn-of-the-era Judaism, so it seems likely that the poem's original meaning was something less concrete, perhaps that the servant's influence lived on after him.[5] The poem also emphasizes the failure of the servant's contemporaries to recognize his true stature, at least in part because of his unappealing appearance (Isa 52:14, 53:2–4, 8).

The features of Isaiah 53 just noted are central to the explicit identification of Jesus with the servant evident in ancient Christian literature as early as Justin's *Dialogue with Trypho* in the middle of the second century.[6] But there is considerable debate about how far back that identification goes. Suffering is a crucial element of the earliest accounts of Jesus's career, and some scholars are convinced that Isaiah 53 played a major role in shaping the understanding found in the letters of Paul, the gospels, and other early works included in the New Testament; indeed, some suggest that Jesus himself understood his career in those terms.[7] Other scholars, however, think that claims for the impact of Isaiah 53 on the New Testament are overstated.[8]

The more skeptical position about Isaiah 53 and the New Testament finds some support in the paucity of evidence for messianic interpretation of the passage among Jews in the Second Temple period. Martin Hengel's careful survey points to several texts that read the servant's fate in relation to the eschatological suffering of the righteous as a group as well as a couple of texts that describe an eschatological priest in terms drawn from Isaiah 53, but it notes only a single text that may imply a suffering Davidic messiah, the messianic figure most relevant for Christian beliefs about Jesus.[9]

The understanding of the servant as standing for the righteous collectively is attested in Daniel 11–12, the Wisdom of Solomon

1–5, and the Similitudes of Enoch (1 En 37–71). But only in Daniel is it possible, though not certain, that the deaths of the righteous are depicted as benefitting others: the deaths of the *maskilim*, the wise, purify (Dan 11:35), but the Hebrew leaves it uncertain whether it is only the wise who are purified or others as well.[10] These chapters of Daniel respond to the persecution of Antiochus IV, in which people suffered as a result of their piety, an experience that appears to have contributed to the growth among Jews of belief in reward and punishment after death. 2 Maccabees, a somewhat later work responding to the Maccabean Revolt, attributes atoning value for the people as a whole to the suffering and death of the martyrs, though with no sign of the impact of Isaiah 53. It is certainly not implausible that Daniel understood the deaths of the wise in similar terms.[11]

Hengel identifies two texts that suggest an understanding of the servant as eschatological high priest. Both were found among the Dead Sea Scrolls, though neither is a sectarian work. One is 1QIsa[a], the "large" Isaiah Scroll from Qumran. The scroll is dated on paleographical grounds from the mid to late second century BCE. The version of the fourth servant song in this manuscript differs considerably from that of the MT and also from that of the other major witness to Isaiah at Qumran, 1QIsa[b].[12] According to Emmanuel Tov, the scribal characteristics of 1QIsa[a] mark it as a manuscript copied at Qumran.[13] At Isaiah 52:14, in place of MT's *mishhat*, a *hapax* usually translated "marred"—"His appearance was so marred, beyond human semblance"—1QIsa[a] reads *mashahti*, "I have anointed": "So have I anointed his appearance beyond that of any (other) man."[14] The reference to anointing has the advantage of making possible a new way of understanding the opening clause of Isaiah 52:15, "So shall he sprinkle many nations," a clause many translators have found so difficult that they prefer to follow the Greek and understand the verb as something like "astonish."[15] But if God has anointed the servant, the servant may well be a priest, and in that case, the sprinkling becomes comprehensible as an act of purification. Of course, from the point of view of the text-critical preference for the more difficult reading, what I have just described as an advantage might be seen as evidence against the originality of the reading. In this light, the reading *mashahti* looks like an attempt to make sense of both the difficult *mishhat* and the sprinkling.[16]

The second text to depict an eschatological high priest in terms drawn from Isaiah 53 is the Apocryphon of Levi (4Q541), a very fragmentary Aramaic text that shows points of contact with the Aramaic Levi Document and the Greek Testament of Levi. The manuscript dates from around 100 BCE.[17]

> And he will atone for all the children of his generation, and he will be sent to all the children of his [people]. His word is like the word of the heavens, and his teaching, according to the will of God. His eternal sun will shine . . . (frag. 9, col. 1, lines 2–3)[18]

The hero of the text is a not only a priest but also a teacher; yet, like the servant, he is a victim of persecution: "They will utter many words against him, and an abundance of [lie]s; they will fabricate fables against him, and utter every kind of disparagement against him" (frag. 9, col. 1, lines 5–6). The last fragment of the work, which is poorly preserved, begins with a prohibition of mourning (frag. 24, col. 2, line 2), and a few lines later, it promises someone: "You will see and rejoice in eternal light" (frag. 24, col. 2, line 6). Some scholars understand the difficult lines in between to refer to the crucifixion of the priest.[19] The work also contains significant verbal echoes of the book of Isaiah, particularly Isaiah 40–55, where the servant songs appear. The echoes include three participles from the root *k'v*, "pain" (frag. 2, col. 2, line 3; frag. 6, lines 1, 3), which figures so prominently in Isaiah 53:3–4; the use of a Hebrew root in the Aramaic Apocryphon makes it very likely that an allusion to Isaiah is intended.[20]

Hengel also raises the possibility that the speaker of the Self-Glorification Hymn from the Scrolls too could be understood as an eschatological high priest who fulfills the role of the servant, although without attention to suffering.[21] But as Hengel admits, other understandings are also plausible, and the links to Isaiah 53 are not as compelling as in 1QIsa[a] and the Apocryphon of Levi. But even if we leave the Self-Glorification Hymn out of the discussion, 1QIsa[a] and the Apocryphon of Levi demonstrate that some Jews

before the turn of the era looked forward to a high priest who would
fulfill the prophecies of Isaiah 53. Furthermore, despite the fact that
both texts were found among the Dead Sea Scrolls, there is nothing
to mark them or this expectation as sectarian.

The only possible instance of an understanding of the servant as
the Davidic messiah that Hengel can find is the Old Greek translation of Isaiah 53, which strengthens God's promise of reward for
the servant and emphasizes that the reward is still in the future.[22]
Hengel also notes some evidence that the translator identified the
servant with the ideal Davidic king of Isaiah 11, the royal child of
Isaiah 7:14–16 and 9:5, and the Davidic "branch" of Jeremiah 23:5
and Zechariah 3:8.[23] Yet Hengel goes on to suggest very tentatively
that the translator also identified the servant with a historical
figure—Onias III, the martyred high priest of the events leading up
to the Maccabean Revolt—who was undoubtedly anointed but
unmistakably not Davidic.[24] In any case, though Hengel's reading
of Greek Isaiah is suggestive, there is no evidence that its identification of the servant as a Davidic king—if indeed it made such an
identification—was taken up by others, whether in Egypt or
Palestine, until the Jesus movement.

Finally, it is worth noting that Hengel also finds evidence for
early Jewish identification of the servant with a messiah descended
from Joseph in a passage in the Testament of Benjamin (3:8).[25] Here
Jacob tells Joseph that the prophecy of the sacrifice of a blameless
man will be fulfilled in Joseph. The Greek version of the Testament
clearly identifies the figure with Christ, calling him "lamb of God"
and "savior of the world," who will bring salvation to both the
gentiles and Israel. The Armenian version, however, does not include
these obviously Christian elements, and Hengel takes it as reflecting
a pre-Christian Jewish tradition, noting also that the expectation of
a messiah descended from Joseph fits poorly with Jesus's Davidic
genealogy. To me, however, Marinus de Jonge's view of this passage
is more persuasive. De Jonge insists on text-critical grounds that the
Armenian cannot be understood as more original than the Greek.
Perhaps even more important, he argues that the fulfillment of the
prophecy "in" Joseph reflects an early Christian understanding of
Joseph as a type of Christ.[26]

There is some evidence, then, for a messianic interpretation of the servant of Isaiah 53 in Jewish texts of the Second Temple period, but such an interpretation can hardly be said to be widespread. Furthermore, the messiah with whom the servant is most clearly identified is a priestly messiah. The surviving material gives little reason to see the earliest uses of Isaiah 53 in relation to Jesus, such as Paul's formulation in Romans 4:24–25—"Jesus our Lord . . . was put to death for our trespasses and raised for our justification"—as reflecting a traditional Jewish understanding of the fate of the messiah.[27] Indeed, it is only after the idea of a suffering Davidic messiah is well established in Christian thought that clear evidence for such a messiah is found in Jewish texts, including not only *Sefer Zerubbabel* but several other texts and traditions from the middle of the third century CE to the beginning of the seventh century. It is to the earliest of these that I now turn.

### R. Joshua b. Levi and the Messiah

To judge by the date of the tradents rather than the work in which the tradition is preserved, the earliest post-Christian evidence for Jewish use of Isaiah 53 for the messiah is the story in b. San. 98a of an encounter between R. Joshua b. Levi and Elijah that leads to R. Joshua's meeting with the messiah.[28] R. Joshua was a first-generation Palestinian amora; the story is reported by R. Alexandrai, who likely belonged to the second generation of amoraim.[29] Thus the attributions suggest that the story is Palestinian and dates to the middle of the third century. There is little in the pre-Christian Jewish texts just surveyed to prepare us for the picture of the messiah in this story, and apparently the picture was not shared by all Jews since Origen, who lived in Caesarea in Palestine at the same time that R. Joshua was active, reports that a Jew with whom he debated the meaning of Isaiah 53 claimed that the servant should be identified with the Jewish people as a whole (*Cels.* 1.55), a position for which Hengel's survey provides some support.

The story in the Bavli runs as follows:[30] R. Joshua meets the prophet Elijah and proceeds to ask him two questions: will he,

R. Joshua, enjoy the life of the world to come, and when will the messiah come? Rather than answering the questions himself, Elijah directs R. Joshua to the messiah, who is to be found at the entrance to the city of Rome[31] among the poor and diseased as he awaits the call to undertake his mission; while all his companions unbind, object unspecified, all at once, and then rebind, the messiah unbinds and rebinds, object again unspecified, one at a time so as to be ready at any moment for his call. When R. Joshua meets the messiah, however, he asks only one question: When will the messiah come? The answer he receives—"Today"—is clearly false, as R. Joshua soon complains to Elijah. But Elijah explains that R. Joshua has misunderstood the messiah's words (or rather, word). What the messiah meant was, "Today, if you hearken to his voice" (Ps 95:7).[32] That is, the moment at which the messiah is to come is not predetermined, for it depends not on a divine decision but on the behavior of the Jewish people, a view implied in Elijah's explanation for the messiah's practice of binding and unbinding one by one rather than all at once. What is more, the messiah also answered the question R. Joshua did not ask, for by greeting R. Joshua as "son of Levi" he indicated that both R. Joshua and his father would inherit the life of the world to come. The story does not provide any information about the messiah's genealogy. Still, in a story of rabbinic provenance, a messiah should be understood as Davidic unless otherwise stated.

The story's debt to Isaiah 53 is evident not only in the messiah's lowly station but also in the language used to describe his companions, who "suffer illnesses," Aramaic words cognate with two key terms that appear in a single verse of Isaiah 53, though not side by side: "Surely he has borne our illnesses (*ḥolayenu*) and suffered (*sevalam*) our pains; yet we thought him afflicted, struck by God, and tormented" (Isa 53:4).[33] Since the messiah, like the poor, binds and unbinds, the story implies that he too suffers illnesses. The story does not clarify why the poor and the messiah need to bind and unbind, but the activities probably reflect an understanding of the term "afflicted" (*nagu'a*) in the description of the servant just quoted as suffering from skin afflictions since the root *ng'* is used of skin afflictions throughout Leviticus 13–14. In keeping with this

understanding, the New Jewish Publication Society (NJPS) translation makes the interesting suggestion that the description of the
servant as "like one who hides his face from us" (Isa 53:3) alludes
to the Torah's requirement that a person with skin afflictions warn
away passersby (Lev 13:46).[34] The fact that skin afflictions are
notable for their impact on appearance fits well with Isaiah 53's
emphasis on the servant's repulsive appearance: "So marred was his
appearance, unlike that of man, / His form, beyond human semblance . . ." (Isa 52:14, NJPS); "He had no form or beauty, that we
should look at him: / No charm, that we should find him pleasing"
(Isa 53:2, NJPS).

Scholars debate whether the servant poem intends to mark its
hero as suffering from skin afflictions,[35] but the story of R. Joshua
b. Levi is not the only evidence for ancient readers who drew that
conclusion. The Vulgate, which translates *nagu'a* of Isaiah 53:4 as
*leprosum*, clearly made the association. More relevant for our purposes is the tradition that the messiah will be called "the leper of the
house of Rabbi," which appears in the course of a discussion of the
name of the messiah (b. San. 98b) in the same collection of eschatological traditions in which the story of R. Joshua b. Levi appears.
The tradition is in Aramaic, and the word for leper, *ḥivvara*, from
the root "white," is not related to *nagu'a*; nonetheless, the tradition
cites Isaiah 53:4 in support of the name. The passage as a whole is
difficult to date. Several of the suggestions for the name of the messiah are attributed, but the attributions appear to be intended for
comic affect. Thus, the house of R. Shela claims the messiah's name
is Shilo, the house of R. Yannai claims that it is Yinnon, and the
house of R. Hanina claims that it is Hanina. There is no obvious
comic element to the tradition about the name "leper," however; it
is attributed to "the rabbis," and the family of Rabbi, R. Judah the
Patriarch, claimed Davidic descent.

A variant of the tradition naming the messiah "leper" is preserved
in Raymundo Martini's *Pugio Fidei*. There "the house of Rabbi"
says the messiah's name will be *ḥulya'*, Aramaic for sickness, and
then cites Isaiah 53:4, in which, as we have seen, the Hebrew cognate of that word appears: "He has borne our sicknesses (*ḥolayenu*)."
Some scholars prefer the reading of the *Pugio Fidei*, arguing that

the name it supplies is a better fit for the verse from Isaiah.[36] So too the "house of Rabbi" makes more sense as the source of the saying, parallel to the other rabbinical houses to which names of the messiah are attributed, than as the origin of the afflicted messiah.[37] Or perhaps, as Abraham Epstein suggested long ago, the passage in the Bavli conflates two different traditions, one naming the messiah "leper," the other, "sickness," each with an appropriate proof text.[38] For the story of R. Joshua's encounter with the messiah, however, it does not really matter whether the messiah is to be understood as suffering from skin afflictions or from some other condition that requires bandages. The important point is the gap between his true status and the way he appears to onlookers. It is just such a gap that Isaiah 53 laments: "He was despised, shunned by men. . . . He was despised, we held him of no account" (Isa 53:3, NJPS).

The location in which R. Joshua finds the messiah also deserves some emphasis. The redeemer of Israel from the yoke of the evil empire awaits his mission at the heart of that empire. But equally worthy of note, this story, like the birth story discussed in the previous chapter, assumes that the messiah's birth has taken place long before the arrival of the eschaton.

In Chapter 2, I argued that the Yerushalmi's version of the story of the disappearing baby messiah represents a rabbinic criticism of popular tradition. Despite its apparently more positive tone, the story of R. Joshua also appears to reflect rabbinic discomfort with a tradition too enthusiastic about messianic possibilities for the rabbis' taste since it concludes by undercutting the messianic hope implicit in the tradition it reports: the messiah may already be waiting in Rome for the call to undertake his eschatological mission, but the call will not come until Israel obeys God's commands.[39]

## Justin, Clement, and Origen on Christ's Physical Appearance

As discussed earlier, there is little in the literature of the Second Temple period to prepare us for the suffering messiah of the story of R. Joshua, and there is certainly no precedent in that literature for the story's emphasis on the messiah's humble appearance. No Christian text I know suggests that the messiah suffered from skin afflictions—one could hardly do so since the Gospels do not make any mention of such a condition—but, in contrast to the Jewish texts of the Second Temple period, several Christian texts of the first three centuries are concerned with the implications of Isaiah 53 for Jesus's appearance. Thus, according to Justin, when Jesus went to the Jordan to be baptized by John:

> He appeared without comeliness, as the Scriptures declared; and He was deemed a carpenter (for He was in the habit of working as a carpenter when among men, making ploughs and yokes; by which He taught the symbols of righteousness and an active life). (*Dial.* 88)[40]

Justin justifies Jesus's low-status profession by explaining its significance, but the absence of "comeliness" requires no justification since it was predicted by "the Scriptures," which must mean Isaiah 53. For Justin, then, the messiah's unprepossessing appearance is a given that does not require discussion. So too, toward the end of the second century, Clement of Alexandria cites Isaiah 53:2 as evidence that Christ's appearance was ugly, "Yet who is better than the Lord?" (*Paed.* 3.1.3).[41] Rather, Christ's lack of "beauty of the flesh" demonstrates that the true beauty of the soul is good deeds while the true beauty of the body is immortality.

But if Christians were comfortable with the idea that Jesus's appearance left something to be desired, outsiders apparently used this picture against them. According to Origen, Celsus claimed that Jesus's physical shortcomings called into question his claim to divinity:

> It is impossible that a body which had something more divine than the rest should be no different from any other. Yet Jesus' body was no different from any other, but, as they say, was little and ugly and undistinguished. (*Cels.* 6.75)[42]

In his response to Celsus, Origen admits that Isaiah 53:1–3 depicts the messiah as ugly although he insists that there is no scriptural support for Celsus's claim that Jesus's body was little and undistinguished. Furthermore, if Celsus accepts the evidence of Isaiah 53, why, Origen asks, does he ignore Psalm 44 (Greek; Psalm 45 in the Hebrew), which refers to the beauty of the king (*Cels.* 6.75)? Indeed, the range of physical attributes attributed to the Lord's anointed in Hebrew Scripture points to a truth revealed in the account of the transfiguration in Matthew 17: Jesus's appearance reflects the capacity of those looking at him rather than the actual character of his body. Only his followers can see his true beauty; to others, he appears entirely lacking in beauty, as Isaiah prophesied. Finally, Origen concludes, the real import of the passages he has just considered has to do not with perception of Jesus's physical appearance but with apprehension of the divine Logos embodied in Jesus, of which only Christians can see the true divinity (*Cels.* 6.76–77).[43]

As already noted, Origen was a contemporary of R. Joshua and lived in Caesarea in Palestine. A considerable body of scholarship demonstrates points of contact between Palestinian rabbinic literature and the writings of Origen.[44] Origen's commentary on Isaiah is unfortunately lost so we do not know how he treated Isaiah 53 when he was not trying to rebut the arguments of a hostile pagan. But the picture of the messiah in the story of R. Joshua has more in common with the straightforward acceptance of Christ's lack of physical beauty in Justin and Clement of Alexandria than with Origen's Platonizing understanding of Christ's appearance in *Against Celsus,* despite the greater chronological and geographical distance between the teller of the R. Joshua story on the one hand and Justin and Clement on the other, which strengthens the impression that the similarities reflect independent efforts to work out morally elevating implications of a difficult but powerful prophecy.

### *Sefer Zerubbabel* and the Suffering Servant

Unlike the story about R. Joshua, *Sefer Zerubbabel* includes an account of the triumph of its Davidic messiah, yet its description of the messiah's appearance before his triumph clearly draws on traditions like those used by the story of R. Joshua. When Zerubbabel first lays eyes on Menahem, he perceives him as "a man despised, severely wounded, and in pain."[45] The word I have translated "despised" is *nivzeh*; its occurrence twice in a single verse (Isa 53:3) makes it a defining characteristic of the servant's appearance.[46] The significance of the passive participle is worth emphasizing: it expresses the perception of others rather than some inherent characteristic of the figure. The middle phrase in *Sefer Zerubbabel*'s description of Menahem, *petsu'a daka'*, which I have translated as "severely wounded," plays on the description of the servant as "crushed," *meduka'*, by our sins (Isa 53:5). But the phrase is drawn not from Isaiah 53 but from Deuteronomy: "He whose testicles are crushed (*petsu'a daka'*) or whose male member is cut off shall not enter the assembly of the Lord" (Deut 23:2).[47] The understanding of *petsu'a daka'* as referring to crushed testicles is supported by the parallel phrase, "[he] whose male member is cut off." By itself, however, *petsu'a daka'* means something like, "wounded by crushing";[48] it does not on its own refer to the male member,[49] and in the absence of any other indication, there is no reason to understand *Sefer Zerubbabel* as suggesting that the messiah is a eunuch. Rather, as my translation indicates, the phrase serves to emphasize the severity the messiah's wounds. Finally, I understand *makh'ov*, the third element of the description of the messiah in *Sefer Zerubbabel*, as in construct with "man" at the beginning of the description: "a man despised, severely wounded, and in pain." Thus I take it to echo the description of the servant as "a man of pains (*makho'vot*)" (Isa 53:3); in *Sefer Zerubbabel*, however, "pain," *makh'ov*, is in the singular.

Unlike R. Joshua, who had the benefit of Elijah's description, Zerubbabel had not been forewarned of the messiah's unsuitable appearance. Thus when the unprepossessing figure before him identifies himself as the messiah, Zerubbabel is left silent in astonishment. Menahem is at first enraged by Zerubbabel's inability to perceive his true stature, but he soon takes pity on his obviously terrified interlocutor, comforts him, and demonstrates that he is able to appear as a handsome young man.[50]

Later in *Sefer Zerubbabel*, the revealing angel tells Zerubbabel that when Menahem arrives in the valley of Arbel and announces his mission to the elders and sages who have survived the depredations of Gog and Armilos, he will receive a similar reception: they "will look at him and despise (*yavozu*) him" because they will see him as "a man despised (*nivzeh*) in worn-out clothes."[51] The debt to the language of Isaiah 53:3 cannot be missed, and just as Isaiah 53 describes the failure of the servant's contemporaries to perceive his true greatness, *Sefer Zerubbabel* depicts members of the Jewish community of the eschaton as incapable of recognizing the messiah when they first encounter him. But while in Isaiah 53 the people as a whole ("we") fail to recognize the greatness of the servant, in *Sefer Zerubbabel* the emphasis is on the failure of the Jewish elite, "the elders and sages" to whom Menahem announces his identity.

"Sages," *ḥakhamim*, is a favorite rabbinic self-designation and thus of particular interest for discerning *Sefer Zerubbabel*'s attitude toward the rabbinic elite of its own day. As just noted, the sages sometimes appear together with elders, but each group also appears separately. It is the sages who go out to meet Menahem; he addresses the announcement of his messianic mission to both groups; it is the elders alone who are said to despise him, although a marginal note in the *Sefer Hazikhronot* manuscript adds "and sages";[52] and, finally, it is the elders together with the rest of Israel who are said to believe in him when they see the resurrection of Nehemiah. The marginal note in particular suggests that "sages" and "elders" are used more or less interchangeably in the *Sefer Hazikhronot* manuscript.[53] Thus it seems reasonable to conclude that the object of *Sefer Zerubbabel*'s criticism is indeed the rabbinic elite. Yet the fact that *Sefer Zerubbabel* has already shown Zerubbabel himself failing to recognize the messiah softens the criticism. As we shall see in Chapter 4, Pesiqta Rabbati offers even stronger criticism of those who prefer Torah to God's kingdom in its homilies about the messiah Ephraim.

## *Sefer Zerubbabel* and the Story of R. Joshua

Like the story of R. Joshua in the Bavli, *Sefer Zerubbabel* describes a messiah of humble appearance stationed in Rome as he awaits the eschaton, and scholars have generally assumed that *Sefer Zerubbabel* here draws on the Bavli.[54] It is quite possible that the story of R. Joshua was known to the author or authors of *Sefer Zerubbabel*, although likely not as part of the Bavli, which might not yet have reached its final form and would probably not have been available in the Byzantine Empire in the early seventh century outside of very limited circles.[55] Still, the story, which presumably dates back to third-century Palestine, might have circulated orally among Jews in the Byzantine Empire. But while the story of R. Joshua and *Sefer Zerubbabel* both describe their messiah in terms drawn from Isaiah 53, they make use of different features of Isaiah's picture of the servant. The story of R. Joshua describes the messiah as suffering some kind of physical ailment, likely skin afflictions, while *Sefer Zerubbabel* emphasizes the response of others to the messiah's humble appearance through the use of the passive participle *nivzeh*. Furthermore, *Sefer Zerubbabel* does not contain the most memorable detail of the rabbinic story, the messiah's binding and unbinding. It is true that the Hebrew verb *Sefer Zerubbabel* uses to describe the messiah's imprisonment in Rome (*'sr*) is cognate with the Aramaic verb used by the story of R. Joshua for the binding performed by the messiah and his companions.[56] Yet since the texts make use of different aspects of the root's semantic range, it is probably coincidence that it appears in both.[57]

Thus, while *Sefer Zerubbabel* and the Bavli's story of R. Joshua clearly share an understanding of the messiah in terms of the suffering servant, it is more likely that they reflect independent developments of popular traditions that embraced such a picture than that *Sefer Zerubbabel* is indebted to the story in the Bavli. As already discussed, the Bavli story ends by insisting that the messiah's coming depends on Israel's obedience to God, hardly good news for those yearning for the new era. The subversion of what at first appears to be a much more hopeful message suggests that the story is not a rabbinic invention but a widely known tale that the rabbis adapted, or rather, undercut, for their own purposes. Centuries later *Sefer Zerubbabel* embraced a form of the story in which the messianic optimism was still evident.

## The Messiah in Rome

One notable connection between the story of R. Joshua in the Bavli and *Sefer Zerubbabel* is the location where the messiah awaits the eschaton: Rome, which for *Sefer Zerubbabel* meant Constantinople. Like the description of the messiah's appearance in terms drawn from Isaiah 53, I take this shared element not as an indication of the dependence of *Sefer Zerubbabel* on the story in the Bavli but rather as an indication of the content of a popular tradition that was their common source. But it is worth considering briefly Alexei Sivertsev's understanding of the messiah's presence in Rome in *Sefer Zerubbabel* as another instance of Jewish adaptation of Byzantine imperial ideology.

In Sivertsev's view, we should read Menahem's imprisonment in Rome in light of the Byzantine legend that Constantine took the palladium of Troy from Rome, where it had rested since the arrival of Aeneas, and brought it to Constantinople, where he placed it in the forum under a column that would bear his statue. The legend is part of a larger project of appropriating the greatness of the old Rome for the new Rome.[58] Sivertsev also notes the sixth-century Byzantine historian Procopius's attention to his hero Belisarius's return to Constantinople of treasures taken from Rome by the Vandals and Goths, including vessels of the Jerusalem Temple that had been brought to Rome after its destruction. These vessels, Procopius reports, were immediately sent on to churches in Jerusalem on the advice of a Jew who claimed that it was their presence in Rome that permitted the successful barbarian invasions. In Sivertsev's view, *Sefer Zerubbabel* plays on the idea of the transfer of Rome's treasures to Constantinople by depicting Menahem himself as a sort of palladium, the secret source of the power of the new Rome. But, like the presence of the temple vessels in the old Rome, his presence in the new Rome will ultimately prove its undoing.[59]

I do not believe, however, that Sivertsev's reading of Menahem as palladium can be sustained.[60] To begin with, the idea that the messiah awaits his mission in Rome goes back at least as early as the third century, as the story of R. Joshua demonstrates. It would certainly be possible to argue that *Sefer Zerubbabel* took this earlier tradition and transformed it in response to Byzantine ideas about the transfer of the treasure of Rome to Constantinople, but there is nothing in *Sefer Zerubbabel* to suggest a concern for the such treasure, not even temple spoils; after all, the Third Temple eventually descends from heaven, presumably fully equipped. I find more persuasive the suggestion of Ra'anan Boustan that *Sefer Zerubbabel*'s placement of the messiah in Rome should be read as an inversion of the Christian messianic scenario, in which the messiah's death in Jerusalem sets the new movement, led by the Holy Spirit, on a path to Rome.[61] Finally, while the idea that the messiah awaits the dawn of the eschaton in Rome is initially shocking, its logic is compelling. Until he is able to begin his mission of redemption, the messiah too is subject to the evil empire, but when ultimately he bursts forth from his imprisonment, Roman rule will be at an end.

### The Resurrection of Nehemiah

I return to *Sefer Zerubbabel* at the moment when the elders and sages fail to recognize Menahem as messiah. Again he burns with anger just as he did when Zerubbabel first met him, and again he modifies his appearance in response to his audience's skepticism about his identity, this time by trading his worn-out clothes for a garment of vengeance and a mantle of zeal.[62] But this time, as the eschatological drama is reaching its climax, what ultimately convinces the people of Israel to believe in Menahem is not his change of appearance but the resurrection of the messiah descended from Joseph, which he accomplishes together with Elijah the prophet:

> Then he will go to the gates of Jerusalem, and Elijah the prophet will be with him. They will awaken Nehemiah b. Hushiel and bring him back to life at the gates of Jerusalem. Then Hephzibah, the mother of the messiah, will come and hand over to him the staff by which the signs were performed. All Israel [and] the elders of Israel will go,

and the children of Israel will see that Nehemiah is alive and standing on his feet. They will believe at once in the messiah.[63]

Bringing the dead back to life is certainly an impressive miracle, and this alone is perhaps enough to explain the impact of the resurrection of Nehemiah b. Hushiel on the people of Israel, even if the fact that Menahem performs it together with Elijah, who already had a resurrection to his credit during his pre-ascent career (1 Kgs 17:17–24), detracts a little from Menahem's glory. But it is also striking that according to ps.-Ephrem's Sermon on the End, a Syriac work that reached its final form sometime shortly after the Muslim conquest, it is precisely the ability to bring the dead back to life that distinguishes the true Christ from the antichrist. The "Son of Destruction" who comes at the end of days will be able to perform a series of miracles in which nature obeys him and he effects wonderful cures, but he will not be able to resurrect the dead.[64] *Qissa-yi Daniyal*, a Judeo-Persian Danielic work likely from the ninth century, also makes a point of its false messiah's inability to resurrect the dead, though there are other signs he fails to perform as well.[65] To complicate matters, this false messiah is apparently the messiah descended from Joseph, for *Qissa-yi Daniyal* gives this messiah a role elsewhere reserved for the antichrist. The work would certainly reward further study.

The resurrection of the messiah descended from Joseph by the Davidic messiah appears in two seventh-century Jewish texts in addition to *Sefer Zerubbabel*, both piyyutim mentioned in previous chapters. In "*'Oto ha-yom*," "That Very Day," the piyyut in which Hephzibah is identified with the staff (see Chapter 2), the Davidic messiah's resurrection of his messianic predecessor serves to inspire the people to believe in him (lines 55–56) just as it does in *Sefer Zerubbabel*.[66] "*Ha'et lig'or*," "The Time to Rebuke," the piyyut that mentions the restoration of sacrifice under Persian rule (see Chapter 1), reports that the Davidic messiah brings the messiah who preceded him back to life (line 97) without commenting on the impact of the deed on bystanders.[67] While I argued earlier that "*'Oto ha-yom*" draws on *Sefer Zerubbabel*, it does not follow it at every point, and there is no evidence of a direct relationship between

*Sefer Zerubabbel* and *"Ha'et lig'or."* Thus the inclusion of the Davidic messiah's act of resurrection in the piyyutim suggests a more widely shared understanding of the significance of the messiah's ability to resurrect the dead among Jews in the seventh century. The Sermon on the End was composed shortly after the Muslim conquest, but it is not implausible that its view that the antichrist would be unable to resurrect the dead was already in circulation among Christians at the time *Sefer Zerubbabel* and the piyyutim were composed. It would certainly provide a compelling backdrop for *Sefer Zerubbabel*'s understanding of the ability to bring the dead back to life as the deed that ultimately persuades the skeptics of Menahem's true identity.

*Sefer Zerubbabel*'s depiction of Menahem b. Ammiel is deeply indebted to the suffering servant of Isaiah 53. While there is some evidence in texts of the Second Temple period for the use of elements of Isaiah 53 for a priestly messiah, the first clear instance of Jewish use of the poem for a Davidic messiah comes only after the association is well established in Christian texts, in the third-century story of R. Joshua b. Levi's encounter with the messiah at the gates of Rome. But a central focus of the use of Isaiah 53 in both the story of R. Joshua and *Sefer Zerubbabel* is the description of the messiah's body, a rather secondary concern of Christian texts. In my view, the two Jewish texts are best understood as independent developments of popular traditions about a suffering messiah. The insistence of the story of R. Joshua that the messiah's arrival depends on pious behavior presumably reflects a rabbinic effort to tamp down the expectations of those traditions; the more robust messianism of *Sefer Zerubbabel* is likely more in keeping with the original intent of the traditions.

# CHAPTER FOUR

# The Servant-Messiah beyond
## *Sefer Zerubbabel*

AS WE SAW in Chapter 3, Isaiah 53 is crucial to both the Bavli's story of R. Joshua b. Levi's encounter with the messiah and *Sefer Zerubbabel*'s picture of Menahem b. Ammiel, but neither of these texts takes up one of the most distinctive features of the poem: the idea that the servant's suffering is on behalf of others and effects atonement for them. The idea of vicarious suffering is, however, central to two texts roughly contemporary with *Sefer Zerubbabel* to be discussed in this chapter: "*'Az milifnei vereishit*," "Then, Before 'In the Beginning,'" a piyyut for the qedushah of the musaf service of Yom Kippur by the great Palestinian payyetan Eleazar be-rabbi Qillir, and Pesiqta Rabbati, a collection of homilies for the holidays and special Sabbaths of the year.[1] "*'Az milifnei vereishit*" uses the messiah's suffering to assure worshippers on the Day of Atonement that they will be forgiven by his efforts if not their own, while three interrelated homilies of Pesiqta Rabbati (34, 36, and 37) describe the messiah's suffering on behalf of the people of Israel in the service of their eschatological redemption. The two works appear to have come to their interest in vicarious suffering by different paths, but as we shall see, both are clearly aware of the significance of the idea for Christians.

The third text discussed in this chapter, Targum Jonathan, the semi-official Aramaic translation of the prophets, explicitly identifies the servant as the messiah in its rendition of Isaiah 53, but it denies that the servant suffers. I shall argue that its distinctive approach to the servant poem constitutes further evidence for widespread Jewish embrace of the identification of the servant with the Davidic messiah.

## " *'Az milifnei vereishit*"

" *'Az milifnei vereishit*" treats seven things created before the world, drawn from lists of such items found in rabbinic literature: the Torah, the throne of glory, the forefathers, Israel, the temple, the messiah, and repentance.[2] In keeping with its setting in the Yom Kippur liturgy, the piyyut uses each of the seven things to reassure the assembled worshippers that the possibility of atonement is built into the very structure of the universe.[3] The piyyut consists of four stanzas. Each of the first three treats two items from the list; the last stanza, appropriately for the Day of Atonement, is devoted entirely to repentance. The messiah appears in the third stanza, together with the temple.

Rabbinic lists of things created before the world generally include the name of the messiah rather than the messiah himself.[4] This fact helps to explain the piyyut's use of the name Yinnon for the messiah; the name derives from a playful misreading of Psalm 72:17, "Before the sun may his name increase (*yinnon*)," as "Before the sun [was created] Yinnon is his name," attributed, as we saw in Chapter 3, to the house of Yannai (b. San. 98b, Lam. Rab. 1:51), presumably with comic intent. Yet, according to the piyyut, not only the name but the messiah himself is already in existence. The piyyut does not claim that the messiah was created before the world, nor does it say exactly when he came into existence, but he is certainly alive before the unfolding of the eschatological drama, for he is described in language drawn from Isaiah 53's account of the suffering servant as already bearing the sins of Israel and suffering for his people:

Our sins and the yoke of our transgressions he carries, and "he is wounded by our transgressions" (Isa 53:5).

He bears on his shoulder our wrongdoings (see Isa 53:11–12), to find forgiveness for our sins.

There has been healing for us in his wound (see Isa 53:5). [Now] it is time to create him eternally as a new being. (lines 8–10)

But while the messiah of "*'Az milifnei vereishit*" already exists, he is not exactly present, as we learn in the line preceding those just quoted: "Our righteous messiah has turned from us (see Isa 53:3), we have been made to shudder, and there is no one to cause us to be found righteous (see Isa 53:11)" (line 7). The piyyut's language recalls Isaiah 53's description of the servant as being "like one who hides his face from us" (*kemaster panim mimenu*) (Isa 53:3), discussed in the previous chapter. The piyyut's *panah*, "turned," comes from the same root as Isaiah's *panim*, "face," while the piyyut's *menu*, "from us," is a poetic form of Isaiah's *mimenu*. Moses hides his face as he stands before the burning bush (Exod 3:6), but elsewhere in the Bible, only God hides his face, with the metaphor usually suggesting that God is potentially available even when he has turned away in anger.[5] It is also worth noting that the servant is not said to hide his face but only to be "*like* one who hides his face."[6] Thus the words "*'Az milifnei vereishit*" chooses to describe the messiah's turning away strengthen the picture that emerges from the description of the messiah's current suffering on Israel's behalf: the messiah is available even if not obviously present.

By the end of the stanza, we learn where the messiah has gone on turning away: "From the circle (of the earth) (Isa 40:23) raise him, from Se'ir draw him up" (line 11). Se'ir is the abode of Esau (Gen 36:8–9) and thus a way of indicating Rome since the rabbis understand Esau as the ancestor of the Romans. The choice of Se'ir rather than the more common Edom may reflect the piyyut's setting in the Yom Kippur liturgy. *Sa'ir*, one of the biblical words for goat, appears repeatedly in the description of the ritual for Yom Kippur in Leviticus 16 and is identical in its consonants to Se'ir.[7] Like the messiahs of the story of R. Joshua and *Sefer Zerubbabel*, the messiah of "*'Az milfinei vereishit*" is alive long before the end, and he awaits the eschaton in the same place they do.

But though the messiah of "*'Az milfinei vereishit*" has turned away to Rome, he continues to bear Israel's sins and to provide healing for his people through his wounds (lines 9–10). If he were truly absent, the piyyut tells us, the consequences for Israel would be devastating: without him "there is no one to cause us to be found righteous (*letsaddeqenu*)." The piyyut's debt to Isaiah 53:11— "... By his knowledge my servant ... shall cause many to be found righteous (*yatsdiq*)"—is evident.[8] The messiah's contribution to a favorable judgment is particularly relevant to the occasion of the piyyut's recitation on Yom Kippur.

The claim that only the messiah causes Israel to be found righteous stands in a certain tension with the appeal of the eleventh blessing of the daily Amidah: "You, Lord, alone reign over us with lovingkindness and mercy and cause us to be found righteous (*tsaddeqeinu*) in judgment." Here it is God himself who causes Israel to be found righteous, and, as the blessing emphasizes, only God. Some of the ancient Jews who recited this prayer would likely have been aware of the Christian claim that human beings are found righteous, or as it is usually translated in this context, justified, only through faith in Christ. These claims go back to the letters of Paul, the earliest surviving texts by a follower of Jesus.[9] Paul wrote in Greek, but the root *dikaio-* that figures so prominently in his letters is the standard equivalent for the Hebrew root *tsdq* in the Greek translation of the Hebrew Bible.[10] It is also significant that Paul's formulation in Romans of the principle of justification through Christ may indicate a debt to Isaiah 53: "Jesus our Lord ... was put to death for our trespasses and raised for our justification (*dikaiōsin*)" (Rom 4:24–25, RSV); "For as by one man's disobedience many were made sinners, so by one man's obedience many will be made righteous (*dikaioi*)" (Rom 5:19, RSV).[11]

What Paul attributes to Christ, "*'Az milifnei vereishit*" attributes to the Jewish messiah. The Amidah, on the other hand, attributes it to God. The earliest form of the Amidah, the central prayer of the Jewish liturgy, dates to the beginning of the rabbinic era or perhaps even to the late Second Temple period, but the versions that have come down to us are somewhat later. Thus it is possible that the wording of the blessing is at least in part a response to the Christian claim of justification in Christ.[12] Certainly both the Amidah and "*'Az milifnei vereishit*" become more pointed if they are read in light of the Christian claim.

It did not take long after Paul wrote for some Christians to become nervous about Paul's claim that faith in Christ by itself is sufficient for salvation, and subsequent writers offer different ways of balancing faith and works. Neither the Amidah nor "*'Az milifnei vereishit*" suggests any awareness of this debate. For them, the important point is the identity of the one who brings about the positive judgment: for the Amidah, God himself; for the piyyut, the Jewish messiah, a claim the piyyut probably understands as supplementing the Amidah's view rather than contradicting it. Indeed, on the Day of Atonement, an occasion marked by repeated listing of Israel's sins with God depicted as judge, the desire for help from another quarter is quite understandable. The Amidah refers to God's lovingkindness and mercy, but the piyyut goes beyond it by depicting the messiah as bearing Israel's sins in order to find forgiveness for the people.

Despite the impression of familiarity it produces, the phrase "our righteous messiah" and variants (e.g., "my righteous messiah," "your righteous messiah") is not common in rabbinic literature. David is called "your righteous messiah" in the qedushah for the morning service on Sabbaths and festivals, although here, in contrast to "*'Az milifnei vereishit*," "messiah" has the biblical sense of "anointed" without the eschatological component that develops later. The only rabbinic work to use the designation for the eschatological redeemer is Pesiqta Rabbati in its homilies about the suffering messiah.[13] It is not impossible that "*'Az milifnei vereishit*" and Pesiqta Rabbati were independently inspired by the liturgical use, which they then developed in the same way, but given the other similarities between the messiahs of the two works, some already noted and others to be discussed shortly, the shared expression may well indicate a common milieu. But it must be emphasized that as "*'Az milifnei vereishit*" uses "*meshiaḥ tsidqenu*," the designation points not to the messiah's righteousness but to his role in allowing Israel to be judged righteous; in this context, it might appropriately be translated "messiah of our justification."

### Suffering Messiahs and Dying Messiahs

Just as Isaiah 53 describes the servant's suffering as benefitting his contemporaries, "*'Az milifnei vereishit*" insists on the benefit Israel has derived from the messiah's suffering: "There has been healing for us in his wound" (line 10a). It follows this notice with a declaration that is really an exhortation: "It is time to create him forever as a new being (*beriyyah ḥadashah*)" (line 10b).[14] But what does it mean for the messiah to be created as a new being?

"*'Az milifnei vereishit*" was written for the Yom Kippur liturgy, and the phrase "new being" is elsewhere associated with the experience of the Days of Awe. A rabbinic tradition has God pronounce those who survive the judgment of Rosh Hashanah "new beings,"[15] while a homily in Pesiqta Rabbati (40§21) describes God as creating anew on Yom Kippur those who have repented. But these uses do little to explain the need for the messiah to be created anew. For that I turn to Pesiqta Rabbati 31, which makes explicit the connection between suffering and new creation that is only implicit in the piyyut.[16] Unlike the homilies about the messiah Ephraim, which, as we shall see, place his suffering in the final week of years before the end, this homily understands the messiah to be suffering for the sins of each generation. Because of the suffering he has endured (Pes. Rab. 31§§26–27),[17] God promises to create the messiah anew, presumably as the eschaton is dawning since until then human sins will cause the messiah to continue to suffer. The passage could be understood in a metaphorical sense: when the messiah's suffering ceases, he will be in effect a new being. Such a metaphorical understanding stands behind the use of "new creation" in the traditions about Rosh Hashanah and Yom Kippur.

But a more literal understanding is also possible. While Pesiqta Rabbati 31 does not say anything about the damage inflicted on the messiah's body by his suffering, Isaiah 53 certainly provides ample resources for such a depiction for any reader who understands the servant in messianic terms, resources exploited, as we have seen, by both the story of R. Joshua in the Bavli and *Sefer Zerubbabel*. Furthermore, as the servant poem tells us at some length, the servant is eventually put to death (Isa 53:7–12). It is noteworthy that this aspect of the servant's career is never transferred to the suffering messiah, although it is not hard to understand why, given the place of the Christian messiah's execution in his story.[18] It is also important to remember that while Isaiah 53 appears to imply some kind of afterlife for the servant, or at least an ongoing impact on the world after death (Isa 53:10-11), it does not even hint at resurrection, not surprisingly, given its date at the end of the exilic or beginning of the Second Temple period.[19] *Sefer Zerubbabel* contains a dying messiah who is eventually resurrected, but this is the messiah descended from Joseph, and he is subordinate to the messiah descended from David, the suffering messiah, who brings him back to life. In this light, both the promise to create the messiah anew in Pesiqta Rabbati 31 and the call to do so in "*'Az milifnei vereishit*" should perhaps be read as a way to have a suffering messiah restored to new life just as Christians had without actually having to kill him off.

With this possibility in mind, I want to note a feature of the description of the messiah's suffering in "*'Az milifnei vereishit*" that is not drawn from Isaiah 53 and does not find a parallel in any of the later texts I have invoked to illumine the piyyut: the placement of the messiah's yoke on his shoulder (lines 8–9). In biblical usage the yoke is borne on the neck.[20] So too in Pesiqta Rabbati God's warning to the suffering messiah Ephraim that he will have to bear a yoke of iron (Deut 28:48) (36§4) is fulfilled by his bearing iron bars on his neck (36§6). I would suggest that the explanation for the piyyut's placement of the yoke on the shoulder can be found in Genesis Rabbah's comment on the description of Isaac bearing the wood for his sacrifice in Genesis 22: "Like the one who carries his cross on his shoulder" (Gen. Rab. 56:3). The word for shoulder in Genesis Rabbah is *katef* while in "*'Az milifnei vereishit*" it is *shekhem*, and there is no reason to think that "*'Az milifnei vereishit*" has the passage in Genesis Rabbah in mind. Rather, the two instances suggest that the association of the cross with the shoulder was more widespread. Taken together with the call to create the messiah anew, the allusion to the cross hints at a picture of a messiah who not only shares the suffering of the Christian messiah but also his death and return to life.

## Pesiqta Rabbati

I turn now to the suffering messiah of homilies 34, 36, and 37 of Pesiqta Rabbati. We have seen that "'*Az milifnei vereishit*" connects the messiah to the time of creation through the tradition that the name of the messiah existed before the world. In Pesqita Rabbati, the messiah himself is already in existence if not before the world, then soon after its creation. Homily 36 describes God's negotiations with the messiah about the suffering he will need to undergo to bring about the redemption of Israel. During these negotiations the messiah is found under the throne of glory together with all the people of Israel who will someday come into being (Pes. Rab. 36§4).[21] In the rabbinic lists and "'*Az milifnei vereishit*," the throne of glory is one of the things created before the world, but since the homily notes that the light of the first day of creation is already stored under it to be revealed in the messianic era (Pes. Rab. 36§2), the discussion between God and the messiah must take place after the first day. Still, the presence of the beings awaiting their birth under the throne might suggest that the sixth day, the day on which humanity is created, has not yet arrived; in any case, it adds to the impression that the moment is very early in the history of the world.

Peter Schäfer has recently argued that Pesiqta Rabbati's picture of the messiah present from so early in the process of creation reflects the impact of the Christian identification of Christ with the logos or wisdom of God through which the world was created, as, notably, in the prologue to the Gospel of John.[22] Of course, other texts considered in this chapter and the previous one also picture the messiah in existence long before he manifests himself in the course of the eschatological drama. But neither *Sefer Zerubbabel* nor the story of R. Joshua b. Levi associates the messiah with the era of creation; indeed, *Sefer Zerubbabel* places the messiah's birth at a specific moment in Israel's history. Nor, despite its focus on things created before the world, does "'*Az milifnei vereishit*" suggest that the messiah himself, as opposed to his name, was already in existence then. To look beyond texts concerned with the suffering messiah, Genesis Rabbah (2:4) understands the spirit of God moving on the face of the waters (Gen 1:2) as pointing to the spirit of the messiah, but this interpretation, like the lists on which "*'Az milifnei vereishit*" drew, asserts not that the messiah was already in existence before creation but rather that he was always part of God's plan; after all, the four kingdoms of Daniel to which emptiness, void, darkness, and abyss are said to point surely did not precede the creation of the world. Thus Schäfer seems to me correct to treat the parallels between Pesiqta Rabbati 36's picture of the messiah under the throne and Christian ideas as distinctive. What is more, they are only part of a larger complex of motifs and ideas that reflect the profound impact of Christian ideas on these homilies.

The name of the messiah according to Pesiqta Rabbati 36 and 37 is Ephraim, and the citation of the verse "I have become a father to Israel, and Ephraim is my first-born" (Jer 31:8) in Pesiqta Rabbati 34§8 suggests that the name Ephraim for the messiah is assumed in this homily as well. In any case, the choice of the name for a suffering messiah clearly reflects Jeremiah 31:8–19 with its depiction of Ephraim's chastisements alongside his designation as God's first-born son.[23] But it is important to emphasize that Ephraim is the messiah's personal name, not a patronymic as scholars sometimes take it to be;[24] in fact, Ephraim is clearly identified as the messiah descended from David (Pes. Rab. 36§6). What is more, as Michael Fishbane points out, Pesiqta Rabbati 34 insists that there is only one messiah: "There is no other with him" (Pes. Rab. 34§8).[25] This comment strongly suggests awareness of a two-messiah schema, which in the seventh century inevitably involved a Davidic messiah and a messiah descended from Joseph, presumably through his more important son Ephraim; in later texts, the messiah is often called son of Ephraim rather than son of Joseph. Thus Pesiqta Rabbati's use of the name Ephraim for the Davidic messiah may be intended to represent him as fulfilling all messianic hopes.

The subject of the negotiations between God and the messiah is whether the messiah is willing to suffer on behalf of the beings stored with him under the throne of glory (Pes. Rab. 36§4). God warns that as a result of their sins, the messiah will have to bear a yoke of iron (Deut 28:48); that he will be like a calf whose eyes are darkened as he is choked by his yoke (see Jer 31:17, an Ephraim passage );[26] and that his tongue will cleave to the roof of his mouth (Ps 22:16). The allusion to Psalm 22 is particularly worthy of note; as several scholars have pointed out, this psalm, which figures also in the two subsequent accounts of the messiah's suffering in Pesiqta Rabbati, plays an important role in the passion narratives of Matthew and Mark.[27]

The suffering God describes to Ephraim is indeed terrible, but in contrast to the ongoing suffering already experienced by the messiahs of the story of R. Joshua, *Sefer Zerubbabel*, and, most emphatically, "'*Az milifnei vereishit*," Ephraim's suffering will not begin until the dawn of the eschaton (Pes. Rab. 36§6) and will be of only limited duration, a week of years (Pes. Rab. 36§4). Furthermore, Ephraim is offered a chance to refuse God's offer. If he is not willing to undertake the suffering, God will simply eliminate the beings whose sins would cause it. Ephraim responds with his conditions: he embraces the suffering "with joy and gladness" as long as not a single Israelite, living or dead, be lost, not even one of those God had considered for creation but ultimately decided not to create (Pes. Rab. 36§4). God is so pleased by Ephraim's response that he provides him with his own throne of glory borne by four living creatures (Pes. Rab. 36§4).[28] Here too, Schäfer notes, Pesiqta Rabbati shows the impact of Christian ideas. While rabbinic exegesis typically understands the first-person plurals of Genesis 1:26, "Let us make man in our image," as God's consultation with the angels about whether to undertake the creation of humanity, Christian exegetes read the verse as God's consultation with his son, who served as cocreator and sustainer of creation.[29]

In this regard, Pesiqta Rabbati can be said to reflect a higher Christology, if I may use that term, than the other texts just considered. The story of R. Joshua is too brief to offer much evidence, but there is nothing in its picture of the messiah other than his ongoing existence that marks him as superhuman. The most impressive deed of *Sefer Zerubbabel*'s Menahem is the ability to bring the messiah descended from Joseph back to life, a deed that confirms his messianic status, though, as we saw, he performs that deed together with Elijah. "'*Az milifnei vereishit*," which, like Pesiqta Rabbati, understands the messiah's suffering to atone for Israel's sins, offers the closest parallels to Pesiqta Rabbati's claims, but the piyyut asserts not that Yinnon himself was in existence from before the creation of the world, but only his name. In the piyyut, Yinnon causes the people of Israel to be judged righteous, but in Pesiqta Rabbati,

Ephraim makes it possible for them to exist. Ephraim gets a throne like God's own; Yinnon does not.

Yet despite what I have just called a high Christology, the physical suffering of the messiah is described in more detail in Pesiqta Rabbati than in the other texts to which I have just compared it. The suffering is described three times, first in the negotiations between God and Ephraim, then in the account of the actual suffering, and finally in the patriarchs' praise of the messiah for his devotion to their descendants. Interestingly, the description of the suffering Ephraim actually endures is considerably briefer than God's warning about it. Iron beams are placed on Ephraim's neck until he is bent low (Pes. Rab. 36§6),[30] and in the intensity of his suffering, he cries out to God that he is only flesh and blood and lacks the strength to endure his ordeal, for which the midrash provides a proof text from Psalm 22: "My strength is dried up like a potsherd" (Ps 22:16) (Pes. Rab. 36§6). The patriarchs' praise appears in the following homily (Pes. Rab. 37§2): Ephraim endured the mockery of the nations of the world (Ps 22:8); he sat in darkness (Isa 42:7);[31] his skin stuck to his bones and his body became as dry as wood (Lam 4:8); his eyes darkened with fasting; and his strength dried up like a potsherd (Ps 22:16). Here again, Psalm 22 plays an important part in shaping the description of the messiah's suffering. It seems hard to avoid the conclusion that the figure of Ephraim is significantly indebted to the suffering servant of Isaiah 53, yet it is noteworthy how little explicit use Pesiqta Rabbati makes of that chapter.[32] Instead it prefers to allude to and quote from a psalm that plays an important role in the passion narratives, thus dramatically appropriating central elements of the Christian picture of the messiah.

## The Suffering Messiah and the Jewish Elite

One important conclusion we can draw from "*'Az milifnei vereishit*" is that by the early seventh century, the idea of a messiah who suffered on behalf of the people of Israel and gained atonement for them was so widely accepted that it could claim a place in the Yom Kippur liturgy.[33] Yet both *Sefer Zerubbabel* and Pesiqta Rabbati 34 locate themselves as dissenting from the dominant order with their implicit or explicit criticism of the learned elite of their own day. In Chapter 3, I suggested that *Sefer Zerubbabel*'s criticism of the sages and elders for their failure to recognize the messiah when they first encounter him was softened to some extent by the fact that Zerubbabel has already been depicted making the same mistake. Like *Sefer Zerubbabel*'s, Pesiqta Rabbati's criticism of the rabbinic elite is indebted to Isaiah 53, and while it is harsher than *Sefer Zerubbabel*'s, in the end, it too is softened at least somewhat.

The heroes of Pesiqta Rabbati 34 are the "mourners for Zion," who yearn for redemption while other Jews "despise (*mevazin*) (Isa 53:3) and mock (*mal'igin*) (Ps 22:8) them" (Pes. Rab. 34§2).[34] Recent scholarship has been rightly reluctant to identify these mourners for Zion with the ninth- and tenth-century Jerusalem Karaites who called themselves mourners for Zion; both the dating and the appearance of the traditions about them in a rabbinic work such as Pesiqta Rabbati make such an identification implausible.[35] Philip Alexander has recently offered a different suggestion: mourning for Zion reflects a "priestly spirituality" belonging to an ongoing priestly tradition that developed apart from the rabbinic movement and was adopted by the Karaites; the appearance of material from this tradition in rabbinic literature is a result of the Jewish "apocalyptic revival" of the sixth to ninth centuries.[36] I am skeptical about Alexander's claims for such a priestly tradition, and it seems to me that at this stage of our knowledge, it is best to be extremely cautious in attempting to relate the mourners of Pesiqta Rabbati 34 to any group beyond the homily.

To return to Pesiqta Rabbati 34, it is important to note that there it is the mourners for Zion who are the object of the contempt endured by the servant in Isaiah 53 and the messiah in *Sefer Zerubbabel*. But as the model of Isaiah 53 leads us to expect, the mourners are ultimately vindicated by God. God sends angels of destruction to punish the mockers (Pes. Rab. 34§5), and, most telling for our purposes, he informs the "righteous of the world," who are devoted to God's Torah but not to his kingdom, that he prefers the mourners to them (Pes. Rab. 34§6).[37] This is indeed a remarkable preference for God to express in a work in the rabbinic tradition.[38] It is worth noting, however, that the expression of this preference is restricted to Pesiqta Rabbati 34.[39] Neither Pesiqta Rabbati 36 nor Pesiqta Rabbati 37 mentions the mourners for Zion, and Pesiqta Rabbati 37 clearly embraces Torah experts: it is "the righteous ones, the pious ones, the holy ones, the heroes of (*gibborei*) Torah" who look on the messiah under the bejeweled canopies God has set up for him (Pes. Rab. 37§5).[40] And even Pesiqta Rabbati 34 acknowledges the value of Torah study. When "the righteous of the generation" toss down their *tefillin* and confess that they have gone astray like sheep (Isa 53:6) in having failed to understand the significance of the disasters that announce the arrival of the messiah, God forgives them, for the merit of Torah stands by anyone who possesses it and God grants the merit of Torah even to those who do not possess it (Pes. Rab. 34§4).[41]

Aside from their embrace of a suffering messiah and their criticism of the rabbinic elite, *Sefer Zerubbabel* and Homily 34 of Pesiqta Rabbati do not have much in common. Their eschatological scenarios and their understandings of the task of the messiah are very different. *Sefer Zerubbabel* breaks with the genre conventions of rabbinic literature, while the homilist of Pesiqta Rabbati embraces them. But these differences make their shared sense that the rabbis of their day were not sufficiently concerned with the coming of the messiah all the more significant. Above I suggested that the relationship between the picture of the messiah in the story of R. Joshua and the picture in *Sefer Zerubbabel* reflects their common debt to traditions circulating among Jews in the centuries after the rise of Christianity. It is possible that those traditions included the messiah's rejection by the Jewish elite; this is an element that rabbinic storytellers would surely have chosen to suppress even if they knew it. But the intensity of Pesiqta Rabbati's condemnation of those who are insufficiently enthusiastic about the messiah could also suggest a particular contemporary division between messianic enthusiasts and less eschatologically minded Jews that we can no longer recover but that is also reflected, if with less vehemence, in *Sefer Zerubbabel*.

## Targum Jonathan to Isaiah 53

Finally, I would like to turn to Targum Jonathan to Isaiah 53.[42] It leaves no doubt that the subject of the fourth servant poem is the messiah: "Behold, my servant the messiah shall prosper" (Tg. Jon.

Isa 52:13). But it goes on to offer an interpretive translation of Isaiah 53 that depicts the servant-messiah as the triumphant rebuilder of the temple, teacher, intercessor, and redeemer of his people from exile, while completely eliminating his suffering, although perhaps not his death (Isa 53:12), a point to which I shall return. Some scholars have suggested that the translators were engaged in a polemic against Christian use of Isaiah 53. Their critics respond that any apparent points of contact with Christian positions can be explained by internal Jewish developments; indeed, some even suggest that Targum Jonathan preserves the very traditions that contributed to the emergence of the Christian ideas in the first place.[43]

Before proceeding to a discussion of the passage, a few words are in order about the date of Targum Jonathan, which is obviously of considerable importance for the question of its relationship to Christian literature and ideas. Although it originated in Palestine, Targum Jonathan served as the semi-official Aramaic translation of the prophets in the synagogues of Babylonia.[44] It is clear that it did not reach its final form until after the Muslim conquest, but it is also clear that most of it is significantly earlier.[45]

A process of development over several centuries is certainly plausible for a work in an originally oral genre, but it is extremely frustrating for scholars, who would like to be able to specify a historical context. In his study of Targum Jonathan to Isaiah, Bruce Chilton applies an approach devised to overcome the difficulties involved in dating particular elements of the targum, delineating what he sees as the central concepts of Targum Jonathan to Isaiah and comparing them to other ancient Jewish evidence in an effort to determine the historical setting in which they emerged.[46] His conclusion is that the composition of Targum Jonathan to Isaiah, and indeed of much of Targum Jonathan, took place in two stages, the first between the destruction of the Second Temple and the Bar Kokhba revolt, and the second sometime during the third through fifth centuries.[47]

I find this approach deeply problematic. Judgments based on linguistic criteria are of course not entirely objective, but a system of dating based on a scholar's decisions about the appropriate historical context in which to place what the same scholar has chosen as key concepts of the text runs the risk not only of circularity but of unchecked subjectivity.[48] In the absence of any literary grounds for arguing for two-stage composition in Targum Jonathan to Isaiah, I prefer to work on the assumption that the text took shape over a long period of time, with material added as late as the early Muslim period, and to avoid making claims about Targum Jonathan's relationship to other works that depend on precise dating.

I turn now to Targum Jonathan's interpretation of the suffering servant as a triumphant messiah who defeats the nations (Tg. Jon. Isa 52:15, 53:7), rebuilds the temple (Tg. Jon. Isa 53:5), brings the people back from exile (Tg. Jon. Isa 53:8), and liberates the land of Israel from gentile rule (Tg. Jon. Isa 53:8). The targum succeeds in erasing the biblical text's picture of the servant's suffering through some remarkable transformations of the Hebrew text as, for example, thus:

| *Hebrew*[49] | *Targum Jonathan*[50] |
|---|---|
| He was wounded for our transgressions, he was bruised for our iniquities. . . . (Isa 53:5) | And he will build the sanctuary which was profaned for our sins, handed over for our iniquities. . . . |
| He was oppressed, and he was afflicted, yet he opened not his mouth; like a lamb that is led to the slaughter, and like a sheep that before its shearers is dumb, so he opened not his mouth. (Isa 53:7) | He beseeches, and he is answered, and before he opens his mouth he is accepted; the strong ones of the peoples he will hand over like a lamb to the sacrifice, and like a ewe which before its shearers is dumb, so there is not before him one who opens his mouth or speaks a saying. |

Targum Jonathan also eliminates the servant's humiliation and physical deficiencies by applying some elements of the depiction of the servant to the people of Israel (Tg. Jon. Isa 52:14) and the nations (Tg. Jon. Isa 53:3) and transforming others into praise (Tg. Jon. Isa 53:2):

| *Hebrew* | *Targum Jonathan* |
|---|---|
| . . . His appearance was so marred, beyond human semblance, and his form beyond that of the sons of men. . . . (Isa 52:14) | . . . [The house of Israel's] appearances were so dark among the peoples, and their aspect beyond that of the sons of men. . . . |
| . . . He had no form or comeliness that we should look at him, and no beauty that we should desire him. (Isa 53:2) | . . . His appearance is not a common appearance and his fearfulness is not an ordinary fearfulness, and his brilliance will be holy brilliance, that everyone who looks at him will consider him. |
| He was despised and rejected by men; a man of sorrows [lit., pains], and acquainted with grief [lit., sickness]; and as one who hides his face from others, he was despised, and we esteemed him not. (Isa 53:3)[51] | Then the glory of all the kingdoms will be for contempt and cease; they will be faint and mournful, behold, as a man of sorrows and appointed for sicknesses; and as when the face of the Shekhinah was taken up from us, they are despised and not esteemed. |

Yet although the targum eliminates all of the messiah's suffering, it appears to leave open the possibility of his death. Most of the Hebrew's allusions to the servant's death are transformed into something quite different (Tg. Jon. Isa 53:7–9, 10), but at the end of the poem, one mention remains:

> Then I will divide him the plunder of many peoples, and he shall divide the spoil, the possessions of strong fortresses; because he handed over his soul to the death, and subjected the rebels to the law; yet he will beseech concerning the sins of many, and to the rebels it shall be forgiven for him. (Tg. Jon. Isa 53:12)

In contrast to Chilton, who translates quite literally, "he handed over his soul to the death," some prefer to take the phrase as an idiom and translate instead "he risked his life."[52] Such a reading seems to be required by context, even if the evidence for such an idiom is not abundant. Still, given the targum's creativity in eliminating the messiah's suffering from the poem, the fact that it allows even the suggestion of death is significant.[53] I suggested above that just as the embrace of the suffering of the messiah in the texts considered here is owed at least in part to the impact of the Christian messianic narrative, so too is the unwillingness of those texts to contemplate the possibility of the messiah's death: the combination of suffering and dying, natural though it is, would have brought the Jewish messiah too close to the Christian one. So perhaps it is precisely the elimination of the messiah's suffering throughout Isaiah 53 that allows the targum to offer a translation considerably closer to the original than one might have expected for this very fraught passage at the end of the servant poem.

The aspect of the messiah's activity in Targum Jonathan to Isaiah 53 most congruent with the picture of the servant in Isaiah 53 is his intercession on behalf of Israel (Tg. Jon. Isa 53:4, 6, 11) and his teaching (Tg. Jon. Isa 53:5, 11), which lead to the forgiveness of Israel's sins.[54] But here too Targum Jonathan goes well beyond what the Hebrew text has to say, repeatedly insisting on the success of the intercession, which is implied but not emphasized in the Hebrew:

| *Hebrew* | *Targum Jonathan* |
|---|---|
| Surely he has borne our griefs [lit., sicknesses] and carried our sorrows [lit., pains]. . . . (Isa 53:4) | Then he will beseech concerning our sins and our iniquities for his sake will be forgiven. . . . |
| . . . Upon him was the chastisement that made us whole, and with his stripes we are healed. (Isa 53:5) | . . . And by his teaching his peace will increase upon us, and in that we attach ourselves to his words our sins will be forgiven us. |
| . . . . And the LORD has laid on him the iniquity of us all. (Isa 53:6) | . . . And before the LORD it was a pleasure to forgive the sins of us all for his sake. |

| *Hebrew* | *Targum Jonathan* |
|---|---|
| . . . By his knowledge shall the righteous one, my servant, make many to be accounted righteous; and he shall bear their iniquities. (Isa 53:11) | . . . By his wisdom shall he make innocents to be accounted innocent, to subject many to the law; and he shall beseech concerning their sins. |

Thus the messiah of Targum Jonathan to Isaiah 53 gains forgiveness for Israel through his verbal intercession and his teaching.

It is important to emphasize that Targum Jonathan's insistence that the messiah it finds depicted in Isaiah 53 does not suffer sets it apart not only from Christian readings of the passage but also from a tradition of Jewish readings that goes back at least to the story of R. Joshua b. Levi from the middle of the third century. One way to make sense of the targum's approach to Isaiah 53 is to suggest that it is responding to the type of criticism, discussed in the previous chapter, that Origen reports Celsus making about Christian beliefs: "It is impossible that a body which had something more divine than the rest should be no different from any other" (*Cels.* 6.75).[55] For Celsus, the Christian understanding of Christ should have made his body impervious to human ailments. Targum Jonathan may not have understood its messiah to be divine in quite the way Christians understood theirs to be, but it is worth remembering that the story of R. Joshua, *Sefer Zerubbabel*, "*'Az milifnei vereishit*," and Pesiqta Rabbati all describe the messiah or his career in ways that imply that he is not an ordinary human being. Thus it seems possible that Targum Jonathan's unwillingness to depict the messiah as suffering or physically deficient was inspired by the kind of sentiment Origen attributes to Celsus. That sentiment could just as well have come from Jews concerned to shore up Jewish messianic claims as from hostile outsiders. The elimination of the servant's suffering and physical deficiencies could thus have been a strategy for holding onto Isaiah 53 as a messianic prophecy. In that case, Targum Jonathan to Isaiah 53 is not a polemic against Christian readings of Isaiah 53 but rather a response to polemics, actual or possible, against Jewish readings—and Christian readings as well, though that was presumably not the translators' concern.

## The Suffering Servant in Ancient Judaism and *Sefer Zerubbabel*

Like the story of R. Joshua and *Sefer Zerubbabel*, "*'Az milifnei ver-eishit*" and Pesiqta Rabbati are deeply indebted to Isaiah 53, but their focus is not on the humble physical appearance of the messiah but rather on the themes of vicarious suffering and atonement that are also central to Christians' understanding of their messiah. "*'Az milifnei vereishit*" repeatedly alludes to Isaiah 53 to demonstrate that atonement is guaranteed to its audience, but its placement of the yoke on the messiah's shoulder appears to be inspired by the cross of the Christian suffering messiah. Pesiqta Rabbati, on the other hand, rarely alludes to Isaiah 53, instead describing the messiah's suffering in terms drawn from Psalm 22, which plays an important role in the gospels' accounts of the crucifixion. Thus, while both "*'Az milifnei vereishit*" and Pesiqta Rabbati respond to Christian appropriation of the figure of the suffering servant, they do so in quite different ways.

*Sefer Zerubbabel* lacks the interest in vicarious suffering and atonement displayed by "*'Az milifnei vereishit*" and Pesiqta Rabbati, but it shares Pesiqta Rabbati's attention to another aspect of Isaiah 53: the poem's description of the servant's rejection by his contemporaries. Furthermore, for both Pesiqta Rabbati and *Sefer Zerubbabel*, not all of the messiah's contemporaries are equally guilty. The fact that two roughly contemporary texts attack the learned elite for lack of messianic enthusiasm may reflect particular contemporary conditions. On the other hand, it is possible that a certain antipathy to the elite was already present in the traditions on which the seventh-century texts drew. It is worth noting that while R. Joshua in the Bavli is able to recognize the messiah because Elijah has warned him about the messiah's humble appearance, he fails to understand the meaning of the messiah's words.

Targum Jonathan to Isaiah 53 stands in striking contrast to the other texts about a suffering messiah considered in this chapter and the previous one. Yet its extraordinary translation of the poem so as to eliminate the servant-messiah's suffering and affirm his triumph should perhaps be read as a reflection of the importance the idea of a suffering messiah had for contemporary Jews. That is, Targum Jonathan to Isaiah 53 should be understood as an attempt to protect

Isaiah 53 as a messianic prophecy by eliminating the features that critics could have pointed to as disqualifying it. If, as seems likely, Targum Jonathan to Isaiah 53 predates the seventh century in something like its current form, it would provide evidence for the importance of the figure of a suffering messiah before the figure was taken up by *Sefer Zerubbbel*, "*'Az milifnei vereishit*," and Pesiqta Rabbati.

Finally, it should be emphasized that *Sefer Zerubbabel* stands apart from the story of R. Joshua, "*'Az milifnei vereishit*," Pesiqta Rabbati, and Targum Jonathan to Isaiah 53 in one very important way: its embrace of a second messiah descended from Joseph alongside the suffering Davidic messiah. The messiah descended from Joseph is not described in the language of Isaiah 53, but he does have one notable feature in common with the suffering servant: he dies. This messiah is the subject of the next chapter.

# CHAPTER FIVE

# The Dying Messiah Son of Joseph

THE PREVIOUS CHAPTERS attempted to place the suffering Davidic messiah of *Sefer Zerubbabel* in context. *Sefer Zerubbabel* did not invent the suffering messiah, and his appearance in two other works roughly contemporary with *Sefer Zerubbabel* suggests that by the early seventh century such a figure was an important element of the Jewish eschatological repertoire. The case is very different for the messiah who is the subject of this chapter, the dying messiah son of Joseph. In the centuries following the Muslim conquest, a messiah who is descended from Joseph and dies in battle becomes a frequent figure in Jewish eschatological scenarios, but *Sefer Zerubbabel* is unique among texts from before the Muslim conquest in offering a coherent account of his career. Some of the Islamic-era texts, as will be discussed in Chapter 6, include only the broad outlines of the story as it is found in *Sefer Zerubbabel*, making it difficult to determine whether they drew on *Sefer Zerubbabel* itself or whether the story reached them through other channels.

But while *Sefer Zerubbabel* is the first place a narrative of the career of the messiah son of Joseph appears, allusions to such a messiah in earlier rabbinic texts make it clear that *Sefer Zerubbabel* did not invent him. Some scholars, as will be discussed shortly, believe that a messiah son of Joseph can be traced all the way back to the Second Temple period. The evidence for this view is neither as clear nor as abundant as its advocates would like, but some have insisted that it would have become impossible for Jews to embrace a dying messiah after the rise of Christianity.[1] Probably the most influential discussion of this messiah in the past half century is a brief article by Joseph Heinemann, who traces the figure back to Simeon Bar Kokhba, the leader of a revolt against Rome in 132–135 CE, arguing that a messiah originally understood as triumphant was transformed into a dying messiah in response to Bar Kokhba's defeat and death.[2] Yet while Heinemann understands the emergence of the figure of the dying messiah among Jews as postdating the rise of Christianity, he regards the question of the possible impact of Christianity on Jewish messianism as already settled in the negative.[3] Altogether, until fairly recently, most scholars have preferred to understand the emergence of a dying messiah in Jewish tradition, whenever it took place, as an internal development that owed nothing to the Christian messianic narrative.

This position reflects the scholarly consensus for most of the twentieth century: while the earliest Christians were deeply indebted to Jews and Judaism, once their ways parted, Jews were immune to the impact of the new movement. But, as previous chapters of this book make clear, more recent scholarship has been more open to the likelihood that a Jewish minority in the Roman Empire would have been deeply affected by Christian ideas, especially after Christianity became the state religion.[4] Thus it is not surprising that some recent scholars have argued that the Christian messiah, whose death was central to the story his followers told about him, was the model for the dying messiah son of Joseph in Jewish literature.[5] The question of whether a dying messiah son of Joseph enters Jewish tradition before or after the rise of Christianity is of considerable importance. If traditions about such a figure were already in existence, they might have contributed to shaping the understanding of Jesus's death among his earliest followers.[6] If, on the other hand, the traditions appeared only in the period after the emergence of Christianity, it seems plausible to understand the figure as reflecting the impact of the Christian story about a messiah who was also son of Joseph, at least from one point of view.[7] It is also possible that Jews and Christians could have both influenced and been influenced by the other group, either sequentially or concurrently. Thus, one scholar has recently suggested that the figure of the messiah son of Joseph develops as a Jewish apologetic response to Christian use of early Jewish traditions about a suffering and dying Davidic messiah that became uncomfortable for some Jews after the emergence of Christianity.[8]

My goal in this chapter is both to illumine *Sefer Zerubbabel*'s use of traditions about the messiah son of Joseph and to shed light on the issues just raised. I begin by examining arguments that place the origins of this messiah in the Second Temple period, arguments by which I remain unconvinced. After that I survey the more certain evidence for the messiah son of Joseph in rabbinic literature. Finally, I consider the relationship between the references to the messiah son of Joseph in rabbinic literature and *Sefer Zerubbabel*'s more extended narrative, arguing that the brief rabbinic mentions presuppose a widely known set of traditions about this messiah on which *Sefer Zerubbabel* drew.

## The Messiah Son of Joseph in the Second Temple Period?

During the last half century or so, scholars have highlighted the diversity of eschatological expectations and the variety of messianic figures among Jews of the Second Temple era.[9] The Davidic messiah may be the most common such figure, but he is certainly not the only one, as his appearance in some texts alongside a priestly messiah indicates. This pairing reflects the fact that in ancient Israel both kings and priests were anointed, making them messiahs in the literal sense, and it goes back as far as Zechariah's prophecies at the very beginning of the Second Temple period, even before the emergence of apocalyptic eschatology. For Zechariah, Zerubbabel, the Persian governor descended from David, and Joshua the high priest (Zech 3–4, 6:9–15) are two "sons of oil" (Zech 4:14).

If dual messianism was an important possibility in the Second Temple period, why not the type of dual messianism we encounter in *Sefer Zerubbabel* and later works? The Torah, after all, provides significant resources for such a picture. According to the narrative of Genesis, the two most important sons of Jacob are Judah and Joseph. Jacob's death-bed blessing of his sons singles out Judah for dominion: "The scepter shall not depart from Judah" (Gen 49:10);[10] the scepter was often read as pointing to the Davidic messiah since David was a descendant of Judah. But in Moses' blessing of the tribes before his death, the words addressed to Joseph suggest dominion for him:

> Let these [blessings] come upon the head of Joseph, / and upon the crown of the head of him that is prince among his brothers. / His firstling bull has majesty, / and his horns are the horns of a wild ox; / and with them he shall push the peoples, all of them, to the ends of the earth; / such are the ten thousands of Ephraim, and such are the thousands of Manasseh. (Deut 33:16–17)

Yet despite the potential of this passage and perhaps other passages in Scripture, I think it is correct to say that there is no clear evidence for a messiah son of Joseph in the literature of the Second Temple period.

Certainly there are scholars who would not agree with this conclusion. One energetic proponent of a Second Temple–era messiah son of Joseph is David C. Mitchell.[11] Indeed, Mitchell believes that this messiah was a dying and rising messiah whose death was understood as a sacrifice to effect atonement on Israel's behalf. If Mitchell were correct, the implications for both ancient Jewish and early Christian messianism would be profound. Unfortunately, Mitchell's scholarship is compromised by his zeal to make the evidence fit his picture. This is particularly evident in his treatment of the two targumic passages that refer to the messiah son of Ephraim.[12] The targumim in which the passages appear were completed in the era after the rise of Islam, as Mitchell admits. But he also notes, correctly, that there is a long-standing scholarly view that some targumim preserve significantly earlier traditions.[13] Perhaps needless to say, deciding which traditions fall into this category is an extremely subjective undertaking fraught with methodological difficulties, as Mitchell's justification for dating the two passages to the pre-Christian era indicates: after the rise of Christianity, he claims, Jews would not have embraced the picture of a messiah slain in Jerusalem or accepted one modeled on Joshua.[14] But surely the premise that Jews never embraced aspects of Christian tradition should be the object of investigation rather than an unexamined assumption. Altogether, it seems to me extremely problematic to turn to traditions from the targumim in an effort to establish the existence of the messiah son of Joseph in the period of the Second Temple.

Mitchell also finds a messiah son of Joseph in three works that undoubtedly date to the Second Temple period: the Book of Dreams (1 En. 83–90), 4QTestimonia, and the very fragmentary 4Q372.[15] The first two merit discussion, but the Joseph who appears there alongside Levi, Judah, and Benjamin in 4Q372 (frag. 1, line 14) is clearly not an individual but a personification of the northern kingdom.[16]

## The Book of Dreams

Of the two remaining works, I turn first to the Book of Dreams, which dates from the second century BCE. Mitchell is certainly correct to point out that Enoch's vision of the history of Israel, in which the human actors are represented by animals, gives an important role to a figure described in terms drawn from Moses' blessing of Joseph.[17] As the final age dawns, Enoch reports the birth of a white bull with large horns:

> And all the wild beasts and all the birds of heaven were afraid of it and made petition to it continually. And I saw until all their species were changed, and they all became white cattle. And the first one became [leader] among them (and that [leader] was a large animal), and there were large black horns on its head. And the Lord of the sheep rejoiced over it and over all the cattle. (1 En 90:37–38)[18]

The bull that becomes the horned creature is widely understood to bear messianic significance, although George W. E. Nickelsburg points out that the fact that the creature is a bull rather than a sheep links him to the patriarchs of the antediluvian period and to Abraham and Isaac, who are depicted by the Book of Dreams as bulls (1 En. 85:3,9; 89:1,9–11), rather than to David, who is depicted as a sheep who becomes a ram (1 En. 89:45–48).[19] In the light of Moses' blessing of Joseph, Mitchell identifies the white bull of the Book of Dreams as the firstling bull of Deuteronomy 33:17 and understands the transformed bull with the large black horns of the Book of Dreams as the horned wild ox of Deuteronomy, an intriguing and not implausible suggestion.

But Mitchell then goes on to claim that the bull of the Book of Dreams is transformed after having been sacrificed, thus aligning him with the messiah son of Joseph, who dies a sacrificial death and returns to life. Against the objection that there is no hint of such a sacrifice in the Book of Dreams, Mitchell insists that a firstling bull is by its nature "an animal destined to violent sacrificial death."[20] Of course it is Deuteronomy, not the Book of Dreams, that calls the bull a firstling. Mitchell never tries to answer the question of why the Book of Dreams would introduce a messianic figure modeled on the blessing of Joseph when neither Joseph nor the northern kingdom plays a significant role there. A more disinterested exploration of these questions would be of considerable value, but the claim that the Book of Dreams provides evidence for belief in a messiah son of Joseph goes beyond what the passage under discussion will support.


## 4QTestimonia

The other work of the Second Temple period in which Mitchell finds a messiah son of Joseph that deserves further consideration is 4QTestimonia (4Q175). This work juxtaposes four sets of passages. The first set is drawn from Deuteronomy and concerns Moses and the prophet like him to be provided for the people after Moses' death. The second consists of Balaam's prophecy from Numbers about the star and scepter that will arise from the people of Israel. The third is Moses' blessing of the tribe of Levi from Deuteronomy. The last passage concerns Joshua, who belongs to the tribe of Ephraim and is thus a descendant of Joseph. The passage comes not from the biblical book of Joshua but from the so-called Apocryphon of Joshua known from the Scrolls.[21] This work, of which only fragments are preserved, is an expansive paraphrase of the biblical book; it does not appear to be of sectarian provenance.[22]

4QTestimonia is usually read as pointing to three figures associated with the end of days: an eschatological prophet like Moses, the messiah, and an eschatological priest.[23] Such a three-messiah schema is not well attested; the most common form of messianic expectation in the Scrolls pairs a messiah of Israel, presumably a Davidide, with a messiah of Aaron.[24] There is, however, some evidence for the figure of an eschatological prophet in the Scrolls.[25] Mitchell argues that 4QTestimonia's juxtaposition of a passage about Joshua with passages predicting a future prophet, king, and priest indicates expectation of a future hero like Joshua or somehow connected to him.[26] In support of his understanding, Mitchell points to rabbinic interpretations of the four craftsmen of Zechariah 2:3, which identify the craftsmen as four eschatological figures, and Targum ps.-Jonathan to Exodus 40:9–11.[27] The earliest appearance of an interpretation of the four craftsmen is in the fifth-century collection Pesiqta of Rav Kahana (5:9),[28] and Mitchell sees the order of the figures there as corresponding precisely to the order in 4QTestimonia.[29] Pesiqta of Rav Kahana names the four figures as Elijah, the king messiah, Melchizedek, and the "anointed of war"; the last figure is understood by some scholars as the messiah son of Joseph, although the reference may be to the priest of Deuteronomy 20:2.[30] The first place that one of the craftsmen is explicitly identified as the messiah son of Joseph is the version of the interpretation in the Bavli (b. Suk. 52b).[31] Mitchell does not note the weakness of the correspondence between Pesiqta of Rav Kahana's Melchizedek, the mysterious non-Israelite priestly king of Genesis 14, and the future priest descended from Levi in the passage from the Blessing of Moses in 4QTestimonia. The passage from Targum Pseudo-Jonathan offers only three figures: the King Messiah from Judah, Elijah the high priest, and the messiah son of Ephraim descended from Joshua. Mitchell argues that the passage is relevant despite its three figures rather than four because Elijah here fills two roles: prophet and priest.[32]

The rabbinic traditions about four eschatological figures are certainly worth considering in relation to 4QTestimonia, but it is even more important to look closely at the text of 4QTestimonia itself. From several points of view, the passage about Joshua stands apart from the other passages. I have already noted that it is drawn not from the book of Joshua but from an Apocryphon of Joshua. Furthermore, the first three passages in 4QTestimonia predict positive figures: a prophet like Moses, a star and scepter from among the people of Israel, and a future priest or a line of heirs to the priesthood. The passage from the Apocryphon of Joshua, on the other hand, does not predict a future counterpart to Joshua. Rather, in the passage quoted, Joshua is the speaker, issuing a curse on anyone who tries to rebuild Jericho and then predicting the coming of a man of Belial who will cause harm to both his people and his neighbors. Perhaps the passage is included in 4QTestimonia to identify the eschatological enemy rather than a fourth eschatological hero. It certainly does not provide pre-Christian evidence for a messiah descended from Joseph.

### Ḥazon Gabriel

Next I would like to discuss briefly *Ḥazon Gabriel*, the Vision or Revelation of Gabriel, an inscription on a limestone stele probably from the Jordan Valley, dated to the first century BCE and first published in 2007.[33] In a series of publications, Israel Knohl has argued that *Ḥazon Gabriel* contains a dying and rising messiah named Ephraim.[34] He has also argued for a pre-Christian Jewish suffering messiah in the so-called Self-Glorification Hymn from the Dead Sea Scrolls, which he reads as the messianic proclamation of Menahem the Essene, who was killed in a short-lived revolt against Roman rule on the death of Herod in 4 BCE, in terms drawn from the suffering servant of Isaiah 53.[35]

The text of *Ḥazon Gabriel* is damaged and incomplete, and recent improvements in deciphering it have raised questions about the readings of two words critical for Knohl's argument. The first of these words Knohl reads as the name Ephraim (line 16). It appears in close proximity to the words "David my servant"; in Knohl's view, this juxtaposition points to a pair of messiahs: one Davidic, the other descended from Joseph.[36] The original editors of *Hazon Gabriel* marked the *p*, *y*, and *m* of *'prym* (Ephraim) as uncertain.[37] More recently, Elisha Qimron and Alexey (Eliyahu) Yuditsky have offered the reading *'mrym*, "words," insisting that the second letter of the word cannot be a *p*.[38]

Knohl originally read the second word crucial to his argument as *h'yh* (line 80). He understood the word to mean "live," although the form is unusual, and argued that it was a command to return to life addressed to the dead messiah Ephraim. Thus, *Hazon Gabriel* would have provided our earliest evidence for a dying and rising messiah.[39] But Knohl now accepts the view of scholars who argue that the word in question should be read as *h'wt*, "the sign."[40] Altogether, I think it is fair to conclude that even if the reading "Ephraim" is maintained, there is no reason to understand the name to refer to a messiah.[41] It is also worth remembering that the one certain case of a messiah named Ephraim in Jewish literature, in Pesiqta Rabbati 34, 36, 37, is indeed a suffering messiah, but, as we saw in Chapter 4, he is also a Davidic messiah. Even after the publication of *Hazon Gabriel*, then, we still lack clear evidence for a messiah son of Joseph in Jewish texts of the Second Temple period.

## Joshua Typology

But even if Jewish texts fail to provide such evidence, Robert A. Kraft has argued that the importance of Joshua typology for the understanding of Jesus in early Christian works such as Justin's *Dialogue with Trypho* deserves consideration for the light it could shed on Jewish sources.[42] The prominence of this typology is not surprising. The Torah, after all, presents Joshua as the prophet like Moses (Deut 18:15–19) who brought the people of Israel into the Promised Land, and his name, which the Christian savior also bore, means "the Lord is salvation." Kraft argues that the early appearance of the typology in Christian sources probably reflects the existence of Jewish messianic expectation centered on a second Joshua. He discusses several passages in Jewish works from around the turn of the era that could suggest expectation of a messiah named Joshua/Jesus. Yet, as he notes, all of the passages form part of works that reach us through Christian transmitters, who could be responsible for the references to Joshua/Jesus, as indeed many scholars have held.[43] For evidence from the Second Temple period that did not undergo Christian transmission, Kraft points to the interpretation of the star and scepter of Numbers 24:17 as Phinehas and Joshua in the *Asatir* (10:45), the Samaritan work that Moses Gaster dated to the third century BCE.[44] More recent scholarship, however, has argued on the basis of language and content for a date in the tenth century CE.[45]

But even if we dismiss the non-Christian material because of the methodological difficulties in evaluating it, Kraft makes a strong case that the elaborate Joshua typology that appears quite early in Christian writings suggests some kind of prehistory of Jewish speculation. Yet it is important for our purposes that of all the texts Kraft considers, it is only the *Asatir* and rabbinic sources, that is, texts that post-date the Second Temple period, that contain a dual-messiah schema. There are obvious reasons why, even if they knew it, Christians would not be interested in carrying forward such a schema, especially if it subordinated the Joshua messiah to another figure as later Jewish tradition subordinated the messiah son of Joseph to the messiah son of David. But the absence in early Christian literature of any indication of awareness of such a picture is noteworthy.[46]

## Rabbinic Literature

Now I turn to the undoubtedly modest but nonetheless clear rabbinic evidence for the messiah son of Joseph. For the purposes of this discussion, I consider only classical rabbinic literature, up to and including the Bavli, since later texts may reflect the impact of *Sefer Zerubbabel*. With the exception of the interpretation of the four craftsmen of Zechariah 2:3 as four eschatological redeemers, discussed earlier in relation to 4QTestimonia, all of the rabbinic traditions about the messiah son of Joseph appear in the fifth-century Palestinian compilation Genesis Rabbah or in the Bavli.[47] In both works, however, there can be no doubt that the dominant messianic figure is the son of David.[48]

## Genesis Rabbah

I turn first to Genesis Rabbah, and I begin with a tradition predicting that Esau, that is, Rome, will fall at the hands of a descendant of Rachel.[49] This tradition appears three times in Genesis Rabbah (73:7, 75:5, 99:2). It is transmitted by R. Phinehas, a fifth-generation amora (late fourth century), in the name of R. Samuel b. Nahman, a third-generation amora (probably late third-early fourth century); the fact that R. Samuel refers to the saying as a tradition suggests that it predates his own time, and perhaps its preservation in Hebrew indicates tannaitic provenance, as Holger Zellentin claims.[50] The tradition does not indicate from which of Rachel's two sons, Joseph and Benjamin, its hero will descend, nor does it designate him a messiah. Indeed, in the first two instances in which the tradition is cited, there is no indication that the defeat of Edom is eschatological, although the identification of Edom with Rome in rabbinic thought points in this direction.

These missing elements are supplied at least implicitly by the context of the third citation of the tradition (Gen. Rab. 99:2), which comes at the end of an anonymous passage that pairs four oppressive kingdoms with the heroes who redeemed Israel from them or will do so in the future. Edom, the last kingdom, is identified with the horned beast that symbolizes the fourth kingdom in Daniel's vision (Dan 7:20). It will fall at the hand "of the anointed of war who comes from Joseph," the tribe described by Moses as having the horns of a wild ox in the passage by now well known to us (Deut 33:17). Genesis Rabbah's explicit association of the anointed of war with the tribe of Joseph here suggests that the Bavli draws on earlier tradition for its identification of one of the craftsmen of Zechariah 2:3 as the messiah son of Joseph rather than the anointed of war, as in the earliest form of the four-craftsmen tradition in Pesiqta of Rav Kahana.

Given the identity of the enemy, it seems likely that the eschatological setting this passage provides is implicit in the other two appearances of the tradition. But if the descendant of Rachel who brings an end to Esau is to be understood as the messiah son of Joseph, it is noteworthy that this tradition does not pair him with the messiah son of David. In the third passage (Gen. Rab. 99:2), where the descendant of Rachel is the last of four heroes of Israel, the first hero is Daniel, a descendant of Judah, but he is made responsible for the fall of Babylonia, which took place far in the past.

The pairing of the messiah son of Joseph with the messiah son of David does, however, appear elsewhere in Genesis Rabbah, in the course of an interpretation of the message Jacob sends to Esau (Gen 32:6, Gen. Rab. 75:6).[51] The unusual singulars in Jacob's boast, literally, "I have bull, ass, flock, male slave, and female slave,"[52] must have been intended by the biblical text as collective nouns but they permit more imaginative readings. Thus "the rabbis" explain "bull" as pointing to the anointed of war on the basis of Deuteronomy 33:17, which uses the same word for its horned first-born bull, while "ass" refers to the King Messiah, that is, the messiah son of David, on the basis of Zechariah 9:9, "Rejoice greatly, O daughter of Zion. . . . Lo, your king comes to you . . . , humble and riding on an ass." The attribution of the interpretation to "the rabbis" offers little help in dating; the interpretation follows interpretations by R. Judah and R. Nehemiah, third-generation tannaim, but its content is not linked to theirs.

To summarize, Genesis Rabbah clearly knows a messiah son of Joseph, and it seems likely that the traditions reporting his defeat of Rome and pairing him with the Davidic messiah are aspects of a larger narrative about him. But Genesis Rabbah provides no hint of the messiah's death, an episode that appears not only in *Sefer Zerubbabel* but in the Bavli as well. It is possible to that Genesis Rabbah has chosen to be silent about an episode it finds disconcerting because it recalls the fate of the Christian messiah.

## The Bavli

As already noted, the Bavli is the earliest text to designate the fourth craftsman of Zechariah 2:3 as the messiah son of Joseph. Its interpretation of the four craftsmen appears on the second side of the folio (b. Suk. 52b) that contains the two most interesting passages in rabbinic literature about this messiah (b. Suk. 52a), though both are very brief. The first passage involves an interpretation of

Zechariah 12:12, "The land shall mourn, each family by itself; the family of the house of David by itself, and their wives by themselves. . . ." Rav cites the verse in the course of a discussion of the "great improvement" (*tiqqun*) in the women's court of the temple mentioned by the Mishnah (m. Suk. 5:2), which the gemara understands as a gallery for women (b. Suk. 51b). The verse from Zechariah provides justification for this change to temple architecture: if even in the last days, at a time of mourning, separation of men and women was advisable, all the more was it advisable in the era of the temple at a time of celebration. The gemara then reports a dispute between R. Dosa and the rabbis about the cause of the mourning Zechariah describes. One side attributes it to the death of the messiah son of Joseph, citing Zechariah 12:10:

> And I will pour out on the house of David and the inhabitants of Jerusalem a spirit of compassion and supplication, so that they will look to me concerning the one they have pierced; they shall mourn for him, as one mourns for an only child, and weep bitterly over him, as one weeps over a first-born.[53]

The other side makes the remarkable claim that the cause of the mourning is the death of the evil impulse. If the order in which the participants in the debate are mentioned is the order in which their comments are reported, it is R. Dosa who attributes the mourning to the death of the messiah son of Joseph and the rabbis who attribute it to the death of the evil impulse.

Rav is a first-generation Babylonian amora, but the identification of R. Dosa is not certain. The best attested rabbi bearing the name is the second-generation (and second-century) tanna Dosa b. Harkinas, but there also appear to have been a fourth-generation tanna and two fourth-century amoraim named Dosa, none well attested.[54] The disagreement between R. Dosa and the rabbis is in Hebrew, which would fit a tannaitic date, but it is not introduced with the standard formula marking a baraita, a tannaitic tradition. To further complicate matters, the parallel passage in the earlier Talmud Yerushalmi (y. Suk. 5:2 [23b]) attributes the opposing opinions to "two amoraim"; perhaps it understood R. Dosa as one of the fourth-century R. Dosas. Furthermore, the passage in the Yerushalmi differs from the passage in the Bavli in some significant ways: it refers to mourning for a messiah without specifying his patronym, and it never says that its dead messiah had been killed. Zellentin argues that since the passage cites Zechariah 12:12, it is not unlikely that it would have had Zechariah 12:10 with its pierced one in mind; thus the Yerushalmi too should be understood to claim that the dead messiah has been killed.[55] Still, it is important to note that, unlike the Bavli, the Yerushalmi never says so explicitly.

The second passage in the Bavli about the messiah son of Joseph follows the discussion of the cause of eschatological mourning. It is a baraita that reports a conversation between God and the Davidic messiah in which God promises the messiah anything he wants in the words of Psalm 2:7–8:

> I will tell of the decree of the Lord: He said to me, "You are my son, today I have begotten you. Ask of me, and I will make the nations your heritage, and the ends of the earth your possession."

Seeing the messiah son of Joseph who has been killed, the Davidic messiah asks God for life. God responds that he has already been granted life: "He asked life of you; you gave it to him, length of days forever and ever" ( Ps 21:5 [21:4, RSV]).[56]

It is hard to read this passage without being reminded of a different messiah. The words of the heavenly voice in Jesus's baptism according to Mark (1:11) and Luke (3:22) allude to Psalm 2:7,[57] while Acts (13:33) and the Epistle to the Hebrews (1:5, 5:5) quote the passage.[58] Like the Bavli's dead messiah, Jesus, as already noted, is, at least from one point of view, son of Joseph.[59] So, too, both messiahs have been slain. It seems unlikely that the parallels are accidental. Rather, I would suggest that the passage in the Bavli can be understood as an attack on Christian claims for Jesus, for if God had granted life to his son the Davidic messiah even before he asked, then Jesus's fate clearly demonstrates that he is not that messiah.

If this passage uses Psalm 2:7 against Christians, perhaps we should also read the application of Zechariah 12:10 to the messiah son of Joseph in the passage about eschatological mourning as an attempt to undercut the Christian application of that verse to the death of Jesus (John 19:34, 37; Rev 1:7). The verse refers to a messiah, but, the passage suggests, that messiah is not Jesus.

## The Messiah Son of Joseph and Jesus

Holger Zellentin, too, has argued that these passages from the Bavli respond to Christian claims.[60] But in his view, the passages do so by identifying the messiah son of Joseph, the "secondary messiah" of Palestinian rabbinic tradition, with Jesus. According to Zellentin, the figure of the secondary messiah developed among ancient Jews independent of Christianity, although not necessarily before it, out of the combination of an eschatological understanding of the priest anointed for war with the role assigned to the descendants of Rachel in the defeat of the sons of Esau; both themes are attested, as we have seen, in Genesis Rabbah. Like Heinemann, Zellentin assumes that the earliest traditions about this messiah imagined him triumphant rather than slain, but he is skeptical about Heinemann's view that it was the failure of Bar Kokhba that led to the emergence of the idea of this messiah's death, arguing that the challenge of Christianity provides a better explanation.[61] In Zellentin's reading, the traditions in the Bavli understand Jesus as the secondary messiah but insist that it is the Davidic messiah, not Jesus, who will bring salvation and whom God takes as his son. The version of the Christian story the Bavli attempts to subvert is that of the Gospel of Luke, in which Zellentin finds the elements in relation to which the Bavli shapes its claims: the rejection of Jesus's Davidic descent in favor of the fatherhood of God, the idea that God will give to those who ask, and a passion narrative deeply informed by Zechariah 12:10–13:1.[62]

Zellentin's argument for the importance of the Gospel of Luke for the Bavli deserves further consideration, although it requires the rabbis to have read Luke as subtly and attentively as Zellentin does. I am not convinced, however, that the rabbis would have been willing to concede as much to Christians' claims for their messiah as Zellentin suggests. The attitude toward Jesus in the passages in the Bavli that mention him or allude to the early Christian story is hardly friendly, as Peter Schäfer has shown; sexual promiscuity, magic, idolatry, and blasphemy feature prominently.[63]

I also question Zellentin's view that the messiah son of Joseph was originally understood as triumphant. It is true that Deuteronomy 33:16–17 provides a biblical basis for such a picture. But against the view that the death of the messiah son of Joseph is a later transformation of a tradition about a triumphant messiah, the brevity of the traditions from Genesis Rabbah means that their failure to mention the death of the messiah son of Joseph can hardly be taken to exclude his death as an element of the story to which they allude.[64] Indeed, it seems possible that Genesis Rabbah purposely omits an element of the story that it finds uncomfortable.

Furthermore, although Genesis Rabbah as a completed work undoubtedly predates the Bavli, the traditions from the Bavli about the death of the messiah son of Joseph may well predate the traditions from Genesis Rabbah that do not mention the death.[65] One passage in the Bavli, as we have seen, is introduced by a first-generation amora and cites a rabbi who is probably a tanna, while the other passage is identified as a baraita. The only tradition from Genesis Rabbah attributed to named figures is transmitted by a fifth-generation amora in the name of a third-generation amora, although it could be earlier, perhaps even tannaitic, since it is referred to as a "tradition" and reported in Hebrew. To be sure, the date of the traditions does not settle the date of the emergence of the ideas they describe, for it is always possible that later traditions preserve earlier ideas. But it is noteworthy that neither passage in the Bavli bothers to explain the death of the messiah son of Joseph; rather, both appear to take it for granted that their audience will understand the situation. This mode of presentation suggests that the story of the death of the messiah was well known and predates the traditions in the Bavli.[66]

## The Messiah Son of Joseph in Rabbinic Traditions and *Sefer Zerubbabel*

The Bavli, composed in an empire in which Christians remained a minority and often a persecuted one, contains traditions that allude to or explicitly address Christian stories, even as they attempt to deflate Christian claims.[67] Thus we should not be surprised that the Bavli has more to say about the messiah son of Joseph than rabbinic works from Palestine, even if one of the traditions it cites is a baraita, a tradition that is tannaitic and thus Palestinian, while the other may be tannaitic as well. That is, at least one of the Bavli's traditions about a dying messiah son of Joseph and possibly both come from Palestine. Yet Genesis Rabbah's traditions about the messiah son of Joseph, which date from the time after the empire had become Christian, do not mention his death. It is also noteworthy that the parallel in the Yerushalmi to the Bavli's discussion of mourning for the death of the messiah son of Joseph does not identify the messiah as son of Joseph nor does it indicate that he has been killed.[68]

The passages about the messiah son of Joseph in Genesis Rabbah and especially the Bavli appear to know more about the messiah son of Joseph than they choose to tell us, but *Sefer Zerubbabel* is the first text to provide an account of his career. Much of its account is broadly compatible with the rabbinic traditions, but there are some significant differences. And while at the time of *Sefer Zerubbabel*'s composition in the early seventh century Genesis Rabbah was long complete and the Bavli was either completed or nearing completion, it would be very hard to explain *Sefer Zerubbabel*'s account on the assumption that it derived its knowledge of the messiah son of Joseph from rabbinic sources alone. As I have suggested in the previous chapters, it seems more likely that both the rabbis and *Sefer Zerubbabel* knew a variety of popular stories about the messiahs, which the rabbis handled with caution while *Sefer Zerubbabel* embraced them and reshaped them according to its particular concerns.

Any attempt at reconstructing the popular stories about the messiah son of Joseph is necessarily speculative, but it seems to me that the evidence discussed earlier in this chapter and in previous chapters allows us to make some suggestions. To begin with, the messiah son of Joseph was clearly understood as subordinate to the messiah son of David. For the rabbis, the Davidic messiah usually appears alone. Only rarely is he juxtaposed with the messiah son of Joseph. In *Sefer Zerubbabel*, where both messiahs play significant roles, it is the Davidic messiah who is the final redeemer, and he clearly demonstrates his superiority to the messiah son of Joseph by

bringing him back to life and by slaying Armilos, the great eschatological enemy.

The popular stories probably referred to the messiah in question as
son of Joseph, as in the rabbinic traditions and *Sefer Zerubbabel*,
rather than son of Ephraim, as in the targumic passages mentioned
earlier in the chapter and in many works that postdate *Sefer
Zerubbabel*. From one point of view, there is little difference between
the two designations since Ephraim was Joseph's son. But the name
Ephraim elicits a different set of associations from Joseph. It recalls
Joshua b. Nun, who came from the tribe of Ephraim (Num 13:8) and
who was viewed by some Christians as a model for the messiah, as
we saw earlier in the chapter. It also evokes prophetic expressions of
God's love for his wayward son Ephraim (Hos 11–14, Jer 31), a personification of the northern kingdom in which Ephraim was the
leading tribe; its association with God's love for his son helps to
explain the otherwise surprising choice of the name for the Davidic
messiah in Pesiqta Rabbati 34, 36, and 37, as discussed in Chapter 4.

But while the earlier sources use the name Joseph rather than
Ephraim for the ancestor of the messiah, they never make clear their
understanding of the significance of this ancestry. One obvious possibility is that descent from Joseph makes this messiah a representative of the northern kingdom, home to both Ephraim and Manasseh,
the tribes that claimed descent from Joseph's sons, just as the
Davidic messiah's descent from Judah identifies him with the
southern kingdom. The ancestry of the second messiah would thus
serve to include the lost tribes of the northern kingdom in the eschatological drama. Yet beyond his ancestry, nothing in the traditions
about this messiah connects him to the lost tribes.[69] The absence of
such a connection leaves open the possibility that the emergence
of a Jewish messiah son of Joseph owes something to the example of
the Christian messiah, whose human father bore the name Joseph.[70]

In *Sefer Zerubbabel*, the messiah son of Joseph, like the messiah
son of David, has a personal name, and like the names Hephzibah
and Menahem b. Ammiel, it is a meaningful name: Nehemiah b.
Hushiel. As we have seen, the name Menahem for the Davidic messiah was in circulation well before *Sefer Zerubbabel*, and it is easy
to see how Menahem for one messiah could have generated

Nehemiah, "God comforts," also from the root *nḥm*, for the other. The name Hushiel, which is not attested in the Bible, means something like "God hastens," another appropriate sentiment for the name of a messianic figure. *Sefer Zerubbabel* is the first place we find this name, or any name, for the messiah son of Joseph, but I see no way to decide whether the name was *Sefer Zerubbabel*'s own contribution or whether it was already found in the stories on which *Sefer Zerubbabel* drew.

Another feature of the biography of the messiah son of Joseph attested only in *Sefer Zerubbabel* is his concealment in the city of Rakkath as the eschatological drama begins to unfold.[71] This feature is perhaps an echo of the Davidic messiah's existence in Rome before his manifestation according to the Bavli and *Sefer Zerubbabel*. As discussed in Chapter 3, the emphasis of these texts is on the messiah's fulfillment of the role of the suffering servant of Isaiah 53 in the years before his appearance as the triumphant warrior of the eschatological drama; the choice of Rome, the seat of the evil empire, for the years of suffering is deeply significant. But this period of concealment also solves the problem caused by the placement of the messiah's birth at the time of the destruction of the temple (whether first or second) by accounting for his whereabouts in the interim. Since the birth of the messiah son of Joseph is nowhere in the extant sources associated with a particular moment in history, it seems likely that the picture of his existence before the eschaton is intended to echo that of the Davidic messiah. As for Rakkath, the city in which the messiah son of Joseph awaits the eschaton, it is not otherwise a place of great significance, but according to *Sefer Zerubbabel*, it is also the city in which Hephzibah's staff was hidden. Thus the placement of the concealed messiah son of Joseph in Rakkath may well be the contribution of *Sefer Zerubbabel*, and perhaps the same is true for the fact of his concealment, though I cannot offer an adequate explanation for why the city was important to *Sefer Zerubbabel*.

The rabbinic traditions and *Sefer Zerubbabel* differ on the role they assign to the messiah son of Joseph. Genesis Rabbah identifies him as the war messiah and credits him with the fall of Rome, and while the Bavli's version of the four-craftsmen tradition never explicitly calls him a warrior, it places him in the spot that Pesiqta of Rav Kahana gives to the war messiah. Neither Genesis Rabbah nor the four-craftsmen tradition refers to the messiah's death, but his role as warrior provides a plausible context for it. The Bavli tradition in which the Davidic messiah asks for life does not find it necessary to explain what caused the death of the messiah son of Joseph, perhaps because it takes this context for granted.

In contrast to the rabbinic texts *Sefer Zerubbabel* depicts Nehemiah b. Hushiel not as a warrior but as a political leader. His achievements consist of gathering the people to Jerusalem, restoring sacrifices, and registering the people by families. *Sefer Zerubbabel*'s avoidance of military activities for Nehemiah allows it to give the military role to Hephzibah, the mother of the Davidic messiah. But like the messiah son of Joseph in the Bavli, Nehemiah b. Hushiel dies in the course of his mission, although the witnesses to *Sefer Zerubbabel* differ on who is responsible for his death: Armilos according to the *Sefer Hazikhronot* manuscript and associated witnesses, and the king of Persia according to the first edition and witnesses associated with it. The assignment of the killing of the penultimate messiah to the penultimate enemy has a certain appropriateness, but the attribution of the death to Armilos has the advantage of providing the ultimate eschatological enemy with an individual crime of major proportions and emphasizing the importance of the messiah son of Joseph as well. As I suggested in Chapter 1, the differences between the witnesses and the rough spots in the narratives at this point may reflect a not entirely successful effort to transform an inherited eschatological scenario focused on Rome alone into one that allows a role for Persia as well, an effort likely undertaken as a result of the Persian conquest of Palestine and Jerusalem in the early seventh century.

Both *Sefer Zerubbabel* and one of the passages in the Bavli emphasize the mourning that follows the death of the messiah son of Joseph. The passage in the Bavli is built around the description of mourning in Zechariah 12:10–12, while *Sefer Zerubbabel* emphasizes the duration of the mourning, forty-one days, longer than the thirty days of mourning for Aaron (Num 20:29) and Moses (Deut 34:8). *Sefer Zerubbabel* also emphasizes the fate of the messiah's corpse. Though it lies before the gates of Jerusalem, no creature will touch it during that period, surely a miraculous sign.[72] The first edition goes on to claim that after forty days God himself will bury it.[73]

According to *Sefer Zerubbabel,* there is a happy ending to the story: Elijah and the Davidic messiah bring the messiah son of Joseph back to life. In Chapter 3 I suggested that the Davidic messiah's role in the resurrection of the messiah son of Joseph is likely to reflect material *Sefer Zerubbabel* inherited from the traditions on which it drew. It is possible that the absence of any reference to the resurrection in the Bavli reflects discomfort with the idea, but the material about the messiah son of Joseph in the Bavli is so limited that it is difficult to draw any conclusions on the basis of what is not found. It is also worth remembering that the return to life of the messiah son of Joseph, though not by the means described in *Sefer Zerubbabel,* could perhaps be taken for granted since the eschaton is widely understood to involve a general resurrection, a point explicit in *Sefer Zerubbabel*; indeed, some of the texts considered in the next chapter report the participation of the messiah son of Joseph in the larger resurrection.

The Christian messiah first suffers and then dies. It is perhaps not surprising that despite the importance of the suffering of the Davidic messiah for the Jewish texts discussed in Chapters 3 and 4, the suffering never leads clearly to death, although "*'Az milifnei vereishit*" may hint at it through its reference to new creation; Targum Jonathan to Isaiah 53, which may also envision the death of the messiah, has eliminated suffering from the account of the messiah's activity. Unlike "*'Az milifnei vereishit*," Pesiqta Rabbati, and Targum Jonathan to Isaiah 53, which know only a single, Davidic, messiah, the Bavli contains traditions about a suffering messiah descended from David and a dying messiah descended from Joseph. But the traditions about the suffering Davidic messiah are never brought into relation with traditions about the dying messiah son of Joseph. The Davidic messiah who comments on the death of the messiah son of Joseph is not said to suffer, nor, as I have just noted, does the Bavli report the resurrection of one messiah by the other. *Sefer Zerubbabel* is the only one of the texts in which the dying messiah son of Joseph and the suffering messiah son of David participate in the same eschatological scenario. But even *Sefer Zerubbabel* is unwilling to attribute suffering, death, and resurrection to a single messianic figure.

# CHAPTER SIX

# *Sefer Zerubbabel* after Islam

IN THIS CHAPTER, I sketch the reception of *Sefer Zerubbabel* through late antiquity and the Middle Ages to the second half of the seventeenth century, when the followers of Shabbetai Zvi, the most important Jewish messianic claimant since Jesus, adapted it for their own purposes, and attempt to account for its ongoing influence despite its failure to anticipate the rise of Islam. I am particularly interested in why some elements of *Sefer Zerubbabel*'s narrative have a more robust afterlife than others and in how the texts that embraced aspects of its eschatological scenario understood the claim to authority implicit in its presentation of itself as a work of prophecy modeled on the book of Ezekiel.

As I have just noted, all but the earliest readers of *Sefer Zerubbabel* would have noticed a major flaw in its schema. *Sefer Zerubbabel* was probably composed during the third decade of the seventh century. By the end of the fourth decade, Jerusalem was in the hands not of Romans or Persians but of Arabs, a new force in world history of which *Sefer Zerubbabel* is entirely unaware. Yet despite its failure to foresee an event of such momentous import, *Sefer Zerubbabel* had a significant impact on later Jewish messianism, although, as just indicated, some aspects of the work proved more influential than others. Thus, Hephzibah virtually disappears even in texts deeply indebted to *Sefer Zerubbabel*, and there is rather little interest in the figure of Menahem b. Ammiel as *Sefer Zerubbabel* imagines him. But the idea that the Davidic messiah would be preceded by a messiah descended from Joseph who would die in the course of the events of the end became a well-known alternative to the more standard rabbinic picture of a single, Davidic, messiah. So too Armilos, the eschatological enemy who is at once an embodiment of Rome and a sort of antichrist, plays an important role even in works written under Muslim rule.

I have chosen to group the texts to be discussed here into clusters based on provenance, genre, or the aspect of *Sefer Zerubbabel* of most interest to them.[1] I hope the groupings will permit me to illumine the most important features of *Sefer Zerubbabel*'s reception. I have taken chronology into account as much as possible, but the dates of many of the texts I consider are uncertain. The first cluster I treat is the very small corpus of texts in which Hephzibah appears: the piyyut "*'Oto hayom*," "That Very Day," discussed in Chapter 2; a brief eschatological scenario based on *Sefer Zerubbabel* found in a twelfth-century Ashkenazic manuscript; and, finally, a passage from the Zohar. Then I turn to two works by leaders of the Jewish community, the synthesis of eschatological traditions by Saadya Gaon in his *Book of Beliefs and Opinions* and the responsum on redemption of Hai Gaon, together with another work attributed to Saadya, a Judeo-Arabic commentary on Song of Songs. Next I turn to a corpus of interrelated eschatological texts from the Islamic era that take the form either of visions attributed to R. Simeon b. Yohai or of lists of ten signs of the end. After considering these three groups of texts, I turn to a different type of evidence for the reception of *Sefer Zerubbabel*: the titles by which it was known in both the very limited number of explicit references to the work and the manuscripts in which it was transmitted. I conclude in the seventeenth century with the reworking of *Sefer Zerubbabel* by the followers of Shabbetai Zvi.

As we shall see, most of the texts that incorporate elements of *Sefer Zerubbabel* into their visions of the end come from Muslim lands from roughly the eighth to the twelfth century, while the earliest evidence for *Sefer Zerubbabel* in Ashkenaz comes from the second half of the twelfth century. It is not implausible that *Sefer Zerubbabel* was an object of interest for centuries in the Muslim world before it made its way to Europe, but it is also possible that the distribution of evidence reflects other factors, including the prevalence of textual activity and the survival of texts in the different cultural spheres. We should also leave open the possibility that further investigation will uncover new evidence.

Finally, I want to emphasize that my discussion of the reception of *Sefer Zerubbabel* is a sketch, a preliminary and necessarily incomplete attempt to map a complex set of developments. Limitations of space prevent me from treating every piece of evidence for knowledge of *Sefer Zerubbabel* or its traditions. I pass over a few texts that add little to the sketch, and I omit supposed allusions that seem too uncertain.[2] Furthermore, several of the texts included deserve more detailed discussion than I can provide here. I would single out for further attention the piyyut "*Bayamim hahem uva'et hahi'*," which I mentioned only in passing here, and the texts attributed to R. Simeon and the sign texts, which call for a fuller treatment in their own right than anyone has yet provided.

## Hephzibah after *Sefer Zerubbabel*

Hephzibah almost disappears in later literature, as just noted, but she plays an important role in the piyyut "*'Oto hayom*," which was discussed in Chapter 2 and which I would like to review briefly here. The piyyut probably dates from shortly after the rise of Islam and thus not long after *Sefer Zerubbabel* was composed.[3] The events leading to the eschaton in "*'Oto hayom*" are said to fulfill "the vision of the son of Shealtiel" (*ḥezyon ben She'altiel*) (line 32); the term *ḥezyon*, "vision," has prophetic associations. The events the piyyut describes follow the narrative of *Sefer Zerubbabel* very closely, although they are recounted much more briefly: Hephzibah defeats the two kings (lines 36–37), the messiah son of Joseph gathers Israel to Jerusalem and restores sacrifice (lines 51–52),

Harmilos (spelled thus) arrives and pierces the messiah son of Joseph (line 54), and, finally, the Davidic messiah comes on the scene and brings the messiah son of Joseph back to life, causing all Israel to believe in him (lines 55–56).

"*'Oto hayom*" does not follow *Sefer Zerubbabel* at every point, and two of the most important differences relate to the depiction of Hephzibah. First, the piyyut takes up *Sefer Zerubbabel*'s picture of Hephzibah as warrior but adds to it by identifying her with the staff she wields. Thus the blossoming of the staff in the wilderness when it belonged to Aaron points to Hephzibah's pregnancy that led to the birth of the messiah (lines 38–44). This picture, as Sivertsev has shown, takes over imagery Christians used of the Virgin.[4] The other difference is a disagreement between the texts about the identity of Hephzibah's son. Both make Hephzibah the mother of Menahem b. Ammiel, but for *Sefer Zerubbabel*, Menahem is the messiah son of David, while the piyyut makes him the messiah son of Joseph (lines 46–47). I argued in Chapter 2 that there are good reasons to view *Sefer Zerubbabel*'s identification as original and suggested that the piyyut's identification should be understood as the response of a puzzled reader to *Sefer Zerubbabel*'s depiction of Hephzibah's close association with the messiah who is not her son.

The next appearance of Hephzibah of which I am aware comes in a brief eschatological scenario that is clearly indebted to *Sefer Zerubbabel*. The passage, which is found in a manuscript from the Rhineland dated between 1160 and 1180, is the earliest evidence for the knowledge of *Sefer Zerubbabel*, directly or indirectly, in western Europe.[5] It names all of the major figures of *Sefer Zerubbabel*— Menahem b. Ammiel, Nehemiah b. Hushiel, and Armilos, as well as Hephzibah—and it allows Hephzibah her military role, which must have been surprising to a Jew in twelfth-century Ashkenaz. Unlike "*'Oto hayom*," the passage notes Armilos's birth from Satan and the stone statue, but it describes the statue as having the appearance of a woman, *'ishah*, rather than a virgin, *'ishah betulah*, as in *Sefer Zerubbabel*. The passage also contains elements that do not derive from *Sefer Zerubbabel*, notably God's revelation of the Davidic messiah in response to Israel's repentance in the course of the difficulties that follow the death of the messiah son of Joseph; as we shall see shortly, Israel's repentance is a crucial element of the eschatological drama for both Saadya and Hai Gaon, although nothing suggests that the passage draws directly on either of them.

I was once inclined to understand Hephzibah's eclipse in texts that embraced other aspects of *Sefer Zerubbabel* as a result of Jewish anxiety about the figure of the mother of the messiah. But as noted earlier, most of those texts were written in Muslim lands. Some Jews living under Muslim rule would have had considerable contact with Christians, but for most Jews living under Islam, the Virgin would have been a less familiar figure and certainly a less powerful presence than she was for *Sefer Zerubbabel*. Thus Hephzibah's absence from later texts may be less the result of anxiety than of loss of interest in such a figure.

The eschatological scenario just described is the only text I know after "'*Oto hayom*" to make Hephzibah a warrior as in *Sefer Zerubbabel* and one of only two to mention her at all. We know that the passage was copied in Ashkenaz, and composition by a Jew living among Christians would fit well with its interest in Hephzibah. It would also fit well with the passage's identification of the mother of Armilos as the statue of a woman rather than a virgin, which adds another layer of insult to *Sefer Zerubbabel*'s mockery of the Christian idea of the virgin birth. It is presumably the same motive that lies behind description of the statue as "a stone in the likeness of a woman" in the abbreviated form of *Sefer Zerubbabel* in Oxford MS Opp. 603 (34a), an Ashkenazic manuscript from the sixteenth century.[6]

As far as I know, Hephzibah makes her final appearance in Jewish literature in the Zohar, the central work of medieval Jewish mysticism, composed in Christian Spain in the thirteenth century. It is only a passing mention: the one who announces good tidings to Zion in Isaiah 40:9, feminine in the Hebrew, is identified as Hephzibah, wife of Nathan son of David, mother of the messiah Menahem b. Ammiel (*Shelah Lekha* 173b). The names and relationships are familiar from *Sefer Zerubbabel*, but there is no indication of Hephzibah's military role. It is perhaps not an accident that Hephzibah's final appearance is in a work deeply interested in Christianity.[7]

### Saadya, Hai, Commentary on Song of Songs

Saadya b. Joseph (882–942) was the dominant Jewish intellectual of the first half of the tenth century. He also served for a time as head of the academy of Sura. In addition to his legal and philosophical works, he translated the Torah and other books of the Bible into Arabic and wrote biblical commentaries and works of Hebrew grammar. Like many of his writings, his great philosophical work, the *Book of Beliefs and Opinions*, was written in Judeo-Arabic rather than Hebrew.[8] Hai b. Sherira (939–1038), whose long life began shortly before Saadya died, served as head of the academy of Pumbedita. His literary production was primarily in the realm of halakhah and includes over a thousand surviving responsa, of which one, on the subject of the final redemption, is the text of interest here.[9] He also wrote grammatical works and piyyutim. The third text in this cluster is a Judeo-Arabic commentary on Song of Songs attributed to Saadya in the manuscripts.[10] Recent scholarship generally does not accept the attribution, although both editors of the commentary see significant points of contact with Saadya's work.[11] It is impossible to date the commentary with any certainty. Yehudah Ratsaby suggests a date in the century after Saadya based on historical allusions in the text.[12] I find such an approach problematic for a work that draws on traditional material. On the other hand, a date roughly contemporary with Hai's responsum fits well with the commentary's eschatology.

### *Book of Beliefs and Opinions*

In treatise 8 of the *Book of Beliefs and Opinions*, Saadya provides a systematic account of Jewish messianism. As befits the work of a legal authority who headed one of the rabbinic academies of his day, it draws primarily on rabbinic tradition, and, perhaps in response to Karaite criticism, it expends considerable effort to provide biblical proof texts for every element of the scenario it presents.[13] But of most interest for our purposes is the way it relates the expectation of a dying messiah son of Joseph to the rabbis' assertion that Israel must repent in order to be redeemed and that God will if necessary force repentance by bringing great troubles on Israel (b. Sanh. 97b). For Saadya, the death of the messiah son of Joseph will be the beginning of those troubles. It will set in motion a series of evils culminating in Israel's expulsion to the wilderness and the abandonment of their faith by many Jews. Finally, after these troubles, Elijah will come to inaugurate the redemption of those who remain loyal. Only at the end of the account and almost as an afterthought does Saadya mention the appearance of the Davidic messiah; his role in the proceedings is not specified. If, on the other hand, Israel repents on its own, the role of the messiah son of Joseph will be far more limited. The messiah son of David will come to redeem Israel without the great troubles, and while it is possible that the messiah son of Joseph will precede him as a herald and perhaps remove the wicked from among the people, it is also possible that in this happier scenario the services of the messiah son of Joseph will not be required at all.[14]

Saadya's account of the career of the messiah son of Joseph in the first scenario includes a number of elements familiar from *Sefer Zerubbabel*'s narrative: the messiah's appearance in the Galilee, his arrival in Jerusalem, his death in the course of Armilos's conquest of Jerusalem, the retreat of the people to the wilderness, and their mourning for the messiah. Yet although Saadya lived under Muslim rule at a time when Jerusalem had been in Muslim hands for centuries, he retains *Sefer Zerubbabel*'s picture of Rome's crucial role in the eschatological drama. Jerusalem must return to Roman rule before the messiah son of Joseph appears so that Armilos can play his familiar part as conqueror of Jerusalem and slayer of the messiah son of Joseph, or at least as the one responsible for the events in which the messiah meets his death. And even in the event that Israel is worthy, one of the deeds of the messiah son of David will be the slaying of Armilos.[15]

On the other hand, Saadya's account lacks some important elements of *Sefer Zerubbabel*'s story. It does not give the messiah a name, and he comes back to life not through the agency of the Davidic messiah, who plays such a minimal role in Saadya's first scenario, but rather at the head of all the dead in a general resurrection.[16] In addition, in Saadya's account, the Jews who abandon Judaism after the death of the messiah son of Joseph have no share in the redemption.[17] This picture stands in some tension with that of *Sefer Zerubbabel*, in which all Jews are redeemed, even those who at first fail to recognize the Davidic messiah.

I see nothing in the eschatology of the *Book of Beliefs and Opinions* that requires that Saadya knew *Sefer Zerubbabel* itself. He might have learned the story of the messiah son of Joseph through oral transmission or from a work such as the Secrets of R. Simeon, to be discussed shortly.[18] It is also possible that he knew *Sefer Zerubbabel* but chose to omit elements of its story that conflict with his own eschatological views. Thus it is noteworthy that he appears to consider the story of the messiah son of Joseph no less authoritative than the passage from b. Sanhedrin that asserts that God will bring disasters on Israel to force it to repent; both are attributed to "our forebears."[19] In other words, Saadya grants the tradition about the messiah son of Joseph, which derives directly or indirectly from *Sefer Zerubbabel*, the same status as a tradition from the Bavli. Surprising though this may be, we shall see that it is far from unusual.

## Hai's Responsum on Redemption

Hai's responsum on redemption is clearly indebted to Saadya's eschatology. Like Saadya, Hai attempts to integrate and harmonize a large and varied body of eschatological traditions, and like Saadya, Hai works hard to provide proof texts for every aspect of his scenario, often the same proof texts Saadya used. Hai's eschatological synthesis includes the elements of *Sefer Zerubbabel*'s narrative that Saadya incorporates, and Hai too insists that Roman rule must be restored before the events of the eschaton can unfold. But in contrast to Saadya, Hai provides only a single eschatological scenario, one in which the deeds of the Davidic messiah include the resurrection of the messiah son of Joseph.

The responsum's inclusion of the resurrection means that Hai knew more of the story of the messiah son of Joseph than Saadya told. Furthermore, Hai included Zerubbabel himself in the events of the eschaton: he will blow the great shofar that announces the resurrection of the dead, a picture Hai introduces as a tradition: *'omrim*, "They say. . . ."[20] Yet while the idea of an eschatological shofar is well attested in rabbinic and post-rabbinic literature, nowhere else to the best of my knowledge is it Zerubbabel who blows it.[21] In *Sefer Zerubbabel*, it is God,[22] and in two Islamic-era eschatological works (to be discussed later in this chapter), both indebted to *Sefer Zerubbabel* though probably indirectly, the angel Michael is given the task.[23] Thus it seems plausible that Zerubbabel's role in Hai's responsum is a sort of acknowledgment of *Sefer Zerubbabel*; Zerubbabel's proclamation of the arrival of the messiah (*yakhriz ben She'altiel*) in the piyyut "*Bayamim hahem uva'et hahi'*," which clearly knows *Sefer Zerubbabel* quite well, may be a similar gesture.[24] Finally, whether his knowledge of *Sefer Zerubbabel* is direct or indirect, Hai, like Saadya, treats the material that derives from it no differently from the rabbinic traditions he incorporates into his eschatological scenario.

### Commentary on Song of Songs

This commentary reads Song of Songs in light of a variety of midrashic traditions, of which some relate the text to moments in Israel's history. Traditions from *Sefer Zerubbabel* appear in the discussion of the end of chapter 7 of Song of Songs, and they are briefly recapitulated, although with some differences in detail, at the beginning of the discussion of chapter 8.[25] The commentary reports elements of *Sefer Zerubbabel*'s narrative of the messiah son of Joseph and Armilos that appear in Saadya's *Book of Beliefs and Opinions* and Hai's responsum, and like Saadya and Hai, the commentary includes proof texts for many features of its eschatological scenario. But the commentary also contains elements of *Sefer Zerubbabel* that do not appear in Saadya and Hai: a confused reference to Armilos's birth from a stone, a list of Armilos's bizarre physical features very close to the one in the *Sefer Hazikhronot* manuscript, the name Menahem. b. Ammiel and what appears to be a corruption of the name Hushiel (the name Nehemiah does not appear), and the rejection of Menahem until he brings the messiah son of Joseph back to life; in the commentary, however, it is all Israel who fail to believe, while according to *Sefer Zerubbabel*, it is only the elders and sages.[26] And not only does the commentary know elements of *Sefer Zerubbabel* that do not appear in the *Book of Beliefs and Opinions*, but also, in contrast to the *Book of Beliefs and Opinions*, it contains only a single eschatological scenario. Thus it is problematic to claim, as do the editors of the commentary, that its use of *Sefer Zerubbabel* counts in favor of its relationship to Saadya.[27]

There are, to be sure, some differences between the commentary and *Sefer Zerubbabel*: in the commentary, the messiah son of Joseph arrives only after Armilos has established himself in Jerusalem; Elijah appears only after the resurrection of the messiah son of Joseph; and the messiah son of Joseph is once called son of Ephraim, presumably a reflection of the usage that became dominant in later texts.[28] Despite these differences, it seems plausible that the commentary's source was *Sefer Zerubbabel* itself, though it is also possible that it was an intermediary text or texts or even oral tradition. Finally, the commentary attributes the material from *Sefer Zerubbabel* to "our rabbis, peace be upon them."[29] This attribution is more explicit than anything in the *Book of Beliefs and Opinions* or Hai's responsum, but it is consistent with them.

## Secrets and *'Atidot* of R. Simeon

The last cluster of texts I want to consider consists of several inter-related visions and lists of signs of the end composed in the centuries following the rise of Islam. I begin with two visions attributed to the great second-century rabbi Simeon b. Yohai: the Secrets of R. Simeon and the *'Atidot*, Future Things, of R. Simeon. The Secrets offers a veiled prophecy of events from the Muslim conquest until the eschaton; it alludes to Umayyad but not Abassid caliphs and thus appears to have been written in the first part of the eighth century, before the ascension of the Abassid dynasty in 750. It is noteworthy that it incorporates material that understands Muhammed himself in positive terms, presumably from very early in the period of Muslim rule. The *'Atidot* provides a somewhat updated version of the Secrets, or, more likely, of a common source. It is found only as part of a larger work that takes history all the way back to Adam, titled by its editor "Midrash of the Ten Kings." The Secrets comes down to us in a complete manuscript, a genizah fragment, and an eighteenth-century first edition, while the *'Atidot* does not survive independently at all.[30]

Like the texts in the previous cluster, both the Secrets and the *'Atidot* incorporate traditions about the messiah son of Joseph and Armilos that appear to be indebted to *Sefer Zerubbabel*. The messiah son of Joseph makes his appearance in upper Galilee (*'Atidot* only) and restores sacrifices, first rebuilding the temple, something he fails to do in *Sefer Zerubbabel*; in addition, fire descends from heaven to consume the sacrifices, thus, presumably, vouching for the acceptability of his activity. With the messiah established in Jerusalem, Armilos arrives. He is described as the son of Satan and a stone (Secrets) or a stone statue (*'Atidot*). A list provides details of his grotesque appearance (Secrets only); the details differ from those in *Sefer Zerubbabel*, however.[31] Finally, the messiah dies in battle and is mourned by the people, although only in the Secrets does he die at the hands of Armilos; in the *'Atidot*, he is slain by the forces of Gog and Magog. Neither work gives him a name.[32]

With the death of the messiah son of Joseph, the scenarios of the two works diverge. The Secrets introduces the narrative I have just summarized by telling us that if Israel is worthy, the messiah son of David will come without the other messiah as his predecessor. If Israel is unworthy and the messiah son of Joseph is required, he will be followed by the Davidic messiah. Yet when after the death of the messiah son of Joseph God reveals the Davidic messiah, the people respond by attempting to stone him because, they say, the messiah has already died and no other messiah is expected. The text cites Isaiah 53:3 both to support the necessity of the Davidic messiah's rejection and to explain his response to it, which is to hide himself. Finally, the people call to God out of their great suffering, and the

Davidic messiah appears once again. This time he goes on to slay Armilos, and the people apparently accept him. The dead messiah is never heard from again.[33]

If the Secrets is correctly dated to the mid-eighth century, its two eschatological scenarios, one if Israel is worthy and one if Israel must be forced to repent, predate Saadya's. But it is also possible that the Secrets' schema is a development of Saadya's position designed to give more emphasis to the role of the Davidic messiah in the event that Israel is unworthy and that it was introduced into the Secrets in the course of its transmission.

The '*Atidot* offers no parallel to the Secrets' account of the career of the Davidic messiah. Rather, God defeats Israel's enemies after the death of the messiah son of Joseph without any help from a Davidic messiah, comforting, *menaḥem*, his people as he gathers them and brings them to Jerusalem.[34] The participle *menaḥem* can of course be a proper name as it is for the Davidic messiah in *Sefer Zerubbabel* and some rabbinic traditions, as we have seen. The '*Atidot*'s attribution of the act of comforting to God may be intended to underline that God is quite capable of performing all eschatological tasks without the messiah's help. The Davidic messiah appears only once in the '*Atidot*, in the course of an eschatological calendar that indicates what will happen if Israel is worthy.[35] There is some confusion on the subject, however, since the '*Atidot* also presents the activity of the messiah son of Joseph during the reign of Armilos as the response to Israel's worthiness.[36] The calendar in the '*Atidot* is based on a passage in b. Sanhedrin 97a listing the events of the final seven "weeks," presumably, weeks of years, and it culminates in the manifestation of the Davidic messiah. Versions of this calendar appear also at the end of the Secrets and in the middle of the Prayer of R. Simeon.[37]

It is clear that the Secrets and the '*Atidot* know many aspects of the narrative of *Sefer Zerubbabel*, but it is less clear whether they are directly dependent on it. It is also important to emphasize that, as for other texts discussed in this chapter, *Sefer Zerubbabel* is not their only source of eschatological traditions. The other sources show up clearly in their pictures of the messianic age, which include a variety of elements from rabbinic and post-rabbinic sources, such as a Jerusalem that descends from heaven (Secrets), an eschatological feast (Secrets), and the return of the exiles from beyond the River Sambatyon (*'Atidot*).[38]

## The Prayer of R. Simeon and the Ten-Sign Texts

Now I turn to the remaining texts of this cluster: the Prayer of R. Simeon, the Signs of R. Simeon, the Ten Signs, and the Signs of the Messiah.[39] None of these texts is easy to date. The Prayer of R. Simeon takes a form of the Secrets as its "starting point," as Bernard Lewis puts it, and offers an updated but distinct prophecy, probably around the time of the First Crusade. It is attested in only a single manuscript.[40] The sign texts are closely related to each other in ways that go beyond their use of material from *Sefer Zerubbabel*. For example, each contains a sign consisting of a rain of blood followed by a sign consisting of a rain of healing dew, and two of them (Ten Signs, Signs of the Messiah) contain a sign consisting of terrible heat from the sun. The significant body of common material suggests that these texts are best understood as independent developments of a reasonably fixed body of traditional material.[41] Thus, while no individual sign text appears to have been particularly well known, the traditions the texts share were more widely available. There are no historical references to help in dating them beyond the mention of Ishmaelites in the Signs of R. Simeon and the use there of the legend of the last Christian emperor first attested in the Apocalypse of ps.-Methodius toward the end of the seventh century; unfortunately, knowledge of this hugely popular apocalypse does not do much to narrow the likely historical context.[42] The Ten Signs and the Signs of the Messiah lack any explicit reference to Arabs or Muslims, but both complain of burdensome taxation, a common complaint about Muslim rule, although they attribute the taxation to a king of Rome.[43]

The most important feature of the Prayer of R. Simeon and the sign texts for our purposes is their story of the confrontation between the messiah son of Joseph and Armilos. The texts all give the messiah son of Joseph the familiar name Nehemiah b. Hushiel.

As for Armilos, the Ten Signs is silent on the subject of his paternity but calls his mother a female statue (*tselem neqevah*), while the Signs of R. Simeon names Satan as the father and a female statue as the mother.[44] The Prayer of R. Simeon and the Signs of the Messiah are more innovative, at least about Armilos's paternity, making him the son of worthless gentiles who have had sexual relations with a statue of a beautiful young girl, *na'arah*;[45] the phrase I have translated "worthless" is *bnei veli'al*, a not uncommon biblical phrase of which a literal translation is "sons of worthlessness."[46] According to these texts, then, the father of Armilos was not Satan but a human being (or human beings!), which suggests that they have failed to appreciate fully the polemical significance of *Sefer Zerubbabel*'s picture in relation to the Christian understanding of Christ. Still, it is worth noting that in some texts of the Second Temple period as well as some early Christian texts, Belial or Beliar becomes a proper name for the leader of the forces of evil.[47] It seems to me unlikely that medieval Jews would have been aware of this meaning, but if they were, the significance of the phrase in our texts would be somewhat different, perhaps reflecting an effort to make the father of Armilos human and satanic at once.

The mother of Armilos according to the Prayer of R. Simeon and the Signs of the Messiah, as just noted, is the statue of a beautiful young girl. The texts add that the statue was created by God himself in his great power (Signs of the Messiah) during the six days of creation (Prayer of R. Simeon).[48] The insistence that the statue is not the work of human hands is presumably intended to explain how it is possible for it to bear a son. But it is not clear to me how to understand the significance of referring to the statue as that of a *na'arah*. In the Bible, a *na'arah* is a girl of marriageable age, although not necessarily a virgin (e.g., Deut 22:13–21, Ruth 2:6). Thus, while the term could be nothing more than a synonym for virgin, it could also be intended to introduce doubt about the status of the figure the statue represents. Unlike the term *'ishah*, "woman," discussed earlier, however, it is not clearly polemical.

The confrontation between the messiah son of Joseph and Armilos described in the Prayer of R. Simeon and the sign texts has roots in *Sefer Zerubbabel*, but it goes beyond anything found there.

The details of the confrontation vary slightly from text to text; my summary attempts to do justice to the different accounts, with variant details in the notes. It is perhaps worth mentioning that in setting the stage for the confrontation, the texts describe Nehemiah's rise without some familiar elements of the story: his appearance in the Galilee and, perhaps more surprising, the resumption of sacrifice. The confrontation begins with Nehemiah already on the scene. Armilos arrives, announces himself as messiah and God, and demands that the gentiles produce the Torah he has given them. They do so, and it apparently supports his claims. Then he summons Nehemiah and the people of Israel with their Torah and demands that they recognize him as God. Nehemiah and his companions refuse, citing the first two of the Ten Commandments: I am the Lord your God; you shall have no other gods before me. Armilos dismisses the contents of the Torah and again demands that Israel recognize him as God as the nations of the world have done. Nehemiah instead denounces him: "You are not God but Satan!" There follows a battle in which many of Armilos's followers die but Nehemiah too is slain.[49]

In *Sefer Zerubbabel*, it is the beautiful stone statue that is explicitly presented as an object of idolatrous worship. The first edition warns that the statue "will be the head of all idolatry," and at the end of their accounts, both the *Sefer Hazikhronot* manuscript and the first edition include an episode in which Armilos takes the statue from the church and insists that all nations worship it.[50] But there are also some hints, at least in the *Sefer Hazikhronot* manuscript, that Armilos aspires to be worshipped in his own right. When Armilos is first introduced, we are told: "Anyone who does not believe in him, he will slay by the sword, and he will slay many of them."[51] The passage also informs us somewhat confusingly that Armilos himself will worship strange gods.[52] Later, after Armilos has killed Nehemiah, "All the nations of the world will go astray after him, except for Israel, who will not believe in him."[53] Neither of these passages appears in the first edition, perhaps because they stand in tension with the idea of the beautiful statue as the head of idolatry.

In the first century of this era, the apostle Paul warned the earliest followers of Jesus that before the return of Christ, the son of perdition would establish himself in the temple and proclaim himself God (2 Thes 2:3–4). Not long after *Sefer Zerubbabel* was written, ps.-Ephrem's Sermon on the End of Time, the Syriac apocalyptic work discussed briefly in Chapter 3 for its insistence that the ability to resurrect the dead is a sign of the true messiah, offered a more detailed prediction of the career of the antichrist with some interesting parallels to the story in the Prayer of R. Simeon and the sign texts. After a series of terrifying cosmic portents, the antichrist will enter in the temple in Jerusalem, where the Jews will embrace him. He will then proclaim: "I, even I, am the Father and the Son! / The First and the Last! / There is no other God apart from me!" At this, however, some Jews will recognize that "the one whom our ancestors restrained / At the top of the wood(en cross) on Golgotha / Is (actually) the redeemer of (all) creatures." The antichrist will then threaten all who reject him with death by the sword.[54] The parallels between Armilos's behavior in the Jewish texts just considered and the antichrist's in ps.-Ephrem are not sufficiently detailed to suggest a direct link between the Jewish texts and ps.-Ephrem. Rather, the presence of episodes in which the antichrist claims divinity in both Jewish and Christian works suggests that such an expectation was widespread. Furthermore, although all of the texts discussed here postdate the rise of Islam, both Jewish and Christian works depict a contest between Judaism and Christianity without any attention to Islam.

But neither *Sefer Zerubbabel* nor ps.-Ephrem provides background for one central aspect of the confrontation between Armilos and Nehemiah: the two Torahs, one belonging to the gentiles, the other to Israel. The logic of the story suggests that the gentiles' Torah is the New Testament, which identifies Christ with God. The attribution of a Torah to gentiles recalls a tradition that appears in two slightly different versions in the Tanhuma in which Christians claim that they are Israel on the basis of their possession of the Torah in Greek only to have God reject their claim. Rather, he insists, his children are those who possess his *mysterion*, the Mishnah, which Christians cannot coopt because it is oral.[55] The Tanhuma as a collection likely dates to the eighth or ninth century, but the tradition about the *mysterion* is attributed to R. Judah b.

Shalom, a Palestinian amora of the second half of the fourth century, active at a time when Jewish concern for Christian supersessionism is hardly surprising.[56] There is no reason to suggest any direct impact of the tradition about the *mysterion* on the episode of the conflict between Armilos and Nehemiah. Indeed, the picture of the Tanhuma, in which Jews can trump Christians' claim to their shared written text with an oral document, stands in tension with the picture of two Torahs, which does not acknowledge the overlap between the Jewish and Christian Bibles but instead depicts the Christian Torah as the wicked inverse of the true Torah. On the other hand, the ultimate message of both pictures is the same: Christians may claim to possess the truth, but their claim is false.

The story of the confrontation of Armilos and the messiah son of Joseph suggests that the debt of the Prayer of R. Simeon and the sign texts to *Sefer Zerubbabel* is indirect, that they draw not on *Sefer Zerubbabel* itself but on a source that expanded *Sefer Zerubbabel*'s story. Such expansion is further evidence for the impact of the story of the messiah son of Joseph, which can be seen in so many of the texts examined. It is important to acknowledge, however, that this hypothetical expanded narrative has not come down to us and that the texts discussed here provide the only evidence for its existence. Furthermore, as I noted earlier, all aspects of the sign texts, not just the ones relevant to the reception of *Sefer Zerubbabel*, deserve more attention than they have yet received. It would be an important contribution to untangle the complicated relations among them and between them and the Prayer of R. Simeon. The previous discussion suggests a particularly close relationship between the Prayer of R. Simeon and the Signs of the Messiah, but the nature of the relationship requires further study. A clearer picture of these relations would surely have implications for our understanding of the use of *Sefer Zerubbabel*.

Finally, let me note that like many other texts discussed here, the Prayer of R. Simeon and the sign texts draw on a range of rabbinic and post-rabbinic sources for their picture of the messianic era. The more limited impact of *Sefer Zerubbabel* on this aspect of the eschatological scenario is by now perhaps to be expected. *Sefer Zerubbabel*'s distinctive contribution to Jewish messianism is its coherent narrative of the events leading up to the end. No such narrative was to be found in rabbinic literature. On the other hand, the rabbis discussed the messianic age itself at a variety of points, and while they did not leave behind an integrated picture, they did provide rich resources for the eschatologically inclined to draw on. Let me emphasize, however, that the texts discussed in this chapter offer no indication that they distinguish between traditions from rabbinic literature as such and other sources.

## Explicit References

In the discussion in this chapter to this point, I have tried to deduce something about the attitudes toward *Sefer Zerubbabel* of the variety of works that draw on it. This has not been an easy task since many of the texts do not seem to have known *Sefer Zerubbabel* directly and few of them offer any clear statement of their understanding of the nature of its authority. In this section, I would like to consider another kind of evidence for how *Sefer Zerubbabel*'s claims to authority were received in the millennium after its composition: the title by which it was known.

I begin with the very small number of references to the work. The earliest is the piyyut "*'Oto hayom*," which, as we have seen, refers to *Sefer Zerubbabel* as "the vision of the son of Shealtiel," *ḥezyon ben She'altiel*, a designation that fits well with *Sefer Zerubbabel*'s attempt to present itself as prophecy. The next is the commentary on the Torah of the great philosopher, commentator, and poet Abraham ibn Ezra (1089–1167), who spent most of his life in Muslim Spain. In his discussion of Exodus 2:22, after objecting to the views on Moses' wife or wives of a book called "The Chronicles of Moses," he writes:

> Altogether I tell you, any book that was written neither by prophets nor by sages according to the tradition is not to be relied on, especially when it contains things that contradict good sense, such as the book of Zerubbabel and also the book of Eldad the Danite and the like.[57]

For ibn Ezra, then, *Sefer Zerubbabel* was neither prophecy, as " *'Oto hayom*" seems to have believed, nor the words of the sages, as Saadya, Hai, and others appear to have understood it; rather, it contradicted good sense.

Writing not long after ibn Ezra in Ashkenaz, Eleazar of Worms (c. 1176–1238), one of the central figures of the *ḥasidei Ashekanz*, the German pietists, uses a different title that reflects a quite different view. In his commentary on the book of Ruth (to 4:11), he cites the *baraita deZerubbabel* as his source for identifying Jonah's Nineveh with Rome; knowledge of such a detail suggests real familiarity with *Sefer Zerubbabel*.[58] In its original sense, a baraita is a tannaitic saying cited in the Bavli that does not appear in the Mishnah, but the term comes to be used as a title for works claiming tannaitic provenance such as *baraita deniddah,* the baraita on laws of menstrual impurity; *baraita deRabbi Ishmael,* the baraita of R. Ishmael; and *baraita demelkehet hamishkan,* the baraita on the construction of the tabernacle. The designation of *Sefer Zerubbabel* as a baraita is consistent with the attitude toward *Sefer Zerubbabel* or its traditions implicit in many of the texts just considered, which appear to accept it as authentic ancient tradition.

Finally, a fourteenth-century Ashkenazic manuscript of kabbalistic works contains a brief, otherwise unknown, text that begins thus:[59]

> These are five book and five orders that ben Sira revealed to Uzziel his son and Joseph his grandson: the Book of Creation [*Sefer Yetsirah*, an early Jewish mystical work], the Book of the Garden,[60] the Book of Grammar, the Book of Pesiqta with Two Faces [*Sefer Pesiqta Betrei 'Apei* ], and *Sefer Zerubbabel*. And in it are five chapters: the chapter of R. Simeon b. Yohai, the chapter of Avot deRabbi Natan, the chapter of the Alphabet of R. Aqiva, the chapter of the construction of the tabernacle, and the chapter of the way of the world [*derekh 'erets*]. Five orders. . . .

The text goes on to report on the use of *Sefer Yetsirah* by Abraham and Shem and then ben Sira and Jeremiah.

While I cannot explain the significance of all the books in the list, it seems to me that the eschatological concerns of *Sefer Zerubbabel* complement *Sefer Yetsirah*'s interest in cosmogony. If, as seems likely, the Book of the Garden treats the Garden of Eden, it would provide individual eschatology in contrast to *Sefer Zerubbabel*'s collective eschatology. I should note that George Margoliouth thinks the *Sefer Zerubbabel* in question must be a different work from the one known to us, presumably because of the five chapters attributed to it by the passage in the manuscript.[61] The texts considered earlier in the chapter make the association of R. Simeon b. Yohai with *Sefer Zerubbabel* quite reasonable, but I cannot suggest a way to make sense of the remaining chapters. Still, I see no reason to assume the existence of an otherwise unattested *Sefer Zerubbabel* containing several known works as chapters. It seems to me more likely that the intention of the author of the list eludes us.

## Manuscripts and Early Editions

*Sefer Zerubbabel* is, perhaps not surprisingly, the most common title in the manuscript. The Byzantine manuscript MS JTS 2325/20 begins by proclaiming in large letters: "This is the book of Zerubbabel b. Shealtiel" (192). Oxford MS Opp. 236a, an Ashkenazic manuscript from the seventeenth century, the latest of the known manuscripts, prefaces its text thus: "With the help of God I begin the book of Zerubbabel b. Shealtiel" (13r); this title appears in characters the same size as the text. The title "*Sefer Zerubbabel*" also appears in the first printed edition of 1519 and in Jellinek's edition. It is impossible in either case to be certain that the title reflects the manuscripts on which the editions are based, but the conclusion of Jellinek's edition presumably reproduces the reading of at least one of his manuscripts: *Seliq Sefer Zerubbabel*, "The book of Zerubbabel is concluded."[62]

The titles in the two remaining manuscripts of *Sefer Zerubbabel* support opposite poles of its claim to authority. The partial table of contents at the beginning of *Sefer Hazikhronot*, the anthology that provides the earliest manuscript of *Sefer Zerubbabel* and the one that has been the most important for our discussion, lists the work as *ḥezyon Zerubbabel*, the vision of Zerubbabel (4r).[63] As we have seen, "*'Oto hayom*" refers to *Sefer Zerubbabel* the same way. A different title in a similar spirit appears later in the manuscript at the head of *Sefer Zerubbabel* itself: "Prophecy and Dream of Zerubbabel b. Shealtiel" (248r). The title is written in smaller letters than the text, and the words are arranged in pairs with large spaces between to fill the line: *Nevu'at vehalom—shel Zerubbabel— ben She'altiel*, Prophecy and Dream—of Zerubbabel—son of Shealtiel.

The other understanding of *Sefer Zerubbabel*'s authority is reflected in the elaborate and somewhat ungrammatical title at the beginning of the abridged version of the work in Oxford MS Opp. 603, an Ashkenazic manuscript dated 1568–71: "*Zeh hasefer Zerubbabel vehiddushim me'Eliyyahu z"l umimelekh hamashiah*," "This is the book of Zerubbabel and innovations from Elijah of blessed memory and from the King Messiah" (32r). The idea of rabbinic innovations, *hiddushim*, attributed to Elijah and the King Messiah is in itself remarkable, to say nothing of the claim that the content of *Sefer Zerubbabel* should be regarded as such. But perhaps it is a mistake to place too much weight on the attributions, which may be intended only to signal the eschatological content of the work. In any case, like Eleazar of Worms's use of the term "baraita," the title associates the work with rabbinic culture. As already noted, such an understanding of *Sefer Zerubbabel* or its traditions is implicit in several of the works indebted to it that were discussed earlier. I should also note that the title, *hasefer Zerubbabel*, is ungrammatical in giving a definite article (*ha*) to a word in the construct state (*sefer*); the lapse may reflect the fact that the word governed by the construct, which would normally take the definite article, cannot do so because it is a proper noun, Zerubbabel. The correct grammatical solution is to avoid the definite article altogether, as do the other witnesses to this title.

### *Sefer Zerubbabel* and the Sabbatian Movement

For most of the millennium after its composition, it probably did not matter much whether its readers considered *Sefer Zerubbabel* to be a baraita or a prophecy. Although the difference between a rabbinic work and a work of prophecy is enormous, for Jews from late antiquity to modernity, both categories were authoritative. But in the middle of the seventeenth century, prophecy took on new importance for the followers of Shabbetai Zvi, the aspiring messiah at the head of the most important Jewish messianic movement since Christianity. In the upheavals surrounding the movement, Jews around the world were sharply divided between supporters and opponents, with prominent rabbinic figures on both sides. The split only deepened after Shabbetai's conversion to Islam in 1666, when many of his followers continued to believe in his messianic mission, as he himself apparently did.[64]

In *Tsitsat Novel Tsvi*, his anti-Sabbatian polemical work, R. Jacob Sasportas, the great contemporary opponent of Sabbatianism, preserves correspondence from followers of Shabbetai in which they cite the "Prophecy of Zerubbabel" in support of their claims. One correspondent invokes the book for its prediction that the great ones and sages of Israel would reject the messiah, despise him, and strike him, and that he would be imprisoned. Another correspondent claims that the work predicts that the messiah would be accused of apostasy, as does Nathan of Gaza, the prophet of the Sabbatian movement and its most important thinker.[65]

*Sefer Zerubbabel* does indeed report the messiah's rejection by the rabbis, though perhaps not with as much emphasis as Sasportas's correspondent suggests, but there is nothing in it that could be construed as hinting at the messiah's apostasy. Following Shabbetai's conversion to Islam, one of his followers undertook to remedy this lack by writing a new revelation to Zerubbabel that takes *Sefer Zerubbabel* as its point of departure.[66] The new work is particularly indebted to Pesiqta Rabbati, the seventh-century midrash (discussed in Chapter 4) with its more detailed account of the suffering of the Davidic messiah and the failure of the learned to embrace him.[67] The Sabbatian text does not support all of the claims of Sasportas's correspondents, but it emphasizes the messiah's imprisonment by God for eight years to punish the unworthy generation, develops the theme of Jewish opposition to the messiah far beyond *Sefer Zerubbabel*'s picture, and at least hints that the messiah would be accused of apostasy.[68] It was eventually introduced into a manuscript of *Hekhalot Rabbati*, a late antique work of merkavah mysticism, which is how it reaches us today.[69]

Sasportas's response to the claims for the "Prophecy of Zerubbabel" was sometimes to deny the very existence of the book and sometimes, more accurately at least for the original *Sefer Zerubbabel*, to deny that it contained what the Sabbatians said it contained.[70] But another option available to opponents of Shabbetai Zvi was to use aspects of *Sefer Zerubbabel* against him.[71] Thus we learn that a Polish rabbi named Nehemiah Cohen challenged Shabbetai's claims to be the Davidic messiah on the grounds that the messiah son of Joseph had to fulfill his mission before the messiah son of David could manifest himself.[72] Christian sources suggest that R. Nehemiah claimed that he himself was the messiah son of Joseph.[73] But while he conveniently bore the same name as the messiah son of Joseph in *Sefer Zerubbabel*, his priestly descent, evidenced by the appellation Cohen, would seem to pose a problem for his claim to be a descendant of Joseph, as some contemporaries commented.[74] Yet whatever the nature of R. Nehemiah's claims, it is clear that *Sefer Zerubbabel* had considerable potential to help the case of opponents of Shabbetai Zvi, as well as supporters.

The Sabbatian reception of *Sefer Zerubbabel* offers a fascinating glimpse of the opportunities and challenges an ancient eschatological work could pose for a movement committed to a living messianic claimant. But the Sabbatian exploitation of the conjunction of *Sefer Zerubbabel*'s presentation of itself as prophecy with the criticism of the rabbinic elite expressed in its narrative should not obscure the irony that, as we just saw, many of *Sefer Zerubbabel*'s readers and transmitters in the millennium after its composition viewed it as a rabbinic work.

## Authority and Narrative

In the end, however, *Sefer Zerubbabel*'s impact on later Jewish eschatology may have had less to do with perceptions of its authority than with the appeal of its story of the messiah son of Joseph and the great eschatological archenemy, Armilos. Jews in Muslim lands, unfamiliar with Christian veneration of the mother of Christ, seem to have lost interest in Hephzibah, and while Jews everywhere undoubtedly remained interested in the Davidic messiah, with the notable exception of the Sabbatian revision, later texts draw very little on *Sefer Zerubbabel*'s picture of Menahem b. Ammiel as a suffering messiah imprisoned in Rome whose glory is at first obscured by his unprepossessing appearance. Here I suspect the explanation is that rabbinic literature provided a large enough body of traditions about the Davidic messiah, including the picture of the suffering messiah in b. Sanhedrin 98b, to satisfy interest in this most important eschatological hero. But for someone interested in the other messiah, the one who gives his life for the Jewish people, rabbinic literature has only a few hints to offer. Nor does rabbinic literature provide an eschatological foe of truly demonic character with the colorful biography and appearance of Armilos. Altogether, I would agree that it was *Sefer Zerubbabel*'s compelling narrative more than its claims to be a prophetic work or its readers' understanding of it as rabbinic tradition that accounts for its long afterlife.

# Conclusion

*SEFER ZERUBBABEL* IS the first Jewish text in which the complementary roles in the eschatological drama of two different messiahs, one descended from Joseph and the other from David, are described in some detail. In this book, I have attempted to illumine this influential eschatological scenario by placing the main actors in that scenario—Menahem b. Ammiel, the Davidic messiah; Nehemiah b. Hushiel, the messiah son of Joseph; and Hephzibah, the mother of Menahem b. Ammiel—in the context of both Jewish and Christian culture of the Byzantine era.

*Sefer Zerubbabel* is deeply informed by its encounter with Christian messianism. Its interest in a mother of the messiah, her role as a warrior, the depiction of the Davidic messiah in terms drawn from the suffering servant of Isaiah 53, the death of the messiah descended from Joseph—all these demonstrate the great attraction some aspects of Christian belief and narrative held for *Sefer Zerubbabel*. Other aspects of Christianity were clearly repugnant to *Sefer Zerubbabel*, as indicated by its depiction of Armilos, the great eschatological enemy, as the son of Satan and a beautiful statue of a virgin. But whether attracted or repelled, *Sefer Zerubbabel* provides powerful evidence for the impact of Christian culture on Jewish messianism.

The literary evidence for Jewish culture in the centuries before *Sefer Zerubbabel* was composed is largely rabbinic. While it has long been noted that *Sefer Zerubbabel* shows significant points of contact with rabbinic literature, such as the name Menahem for the messiah descended from David, the picture of this messiah awaiting the time for his mission in Rome, and the death of the messiah son of Joseph, I have argued for a new understanding of the relationship. I hope to have shown that the shared elements are evidence not for *Sefer Zerubbabel*'s debt to rabbinic literature but rather for popular traditions on which the rabbis and *Sefer Zerubbabel* drew independently. Thus, *Sefer Zerubbabel* allows us a glimpse of the messianic hopes of ordinary Jews in the centuries preceding its composition. The rabbis shared these hopes to a certain extent but also attempted to tamp them down. *Sefer Zerubbabel*, on the other hand, embraced them fully, though it sometimes developed them in distinctive ways that reflect its early seventh-century setting.

Finally, *Sefer Zerubbabel* is the first Jewish work after the apocalypses written in the wake of the destruction of the Second Temple to offer an extended narrative of the end of days. Rabbinic texts tend to break narrative down into small units; *Sefer Eliyyahu*, the other Hebrew apocalyptic work written in response to the wars between the Byzantine and Persian empires, lacks real narrative in part because it imitates rabbinic style. *Sefer Zerubbabel*'s narrative line is by no means straightforward, and it would have benefitted from better editing; it is all too evident that the narrative incorporates a number of preexisting units, and at some points, it offers doublets of speeches or events. Its long history of transmission and its impact on later Jewish messianism despite these infelicities are testimony to the power of its story.

# APPENDIX

Translation of *Sefer Zerubbabel* according to the
*Sefer Hazikhronot* Manuscript

The translation that follows is based on my 1990 translation of the
*Sefer Hazikhronot* manuscript, Oxford MS Heb. d. 11, **248r–251r**.[1]
In revising it, I have consulted images of the manuscript as well as
Lévi's edition. I have corrected mistakes and misreadings in the earlier translation (few and minor, I hope), and I have also attempted to
improve its clarity while maintaining a balance between a usefully
literal rendering and readable English. The margins of the manuscript contain a number of notes, which, based on the handwriting,
Lévi takes to be the work of the copyist;[2] this judgment seems correct to me. I include some of these readings in my notes. *Sefer
Zerubbabel* is full of biblical language and allusions, which I note in
parentheses in the body of the translations. Chapter and verse numbers indicate an explicit quotation or, more often, the incorporation
of a phrase or verse from the biblical text; "see" plus chapter and
verse indicates an allusion. Some of the issues raised in the notes to
the 1990 translation have been addressed in the body of this book,
and I have therefore felt free to omit those notes in the translation
here. But I have also omitted a few notes on subjects not directly
relevant to my arguments in this book, so for some purposes the
notes to the earlier translation may still be useful.

## PROPHECY AND DREAM
## OF ZERUBBABEL B. SHEALTIEL[3] (248r)

The word that came to Zerubbabel b. Shealtiel, governor of Judah, on the twenty-fourth day of the seventh month.[4] The Lord showed me this vision there. I was prostrate in prayer before the Lord my God during the apparition of the vision I saw on the Chebar (river) (see Ezek 1:1). When I said, "Blessed are you, Lord, who revives the dead,"[5] my heart groaned within me saying, What will be the form of the eternal house?[6]

The Lord answered me from the doors of heaven: "Are you Zerubbabel b. Shealtiel, governor of Judah?"

"Your servant," I said.

He answered me and spoke as one person speaks to another (Exod 33:11). I heard his voice, but I did not see his form (see Deut 4:12).[7] Then I rose to prostrate myself as at first, finished my prayer, and went to my house.

On the eleventh day of the month of Adar he spoke to me there, saying, "O Zerubbabel, my servant."

"Your servant," I said.

"Come to me," he said. "Ask and I will tell you."

"How shall I ask?," I answered, "for my end draws near and my days are numbered (Lam 4:18)."

"I will make you live," he said. "Be alive."

Then a spirit lifted me between heaven and earth (see Ezek 8:3) and led me about Nineveh, the great city (Jonah 3:3), which is the city of blood (Ezek 22:2, 24:6,9; see Nah 3:1).

"Woe is me," I said. "My heart has been false (see Hos 10:2), and my soul is very sad." Then I rose from my sorrow to pray and beseech the name of the Lord God of Israel. I confessed all my sins and transgressions for my heart had been false. "O Lord," I said, "I have gone astray, I have sinned, I have transgressed, for my heart has been false. You, O Lord, are the god who made everything by the utterance of your mouth, and by the word of your lips (Ps 17:4) the dead will come to life."

Then he said to me, "Go to the house of disgrace, to the market-place."[8] I went as he commanded. "Turn this way," he said. When I turned, he touched me, and I saw a man despised (Isa 53:3), severely wounded (Deut 23:2), and in pain (see Isa 53:3).[9]

Now that despised man said to me, "Zerubbabel, what is your business here? Who brought you here?"

"The spirit of the Lord lifted me up," I answered, "and deposited me in this place."

"Fear not," he said, "for you have been brought here in order to show you" (Ezek 40:4).

When I heard his words, I took comfort, and my mind was at rest. "Sir," I asked, "what is the name of this place?"

"This is Rome the Great, in which I am imprisoned," he said.

"Sir, who are you," I asked, "and what is your name? What are you looking for here? And what are you doing in this place?"

"I am the Lord's anointed, the son of Hezekiah," he answered, "and I am jailed until the time of the end." When I heard this, I was silent and hid my face. His anger burned within him.[10] I beheld him (Num 24:17) and was afraid.

"Come to me," he said. When he spoke to me, my limbs trembled, but he extended his hand and supported me. "Do not fear," he said, "and let not your heart be afraid." He encouraged me and said, "Why did you fall silent and hide your face from me?"

I replied, "Because you said, 'I am the Lord's servant and his anointed one, and the light of Israel.' "[11] (**248v**) Then he appeared like a young man, a handsome and comely youth. I asked him, "When will the light of Israel come?"

As I was speaking to him, behold, a man with two wings came to me and said, "Zerubbabel, what are you asking the Lord's anointed one?"

"I am asking when the time of salvation will come," I answered.

"Ask me and I will tell you," he said.

"Who are you, sir?" I asked.

"I am Michael," he answered, "who brought good tidings to Sarah.[12] I am the commander of the host of the Lord God of Israel who fought against Sennacherib and struck down 180,000 men.[13] I am the commander of Israel who fought the wars against the kings of Canaan (see Josh 5:13–15). And in the future I shall fight the wars of the Lord at the side of the Lord's anointed, the one sitting before you, against the king with the arrogant face (Dan 8:23) and against Armilos son of Satan, who came forth from the stone statue.[14] The Lord appointed me as commander of his people and those who love him to fight against the commanders of the nations."[15]

Then Michael answered Metatron[16] and said to me, "I am the angel who led [Abraham][17] throughout the land of Canaan and blessed him in the name of the Lord. I am the one who redeemed Isaac and wept over him.[18] I am the one who struggled with Jacob at the ford of Jabbok (see Gen 32:22–32). I am the one who led Israel in the wilderness in the name of the Lord (see Exod 23:20–23). I am the one who appeared to Joshua at Gilgal (see Josh 5:13–15). I am the one who rained down fire and brimstone on Sodom and Gomorrah. For he put his name in me: "Metatron" equals *shadday*, "the Almighty," in gematria.[19] Now you, Zerubbabel b. Shealtiel, whose name is Jeconiah, ask me and I will tell you what will happen to your people at the end of days."

[I asked, "Who is this man here?"] [20]

He answered, "This is the Lord's anointed, who is hidden in this place until the end time. This is the messiah son of David, and his name is Menahem b. Ammiel. He was born at the time of David, king of Israel, and a wind lifted him up and hid him in this place until the end time."

I, Zerubbabel, asked Metatron, the commander of the Lord's host, ["What are the signs that Menahem b. Ammiel will perform?"][21]

He said, "The Lord will give Hephzibah, the mother of Menahem b. Ammiel, a staff for these acts of salvation. A great star will shine before her. All the stars will swerve from their paths. Hephzibah, the mother of Menahem b. Ammiel, will go forth and kill two kings, both with hearts set on doing evil (see Dan 11:27). The names of the two kings are Nof, king of Yemen, who will wave his hand[22] (Isa 11:15) at Jerusalem, and the name of the second, is Iszinan,[23] king of Antioch. This war and these signs will take place on the Festival of Weeks in the third month.

"For the word is true. Four hundred and twenty years after the city and the temple are rebuilt, they will be destroyed a second time. And twenty years after the city of Rome has been built, after seventy kings corresponding to the seventy nations have ruled over her, when ten kings have completed their reigns, the tenth king will come (see Dan 7:20). He will destroy the sanctuary, the daily offering will cease (see Dan 11:31), the nation of the holy ones (Dan 8:24) will be scattered, and he will give them over to the sword, to pillage, (249r) and to panic. Many of them will fall for the sake of their Torah so they will abandon the Lord's Torah and worship their idols. And when they stumble, they will receive a little help (Dan 11:34). From the day that the daily offering ceases and the wicked ones place him whose name is abomination in the temple (see Dan 11:31), at the end of 990 years, the Lord's salvation will take place, [after] the shattering of the power of the holy people (see Dan 12:7), to redeem and to gather them by the hand of the Lord's anointed.

"Now the staff that the Lord will give to Hephzibah, the mother of Menahem b. Ammiel, is made of almond wood, and it is hidden away in Rakkath (see Josh 19:35), a city in Naphtali. This is the staff that the Lord gave to Adam, Moses, Aaron, Joshua, and King David. It is the staff that blossomed and sprouted in the tent for Aaron (see Num 17:23). Elijah b. Eleazar[24] hid it Rakkath, which is Tiberias. A man named Nehmiah b. Hushiel b. Ephraim b. Joseph is also hidden away there."

Then Zerubbabel answered Metatron and Michael the commander, "Sir, I would like you to tell me when the Lord's anointed will come and what will happen after all this."

"The Lord's anointed, that is, Nehemiah b. Hushiel, will come five years after Hephzibah and gather all Israel as one," he said. "They will remain in Jerusalem for forty years. The children of Israel will offer sacrifice, and it will be pleasing to the Lord. He will register Israel by families (see 1 Chr 9:1). Then in the fifth year of Nehemiah and the gathering of the holy ones, Shiroi, king of Persia, will go up against Nehemiah b. Hushiel and Israel, and there will be great trouble for Israel. Hephzibah, the wife of Nathan the prophet, the mother of Menahem b. Ammiel, will go forth with the staff that the Lord God of Israel gave her. The Lord will place a spirit of confusion (see Isa 19:14) in them, and each one will kill his fellow and his brother. And there the evil one will die."

When I heard this, I fell on my face. "O Lord,"[25] I said, "tell me what the prophet Isaiah meant when he said, 'There the calves graze, there they lie down and consume its boughs' " (Isa 27:10).

He said, "The calf is Nineveh, the city of blood, which is Rome the Great."

There I continued to ask about the prince of the holy covenant (see Dan 11:22). He clung to me and they brought me to the house of disgrace and scorn.[26] He showed me a marble stone in the shape of a virgin, and its appearance and form were most lovely and beautiful to behold. "This stone is the wife of Belial," he answered. "Satan will come and lie with it, and a son named Armilos will come forth from it: 'he will destroy the people,' and in the Hebrew language. . . . [27] He will rule over all, and his dominion will reach from one end of the earth to the other. There will be ten letters in his hand.[28] He will worship strange gods.[29] No one will be able to stand before him. Anyone who does not believe in him, he will slay by the sword, and he will slay many of them. He will attack the people of the holy ones of the Most High (see Dan 7:27), and there will be ten kings with him, with might and great strength. He will make war on the holy ones and destroy them. He will kill the messiah son of Joseph, that is, Nehemiah b. Hushiel, and sixteen righteous men will be killed with him. They will exile Israel to the wilderness in three groups. But Hephzibah, the mother of Menahem b. Ammiel, will stand at the east gate so that the evil one may not enter there, in order to fulfill the verse: 'But the rest of the people will not be cut off from the city' (Zech 14:2).

"This war (**249v**) will take place in the month of Av, and there will be trouble in Israel such as there never was before. They will flee to citadels, mountains, and caves; no one will be able to hide from him. All the nations of the world will go astray after him, except for Israel, who will not believe in him. For forty-one days all Israel will mourn Nehemiah b. Hushiel. His corpse will be thrown down before the gates of Jerusalem and broken, but no wild beast will touch it, nor bird nor animal. Then the children of Israel will cry out to the Lord from great oppression and deep trouble, and the Lord will answer them."

When I heard the word in the Lord's prophecy to me, I was very troubled. I rose and went to the canal, and I cried out there before the Lord God of Israel, the God of all flesh (Jer 32:27). Then he sent his angel to me, while the prayer was still on my lips, before I had completed it. The Lord sent his angel to me, and I looked and saw that he was the angel who had told me all those things earlier. I knelt and bowed before him, and he touched me again as he had the first time. He said to me, "What is the matter, Zerubbabel?"

"Sir," I said, "the spirit within me pains me" (Job 32:18).

"Ask," Metatron said, "and I shall tell you before I leave you."

So I continued to question him. "Sir, Metatron, when will the light of Israel come?"

"As the Lord lives, who sent me and made me commander of Israel, I shall tell you the deeds of the Lord," he answered. "For the holy God said to me, 'Go to my servant Zerubbabel and tell him whatever he asks you.' "

Then Michael, who is Metatron, said to me, "Come here and pay attention to everything that I tell you. For the word I speak to you is true, from the words of the living God. Menahem b. Ammiel will come suddenly in the first month, the month of Nisan, on the fourteenth day of the month,[30] and he will stand in the valley of Arbel,[31] which belongs to Joshua b. Jehozadak the priest.[32] All the surviving sages of Israel will go out to him, for only a few will survive the attack and pillage of Gog and Armilos and of the plunderers who plundered them. Menahem b. Ammiel will say to the elders and sages, 'I am the Lord's anointed. The Lord sent me to bring you good tidings and to save you from the hand of these enemies.' But the elders[33] will look upon him and despise him, for all they will see is a man despised, in worn-out clothes, and they will despise him as you despised him. Then his anger will burn within him and he will put on clothes of vengeance as a garment and wrap himself in a mantle of zeal (see Isa 59:17).

"Then he will go to the gates of Jerusalem, and Elijah the prophet will be with him. They will awaken Nehemiah b. Hushiel and bring him back to life at the gates of Jerusalem.[34] Then Hephzibah, the mother of the messiah, will come and hand over to him the staff by which the signs were performed. All Israel [and] the elders of Israel will go and the children of Israel will see that Nehemiah is alive and standing on his feet.[35] At once they will believe in the messiah."

Thus Metatron, the commander of the Lord's host, adjured me. "In truth this matter shall come to pass, for there shall be peaceful understanding between them (Zech 6:13), as in Isaiah's prophecy: 'Ephraim shall not envy Judah, and Judah shall not trouble Ephraim' (Isa 11:13).

"On the twenty-first day of the first month of the completion of 990 (250r)[36] years from the destruction of Jerusalem the Lord's salvation for Israel will come to pass. Menahem b. Ammiel, Nehemiah b. Hushiel, and Elijah the prophet will come and stand at the great sea and will call out[37] in the Lord's prophecy. The corpses of all the children of Israel who threw themselves into the sea to escape their enemies will come forth, and a wave will come up out of the sea, bring them to the surface, and cast them alive into the Valley of Jehoshaphat near the Valley of Shittim (see Joel 4:18). For there the judgment of all nations will take place.

"In the second month, Iyyar, the band of Korah will come up to the plains of Jericho at the Valley of Shittim. They will come to Moses, and the banner of the Korahites will be gathered in.

"On the eighteenth day of the month mountains and hills will quake, the earth and everything on it will shake, and the sea and everything in it.

"On the first day of the third month the dead of the wilderness will come to life, and they will come by family to the Valley of Shittim.

"On the eighteenth of Sivan there will be a great earthquake in the Land of Israel.

"In Tammuz, the fourth month, the Lord God of Israel will descend upon the Mount of Olives, and the Mount of Olives will split (see Zech 14:4) at his rebuke. He will sound a great shofar (see Isa 27:13, Zech 9:14). All the strange gods and temples of images will fall to the ground, and every wall and cliff (see Ezek 38:20) will fall to the ground. The Lord will strike all their plunderers and fight against those nations. Like a warrior he will stir up his zeal (Isa 42:13). The anointed of the Lord will come, that is, Menahem b. Ammiel, and he will breathe on Armilos's face and slay him (see Isa 11:4). The Lord will put men's swords on each other's neck, and there they will fall dead as corpses. The holy people will go forth and see the salvation of the Lord. Eye to eye (Isa 52:8) all Israel will see him as a warrior. There will be a helmet of salvation on his head (Isa 59:17) and he will dress in armor to make war against Gog and Magog and the forces of Armilos. They will all fall dead in the Valley of Arbel. Then all Israel will go forth to despoil their despoilers and pillage their pillagers for seven months (see Ezek 39:10, 12). But some survivors will escape and gather at Zela Haeleph (see Josh 18:28), five hundred men and a hundred thousand dressed in armor [against] five hundred men of Israel, with Nehemiah, Elijah, and you, Zerubbabel, at their head. They will kill all of them, for there one man shall pursue a thousand (see Josh 23:10).

"This will happen in the third war, for there will be three wars in the Land of Israel: one that Hephzibah will wage against Shiroi, king of Persia; another that the Lord God of Israel and Menahem b. Ammiel will wage against Armilos, the ten kings with him, and Gog and Magog; and a third at Zela Haeleph, which Nehemiah b. Hushiel and Zerubbabel will wage. The third war will take place in the month of Av.

"After all this has come to pass, Menahem b. Ammiel will come, and Nehemiah b. Hushiel and all Israel with him. All the dead will come to life, and Elijah the prophet will be with them. They will go up to Jerusalem, and in the month of Av, during which they mourned Nehemiah and in which Jerusalem was destroyed, there will be great joy for Israel. They will offer sacrifices to the Lord, and the Lord will accept them. Israel's offering will be pleasing to the Lord as it was before, in ancient times (see Mal 3:4). The Lord will smell the sweet savor of his people Israel and rejoice greatly. Then the Lord will bring down to earth the temple that was built above, and the pillar of fire and the cloud of incense will ascend to heaven. The messiah will go forth on foot to the gates of Jerusalem, and all Israel after him. The holy God will stand on the Mount of Olives. His awe and his glory will rest upon the heavens and the highest heavens, over the whole earth and its depths, upon all walls, buildings, and foundations. Not a breath will be drawn, for the Lord God will reveal himself before all on the Mount of Olives. The Mount of Olives will split beneath him (see Zech 14:4). The exiles of Jerusalem will ascend to the Mount of (250v) Olives. Zion and Jerusalem will see and say, 'Who begot these for us? And where were these?' (see Isa 49:21). Then Nehemiah and Zerubbabel will answer Jerusalem, 'Here are your children whom you bore and who were exiled from you. Rejoice greatly, daughter of Zion!'" (Zech 9:9).

Again I began[38] to ask Metatron, the commander of the Lord's host, "Sir, show me Jerusalem, how long it is and how wide, and its buildings." So he showed me the walls around Jerusalem, walls of fire (see Zech 2:9), from the great wilderness to the western sea to the Euphrates River (see Deut 11:24). He showed me also the temple building. The temple was built on five mountain tops that the Lord chose to bear his sanctuary: Lebanon, Mount Moriah, Tabor, Carmel, and Hermon.[39]

Then Michael answered,[40] "When 990 years from the destruction of Jerusalem have been completed, I will bring salvation to Israel." Then he explained to me more about the word and the vision, for at the beginning he had said, "If you will inquire, inquire; come back again" (Isa 21:12).

"On the fifth of the week Nehemiah b. Hushiel will come and gather all Israel together. On the sixth of the week, Hephzibah, the wife of Nathan the prophet, who was born[41] in Hebron, will come and kill the two kings Nof and Esrogan. In that year will sprout the root of Jesse, Menahem b. Ammiel. Ten kings will arise from among the nations, and they will not be able to rule even a week and a half out of the year, year after year.[42] These ten kings will rise over the nations during seven years. Their names are as follows, according to their cities and in the order in which they arose:

"The first king is Silqom, and the name of his city is Sepharad, which is Aspamia, the province of the sea. The second king is Hertomos, and the name of his city is Gitnia. The third king is Plios, and the name of his city is Plavis. The fourth king is Galvas, and the name of his city is Galia. The fifth king is Remoshdis, and the name of his city is Moditikha. The sixth king is Moqlanos, and the name of his city is Italia. The seventh king is Okhtinos, and the name of his city is Dormis. The eighth king is Aplostos, from Aramnaharaim. The ninth king is Shiroi, king of Persia. And the tenth king is Armilos son of Satan, who came forth from the stone statue.[43]

"He will rule over all of them. He will come with the kings of Qedar and the children of Qedem and start a war in the Valley of Arbel, and the kingdom will be theirs. He will increase in strength and conquer the whole world. And from there, in Riblah (see 2 Kgs 25:6), which is Antioch,[44] he will begin to plant the sacred posts (*'asherot*) of all the nations and to worship their false gods (*ba'alim*), whom God hates on the face of the earth. In those days there will be no wages for men or for beasts (see Zech 8:10). He will build four altars, and he will anger the Lord by his evil deeds. For forty days there will be a very severe famine (**251r**) on the face of the earth. Their food will be mallow, and they will pick leaves of bushes and broom for their sustenance (see Job 30:4). On that day a fountain will come forth from the house of the Lord and water the Valley of Shittim (see Joel 4:18).

"Then that Armilos will take his mother, the stone[45] from which he was born, out of the house of disgrace of the scorners. From all over the nations will come to worship that stone, offer incense, and pour libations to it. No one will be able to look upon its face because of its beauty. Anyone who does not bow down to it will die, suffering like an animal.

"This is the sign of Armilos: the hair of his head is the color of gold, and he is also green to the soles of his feet. The width of his face is a span. His eyes are deep. He has two heads. He will come up and rule the province with terror. Satan is the father of Belial, and all who see him will tremble.

"Menahem will come up from the Valley of Shittim and breathe on his face to slay him, as it is written, 'He shall slay the wicked with the breath of his lips' (Isa 11:4).[46] The kingdom will belong to Israel, 'and the holy ones of the Most High will receive the kingdom' " (Dan 7:18).

These are the words Metatron spoke to Zerubbabel b. Shealtiel, governor of Judah, in the midst of the exile in the days of the kingdom of Persia. Zechariah b. Anan[47] and Elijah wrote them down in complete exile (Amos 1:6, 9).

# NOTES

## Introduction

1. This account is a summary of the form of *Sefer Zerubbabel* found in the manuscript of *Sefer Hazikhronot*, the Book of Remembrances, in the Bodleian Library of Oxford University, MS Heb. d. 11, ff. 248r–251r. See Chapter 1 for further discussion, and the appendix for a translation.

2. For a new and promising approach to the variety of messiah figures in ancient Jewish and Christian texts, Matthew Novenson, *The Grammar of Messianism: An Ancient Jewish Political Idiom and Its Users* (New York: Oxford University Press, 2017); Novenson's first chapter offers a helpful critical survey of the scholarly literature.

3. See Jacob Neusner, *Messiah in Context: Israel's History and Destiny in Formative Judaism* (Philadelphia: Fortress, 1984), esp. 212–31 (summary); and for a similar picture, though in much shorter compass, Lawrence H. Schiffman, "Messianism and Apocalypticism in Rabbinic Texts," in *The Cambridge History of Judaism*, Vol. 4. *The Late Roman-Rabbinic Period*, ed. Steven T. Katz (Cambridge: Cambridge University Press, 2006), 1053–72; in contrast to Neusner, Schiffman understands tannaitic avoidance of messianism as a response to recent disasters (1063–64).

For discussion of the date of the Bavli, Richard Kalmin, "The Formation and Character of the Babylonian Talmud," in *Cambridge History of Judaism*, vol. 4, 840–42. For the date of the Yerushalmi, H. L Strack and

Günter Stemberger, *Introduction to the Talmud and Midrash*, trans. and ed. Markus Bockmuehl (2nd ed.; Minneapolis: Fortress, 1996), 170–71. For the date of Pesiqta of Rav Kahana, Strack-Stemberger, *Introduction*, 295–96.

4. For a survey of the use of the schema in the rabbinic corpus, Rivka Raviv, "The Talmudic Formulation of the Prophecies of the Four Kingdoms in the Book of Daniel," *Jewish Studies, An Internet Journal* 5 (2006): 1–20 (Hebrew).

5. David Biale, "Counter-History and Jewish Polemics against Christianity: The *Sefer Toldot Yeshu* and the *Sefer Zerubavel*," *Jewish Social Studies* 6 (1999): 130–45; for the understanding of counter-history, 130–32, 137–38.

6. Alexei M. Sivertsev, *Judaism and Imperial Ideology in Late Antiquity* (Cambridge: Cambridge University Press, 2011), 1–8; quotation, 6–7. *Sefer Zerubbabel* plays a major role in two of the five chapters.

7. Himmelfarb, "The Mother of the Messiah in the Talmud Yerusahlmi and Sefer Zerubbabel," in *The Talmud Yerushalmi and Graeco-Roman Culture III*, ed. Peter Schäfer (Tübingen: Mohr Siebeck, 2002), 369–89. Sivertsev graciously acknowledges this discussion (*Judaism and Imperial Ideology*, 93–94).

8. Biale, "Counter-History," 138.

9. I refer particularly to Alexander's two programmatic essays, "The King Messiah in Rabbinic Judaism," in *King and Messiah in Israel and the Ancient Near East: Proceedings of the Oxford Old Testament Seminar*, ed. John Day (Sheffield: Sheffield Academic Press, 1998), 456–73; and "The Rabbis and Messianism," in *Redemption and Resistance: The Messianic Hopes of Jews and Christians in Antiquity*, ed. Markus Bockmuehl and James Carleton Paget (London: T&T Clark, 2007), 227–44. "King Messiah" contains many of the ideas of "Rabbis and Messianism" in preliminary form, but its focus is particularly on the revival of themes from the Second Temple period in later literature.

10. Alexander, "Rabbis and Messianism," 228–34; in "King Messiah," Alexander mentions only the Amidah, which he views as particularly important, and the targumim as possible sources for the later rabbinic incorporation of messianism (471–72).

11. Alexander, "King Messiah," 468–71; "Rabbis and Messianism," 241–43. I cannot accept Alexander's suggestion that one of the reasons for the rabbis' coolness to messianism was that "in their day it was seen largely as a priestly doctrine" ("Rabbis and Messianism," 242).

12. Alexander, "Rabbis and Messianism," 237–40.

13. Ibid., 241 (quotation), 243–44. Alexander sees the revival as related to the rediscovery or at least reemergence of traditions from the Second Temple period ("King Messiah," 264–67; "Rabbis and Messianism," 243).

14. Alexander, "Rabbis and Messianism," 229.

15. For a discussion of the messianism and eschatology of Yose b. Yose, William Horbury, "Suffering and Messianism in Yose ben Yose," in *Messianism Among Jews and Christians: Twelve Biblical and Historical Studies* (London: T&T Clark, 2003), 289–327.

16. Alexander's claim that "their teachings were undoubtedly known in some shape or form to the Rabbis" ("Rabbis and Messianism," 234) has enough qualifiers that it may be true, but this surely does not mean that the (very limited) messsianism of the hekhalot texts is likely to be early enough to testify to popular expectations before the late fifth century.

17. On circumcision and the near sacrifice of Isaac, Martha Himmelfarb, "The Ordeals of Abraham: Circumcision and the *Aqedah* in Origen, the *Mekhilta*, and *Genesis Rabbah*." *Henoch* 28 (2008): 289–310. On Abraham and Christ, Himmelfarb, "Abraham and the Messianism of *Genesis Rabbah*," in *Genesis Rabbah: Text and Context*, ed. Sarit Kattan Gribetz et al. (Tübingen: Mohr Siebeck, forthcoming). Rabbinic adaptation of Christological themes to Abraham and to Jacob as well deserves more scholarly attention than it has so far received.


## 1. Text and Context

1. For an account of the manuscript evidence and the printed editions, John C. Reeves, intro. and trans., "*Sefer Zerubbabel*: The Prophetic Vision of Zerubbabel ben Shealtiel," in *Old Testament Pseudepigrapha: More Noncanonical Scriptures* vol. 1, ed. Richard Bauckham, James R. Davila, and Alexander Panayotov (Grand Rapids, Mich.: Eerdmans, 2013), 449–50.

2. Yehudah Even-Shemuel, *Midreshei ge'ulah* (2nd ed.; Jerusalem: Mosad Bialik, 1954); Salo W. Baron, *A Social and Religious History of the Jews*, 2nd ed. (New York and Philadelphia: Columbia University Press and Jewish Publication Society, 1957–83), 5:354 n. 3; Hillel I. Newman, "Dating *Sefer Zerubavel*: Dehistoricizing and Rehistoricizing a Jewish Apocalypse of Late Antiquity," *Adamantius* 19 (2013): 329.

3. Newman, "Dating *Sefer Zerubavel*," 324 note before n. 1, indicates that he is planning to produce one.

4. The manuscript was previously labeled MS 2797. *Sefer Zerubbabel* appears in fols. 248r–251r. For the date and provenance of the manuscript and the evidence for Eleazar's life, Eli Yassif, *The Book of Memory, That Is, The Chronicles of Jerahme'el: A Critical Edition* (Ramat Aviv: Tel Aviv University, 2001), 13–17 (Hebrew).

5. The translation in the Appendix is a slightly revised form of the translation in Himmelfarb, "Sefer Zerubbabel," in *Rabbinic Fantasies:*

*Imaginative Narratives from Classical Hebrew Literature,* ed. David Stern and Mark Jay Mirsky (Philadelphia: Jewish Publication Society, 1990), 67–90. I would like to thank the Curators of the Bodleian Library for their permission to publish the translation. The folio numbers in references to the Appendix in the notes refer to the folios of the *Sefer Hazikhronot* manuscript, which are indicated in the Appendix.

For another recent English translation with introduction, John C. Reeves, *Trajectories in Near Eastern Apocalyptic: A Postrabbinic Jewish Apocalypse Reader* (Resources for Biblical Studies 45; Atlanta: Society of Biblical Literature, 2005), 40–66; an abbreviated version of the introduction and revised version of the translation appear as Reeves, "*Sefer Zerubbabel,*" 448–66.

6. Israël Lévi, "L'Apocalypse de Zorobabel et le roi de Perse Siroès," in Lévi, *Le Ravissement du Messie à sa naissance et autres essais,* ed. Evelyne Patlagean (Paris-Louvain: Peeters, 1994), 173–204; the article originally appeared in *REJ* 68 (1914): 129–60. Page numbers in the notes here refer to the reprint in the collection of Lévi's essays. Lévi's edition includes a significant critical apparatus drawing on printed editions and other manuscripts as well as a French translation.

7. For the correction, see Chapter 3.

8. For the date and provenance, Malachi Beit-Arié, *Catalogue of the Hebrew Manuscripts in the Bodleian Library: Supplement of Addenda and Corrigenda to vol. I (A. Neubauer's Catalogue),* ed. R.A. May (Oxford: Clarendon Press, 1994), 22. Lévi knows the manuscript by its old designation, MS 160. For his judgment about its relationship to the *Sefer Hazikhronot* manuscript, "L'Apocalypse," 174.

9. For the date and provenance of the manuscript, formerly designated MS 2287, Beit-Arié, *Catalogue of the Hebrew Manuscripts in the Bodleian Library,* 440–41. I thank Natalie E. Latteri for calling the manuscript to my attention and discussing it with me via email, and I look forward to her discussion in her dissertation for the History Department of the University of New Mexico of the interesting scribal features she has noted. Reeves notes and makes use of the manuscript (*Trajectories,* 41, 50–51).

10. Adolph Jellinek, *Bet ha-Midrasch* (3rd ed.; Jerusalem: Wahrmann, 1967), 2:54–57. Jellinek lists the manuscripts as Codices XXII and XXXVIII from the Leipziger Raths-Bibliothek (2:xxii).

11. I examined an image of the fragment online at the Friedberg Genizah Project, http://www.jewishmanuscripts.org/, 4/11/16; a user must set up an account to view images. For a photograph, see also Simon Hopkins, *A Miscellany of Literary Pieces from the Cambridge Genizah Collections: A Catalogue and Selection of Texts in the Taylor-Schechter Collections, Old Series, Box A45* (Cambridge: Cambridge University Library, 1978), 10. My

colleague Eve Krakowski characterizes the script as a semicursive common in the genizah, likely to date from after the tenth century. I would like to thank her for graciously taking time to examine the images of the fragments with me.

12. The first edition was reprinted by Shlomo Aharon Wertheimer; *Batei Midrashot* (2nd ed., ed. Abraham Joseph Wertheimer: Jerusalem: Ktab Wasepher, 1968), 2:497–502. Lévi understood it to represent a different "recension" of *Sefer Zerubbabel* from the form found in the *Sefer Hazikhronot* manuscript ref ("L'Apocalypse," 174). For the delineation of two recensions of *Sefer Zerubbabel* on the basis of the texts' chronology, Newman, "Dating *Sefer Zerubavel*," 328–30, to be discussed shortly.

13. Lévi, "L'Apocalypse," 180 (Appendix, 249r); MS Opp. 236a, 14r; MS Opp. 603, 34r; Jellinek, *Bet ha-Midrasch*, 2:56.

14. Wertheimer, *Batei Midrashot*, 2:499. The passage is confused, but the identity of the evildoer responsible is clear.

15. Ibid., 2:502.

16. Newman, "Dating *Sefer Zerubavel*," 329. I would like to thank Jerry Schwarzbard of the Jewish Theological Seminary Library and Ezra Chwat and Idan Pérez of the Institute of Microfilmed Hebrew Manuscripts of the Jewish National and University Library for their help in obtaining the copy. The copy has been labeled by its modern custodians not with folio numbers as is typical for manuscripts but with page numbers; *Sefer Zerubbabel* takes up three sides, 192–94.

17. Ibid. Newman does not highlight the role of the king of Persia, which is somewhat problematic for his argument, as I shall discuss. For the manuscript, formerly labeled 2642, Adolf Neubauer and A. E. Cowley, *Catalogue of the Hebrew Manuscripts in the Bodleian Library, Volume 2* (Oxford: Clarendon, 1906), 37. The catalogue does not suggest a date for the manuscript, but it identifies the writing of this passage as "Syr. squ. Rabb. char."; aspects of the writing vary from text to text within the manuscript, but all are described as Syrian.

18. For the images, I used the Friedberg Genizah Project online, http://www.jewishmanuscripts.org/, 4/11/16. Note that for both T-S A45.19 and T-S A45.22, the labeling of recto and verso is reversed. See also Hopkins, *Miscellany*, 15 (T-S A45.7), 64–65 (T-S A45.19), 72-73 (T-S A45.22). According to Eve Krakowski, both T-S A45.7 and T-S A45.19 could date from the tenth century; both are more formal hands than T-S A45.5 (see n. 11) or T-S A45.22, which Krakowski also describes as written in a semicursive common in the genizah.

Newman, "Dating *Sefer Zerubavel*," 329, identifies T-S A45.19 as related to the first edition on the basis of the first edition's distinctive chronology. It should be noted that the fragment does not match the first edition perfectly.

19. Hopkins, *Miscellany*, 15. He suggests that the text that followed may have been the eighth section of the *Book of Beliefs and Opinions*, often known as the Treatise on Redemption. On the relationship between *Sefer Zerubbabel* and the Treatise on Redemption, see Chapter 6. Eve Krakowski examined an image of the fragment and reads the Judeo-Arabic as follows: "A book containing the Book of Beliefs and Opinions/of the *shaykh* Joseph b. Yefet"; she understands "of" to mean "belonging to." Krakowski notes that her translation assumes a missing *'aleph* in the first word, *ktb*, which she reads as if it were *kt'b*; she points out that the title "Book of Beliefs and Opinions" is missing five *'alephs*. She also suggests that the second line of the Judeo-Arabic is in a different hand from the first line. I am grateful to Professor Krakowski for devoting time to making sense of the fragment.

20. Lévi, "L'Apocalypse," 177; Appendix, 248v.

21. Peter Schäfer, "Metatron in Babylonia," in *Hekhalot Literature in Context: Between Byzantium and Babylonia*, ed. Ra'anan Boustan, Martha Himmelfarb, and Peter Schäfer (Tübingen: Mohr Siebeck, 2013).

22. Lévi, "L'Apocalypse," 181; Appendix, 249v.

23. Lévi, "L'Apocalypse," 177; Appendix, 248v.

24. Lévi, "L'Apocalypse," 179; Appendix, 249r.

25. Oxford MS Opp. 236a attributes the first list of achievements to Michael (13r) and the second to Metatron (13v); it is perhaps worth noting that it does not match the *Sefer Hazikhronot* manuscript at every point on the names, offering somewhat different attempt at harmonization, e.g. "Metatron, Michael the Prince" (13v–14r). Oxford MS Opp. 603 attributes both lists to Metatron (33r) but later refers to the angel as Michael (33v, 34v). Jellinek's text makes some effort to cut down on the dissonance caused by the existence of two lists by introducing the second with the verb, "*va-yosef*," "he added"; for the first list, the angelic speaker is unnamed, while for the second, he is identified as Metatron (Jellinek, *Bet ha-Midrasch* 2:55). The name Michael appears later in the text (Jellinek, *Bet ha-Midrasch* 2:56).

26. Lévi, "L'Apocalypse," 183, 185 (Appendix, 250r [twice]); Oxford MS Opp. 236a, 14r, 15v.

27. Lévi, "L'Apocalypse," 185–86 (Appendix, 250v); Oxford MS Opp. 236a, 15r.

28. Jellinek, *Bet ha-Midrasch*, 2:57; Oxford MS Opp. 603, 34v.

29. The first comes from Wertheimer, *Batei Midrashot*, 2:498; the second, from MS JTS 2325/20, 192; and the third is found in both T-S A45.19v and T-S A45.22r. The Hebrew of the two fragments differs slightly, however, with T-S A45.22 including the prounoun *hu'* between "I" and the names, giving the statement a somewhat more emphatic character. The margin of T-S A45.7r is missing at a crucial point, but it clearly reads "and Michael, the Prince of the Lord's host," and the letters visible just before

these words could well be *r-w-n*, the last three letters of Metatron. On the verso, the name Metatron for the angel appears clearly. Only a single letter is clearly visible after the name, *w*, "and," which might suggest that "and Michael" follows here.

30. If I am correct in my reading of T-S A45.7v in n. 29, however, it continues to use the name Michael, though as part of the combination "Metatron and Michael."

31. Wertheimer, *Batei Midrashot*, 2:501; MS JTS 2325/20, 193.

32. Newman, "Dating *Sefer Zerubavel*,"328–30; for his disagreement with me, 330 n. 25. Newman does not consider differences among the witnesses close to the *Sefer Hazikhronot* manuscript.

33. Lévi, "L'Apocalypse," 182; Appendix, 249r.

34. Lévi, "L'Apocalypse," 180; Appendix, 249r. Wertheimer, *Batei Midrashot*, 2:499-500. MS JTS 2325/20 lacks the trip to the church.

35. Wertheimer, *Batei Midrashot*, 2:502; MS JTS 2325/20, 194.

36. "Days of Armilos": Wertheimer, *Batei Midrashot*, 2:500; MS JTS 2325/20, 193; death of Armilos: Wertheimer, *Batei Midrashot*, 2:502; MS JTS 2325/20, 194.

37. Peter Schäfer with Margarete Schlüter and Hans Georg von Mutius, *Synopse zur Hekhalot-Literatur* (Tübingen: Mohr [Siebeck], 1981).

38. The earliest instance I know is Jellinek, *Bet ha-Midrasch*, 2:xxi; *Bet ha-Midrasch* was first published 1853–78. Note also the title Lévi gave *Sefer Zerubbabel*: "L'apocalypse de Zerobabel." I must admit that I too called *Sefer Zerubbabel* an apocalypse until I undertook the exploration of its relationship to the genre that I draw on in this section: "Revelation and Rabbinization in *Sefer Zerubbabel* and *Sefer Eliyyahu*," in *Revelation, Literature, and Community in Late Antiquity*, ed. Philippa Townsend and Moulie Vidas (Tübingen: Mohr Siebeck, 2011), 218–25.

39. For an influential description of the apocalypse as a genre, John J. Collins, ed., *Semeia* 14 (1979): *Apocalypse: The Morphology of a Genre*.

40. Himmelfarb, "*Sefer Eliyyahu*: Jewish Eschatology and Christian Jerusalem," in *Shaping the Middle East: Jews, Christians and Muslims in an Age of Transition, 400–800 C.E.*, ed. Kenneth G. Holum and Hayim Lapin (Bethesda, Md.: University Press of Maryland, 2011), 232–38; for the problem of Revelation's availability in the East, 235–36. For the text of *Sefer Eliyyahu*, Moses Buttenwieser, *Die hebräische Elias-Apokalypse und ihre Stellung in der apokalyptischen Literatur des rabbinischen Schrifttums und der Kirche* (Leipzig: Pfeiffer, 1897), 15–26. For an English translation, Reeves, *Trajectories*, 29–39.

41. Lévi, "L'Apocalypse," 175; Appendix, 248r.

42. Ezek 1:5, 1:13, 1:14, 1:16, 1:26, 1:27, 1:28, 8:3, 8:2, 8:4, 10:1, 10:9, 10:10, 10:22, 11:24, 23:15, 23:16, 40:2, 40:3, 41:21, 41:24, 42:11, 43:3.

43. Ezek 7:3, 12:22, 12:23, 12:24, 12:27, 13:16.

44. Lévi, "L'Apocalypse," 175; Appendix, 248 r.

45. Lévi, "L'Apocalypse," 175; Appendix, 248r.

46. Lévi, "L'Apocalypse," 184–85; Appendix, 250r-v.

47. Martha Himmelfarb, *Ascent to Heaven in Jewish and Christian Apocalypses* (New York: Oxford University Press, 1993), 9–13, 72–74.

48. Himmelfarb, "Revelation and Rabbinization," 229–31.

49. Ibid., 230–31.

50. I would like to thank David Stern for his comments about the unusual character of the language of *Sefer Zerubbabel* (at my presentation on *Sefer Zerubbabel* at the Philadelphia Seminar in Christian Origins, April 18, 2013), which encouraged me to look at the language more closely.

51. Thus also Yosef Dan, *The Hebrew Story in the Middle Ages* (Jerusalem: Keter, 1974), 35 (Hebrew).

52. Miguel Pérez Fernández, *An Introductory Grammar of Rabbinic Hebrew*, trans. John Elwolde (Leiden: Brill, 1997), 107.

53. For rabbinic usage, Pérez Fernández, *Introductory Grammar*, 63.

54. Lévi, "L'Apocalypse," 188; Appendix, 251r.

55. Jellinek, *Bet ha-Midrasch*, 2:57; MS JTS 2325/20, 194.

56. *B'omri* twice (Lévi, "L'Apocalypse,"175, 177); *k'shom'i* three times (Lévi, "L'Apocalypse,"176, 180, 181); *b'omar li* (Lévi, "L'Apocalypse," 176).

57. *Har'otekha* (Lévi, "L'Apocalypse," 176).

58. Pérez Fernández, *Introductory Grammar*, 144.

59. All except the last instance in n. 56; Pérez Fernández, *Introductory Grammar*, 58–59, 109–10.

60. *Haspeq lo' hispaqti* (Lévi, "L'Apocalypse," 176); Pérez Fernández, *Introductory Grammar*, 144.

61. *'Egmerah* (Lévi, "L'Apocalypse," 175), *'omrah* (Lévi, "L'Apocalypse," 176); Pérez Fernández, *Introductory Grammar*, 122. On common loss of cohortative meaning, Gary Rendsberg, "Late Biblical Hebrew and the Date of 'P,'" *Journal of the Ancient Near Eastern Society* 12 (1980): 70.

62. *Haggidah* (Lévi, "L'Apocalypse," 180); Pérez Fernández, *Introductory Grammar*, 151.

63. *Tir'eynah, to'marnah,* (Lévi, "L'Apocalypse," 185); Pérez Fernández, *Introductory Grammar*, 106, 122.

64. Pérez Fernández, *Introductory Grammar*, 50.

65. *'Asher*: Lévi, "L'Apocalypse," 175 twice, 176, 179 four times, 181 four times, 182 four times, 183 twice, 184 twice, 185 four times, 187 twice, 188. *She-*: Lévi, "L'Apocalypse," 177 twelve times (mostly in the angel's recitation of his accomplishments), 178 five times, 179, 180, 181 three times, 182 four times, 184 four times, 187, 188.

66. "In the month of Av, during which (*'asher*) they mourned Nehemiah and in which (*she-*) Jerusalem was destroyed, there will be great joy for Israel" (Lévi, "L'Apocalypse," 184; Appendix, 250r).

67. Lévi, "L'Apocalypse," 177; Appendix, 248v.

68. The only words with nonbiblical roots that I have noted are *kat*, group (Lévi, "L'Apocalypse,"181), *siman*, sign (Lévi, "L'Apocalypse,"187), and perhaps *toreph*, indecency (Lévi, "L'Apocalypse," 176, 180, 187). But if *toreph* comes from the root of *teraphim*, household idols, or at least was understood to come from it, it belongs to a different category, words derived from roots attested in the Bible but used in nonbiblical forms: *tsalmah* (Lévi, "L'Apocalypse," 177); *ganuz* (Lévi, "L'Apocalypse," 179, twice); *ganaz* (Lévi, "L'Apocalypse," 179); *leitsut* (Lévi, "L'Apocalypse," 180 [a plausible emendation by Lévi]); *haspeq hispaqti* (Lévi, "L'Apocalypse," 181); *yazi'u* (Lévi, "L'Apocalypse," 187).

69. Words: *beriyah, keivan, ts-vv-ḥ, ris, margaliot, zemaragdin, 'squpah.* Roots: *kns* in the *niph'al, zw'* in the *hiph'il, z'z'* in the *hitpa'el*.

70 In the translation in the Appendix, these borrowed phrases are indicated with a parenthetical "see."

71 The third-person masculine singular imperfect with *vav* consecutive appears six times in *Sefer Zerubbabel* by my count (Lévi, "L'Apocalypse," 177 twice, 179, 180, 181 twice); such a construction appears roughly eighty times in the Bible. The first-person singular imperfect with *vav* consecutive appears twice in *Sefer Zerubbabel* ((Lévi, "L'Apocalypse," 175, 176); there is a single biblical parallel to this usage (Hab 2:2). *Sefer Zerubbabel* also contains an instance of the idiom in the first-person singular perfect (Lévi, "L'Apocalypse," 177); the only biblical parallel to this usage is a third-person singular perfect (Song 2:10).

72. Lévi, "L'Apocalypse," 182; Appendix, 249v.

73. Lévi, "L'Apocalypse,"176–77; Appendix, 248r.

74. Jellinek, *Bet haMidrash*, 2:56, follows the *Sefer Hazikhronot* MS but without a name for the king of Persia. MS JTS 2325/20 shares the first edition's view that the king of Persia kills Nehemiah, but it has a different name for the king (193).

75. Lévi, "L'Apocalypse," 205–12 (=*REJ* 69 [1919]: 108-115). For scholars who follow Lévi as well as a dissenting voice, Reeves, *Trajectories*, 47 n. 48. The 990-year date appears in *Sefer Zerubbabel* at Lévi, "L'Apocalypse," 179, 182, 185; Appendix, 249r, 249v, 250v.

76. Heinrich Graetz, *Geschichte der Juden*, vol. 6 (Leipzig: Leiner, 1894), 52–54. For nineteenth- and early twentieth-century scholarship that follows Graetz on this point, Lévi, "L'Apocalypse," 206 n. 1.

77. Lévi, "L'Apocalypse," 207–12. Lévi also points to Shiroi's place as the ninth king, immediately preceding Armilos, in the list of ten kings at the

end of the work (211) as evidence for the fact that he is already dead (for the passage, Lévi, "L'Apocalypse,"186; Appendix, 250v).

Even-Shemuel, *Midreshei ge'ulah*, 63, proposes a date very close to Lévi's—638—but his argument is rather different. He treats the 990 years as an integral part of the text but argues that the 990 years should be counted from the building of the Second Temple rather than its destruction. It is difficult to see how the text can mean what Even-Shmuel wants it to mean, as Newman notes, "Dating *Sefer Zerubavel*, 329.

78. Lévi, "L'Apocalypse," 208.

79. Newman, "Dating *Sefer Zerubavel*," calls the date of 636 for the beginning of Arab rule "somewhat arbitrary" (328).

80. There is an extensive literature on the wars between the Byzantine and Persian empires. For works with a particular interest in the role of Jews in the events and the impact of the events on the Jews, Andrew Sharf, *Byzantine Jewry from Justinian to the Fourth Crusade* (The Littman Library of Jewish Civilization; London: Routledge and Kegan Paul, 1971), 48–51; Michael Avi-Yonah, *The Jews of Palestine: A Political History from the Bar Kokhba War to the Arab Conquest* (New York: Schocken, 1976), 257–72; Zvi Baras, "The Persian Conquest and the End of Byzantine Rule," in *Eretz Israel from the Destruction of the Second Temple to the Muslim Conquest*, vol. 1: Political, Social and Cultural History, ed. Baras et al. (Jerusalem: Yad Yitzhaq ben-Zvi, 1982), 300–49 (Hebrew); Gilbert Dagron, "Juifs et chrétiens dans l'orient du VIIe siècle. Introduction historique: Entre histoire et apocalypse," *Travaux et mémoires* 11 (1991): 22–28; Robert L. Wilken, *The Land Called Holy: Palestine in Christian History and Thought* (New Haven: Yale University Press, 1992), 202–14; Averil Cameron, "The Jews in Seventh-Century Palestine," *Scripta Classica Israelica* 13 (1994): 78–81; Cameron, "Byzantines and Jews: Some Recent Work on Early Byzantium," *Byzantine and Modern Greek Studies* 20 (1996): 253–57; G. W. Bowersock, *Empires in Collision in Late Antiquity* (Waltham, Mass.: Brandeis University Press, 2012), 31–51.

81. Averil Cameron, "Blaming the Jews: The Seventh-Century Invasions of Palestine in Context," in "Mélanges Gilbert Dagron," ed. Vincent Déroche et al., *Travaux et memoires* 14 (2002): 57–78, argues that the accounts are less revealing about the events than about Christian attitudes toward Jews. For an interesting discussion of the fraught scholarship on the subject, Elliot Horowitz, "The Vengeance of the Jews Was Stronger than Their Avarice: Modern Historians and the Persian Conquest of Jerusalem in 614," *Jewish Social Studies* 4 (1998): 1–39. Horowitz is particularly interested in how Jewish historians handle the Jewish violence reported in the Christian accounts and is considerably less skeptical of their historicity than is Cameron, whose article appeared after his. Jodi Magness, "Archaeological Evidence for the

Sasanian Persian Invasion of Jerusalem," in *Shaping the Middle East*, 85–98, argues that the archeological evidence suggests less extensive destruction than the Christian accounts, many of them significantly later than the events.

82. Avi-Yonah, *Jews of Palestine*, 265–70; Dagron, "Juifs et chrétiens," 26–28; Lutz Greisiger, *Messias-Endkaiser-Antichrist: Politische Apokalyptik unter Juden und Christen des Nahen Ostens am Vorabend der arabischen Eroberung* (Wiesbaden: Harrassowitz, 2014), 46–77. Greisiger considers a wider range of rabbinic and Hebrew apocalyptic literature as potential evidence for a brief period of eschatologically excited Jewish rule, and he offers a quite subtle interpretation, suggesting that the later apocalyptic works read historical events on the basis of eschatological expectations, particularly expectations associated with the messiah descended from Joseph. He also finds more concrete evidence for a Jewish role in provincial administration under the Sassanians in a lead seal with an inscription in Hebrew characters, "Yosina *archon*" (63); for the seal, Ferdinand Dexinger and Werner Seibt, "A Hebrew Lead Seal from the Period of the Sassanian Occupation of Palestine (614–629 A.D.)," *Revue des études juives* 140 (1981): 303–17. It is worth noting, however that the editors of the seal are inclined to understand its owner as the "president of a community in Eretz Israel who wanted to emphasize his position in the years of the Persian rule" (316).

83. Neither Avi-Yonah nor Dagron appears to be aware that in other versions of *Sefer Zerubbabel* Nehemiah dies at the hands of Armilos rather than Shiroi. Avi-Yonah relies on the edition of *Sefer Zerubbabel* in Even-Shemuel, *Midreshei ge'ulah* (*Jews of Palestine*, 269). Dagron does not indicate which text of *Sefer Zerubbabel* he is using ("Juifs et chrétiens," 27 n. 48). Greisiger is much better informed about *Sefer Zerubbabel*, taking into account the different versions and arguing that the attribution of the death of the messiah to Shiroi is original, with Armilos a later replacement for Shiroi (*Messias*, 68–70). Oddly, Greisiger does not include the first edition of *Sefer Zerubbabel* as evidence for the role of Shiroi.

84. Ezra Fleischer, "Solving the Qiliri Riddle," *Tarbiz* 54 (1984–85): 383–427 (Hebrew); see 398–406 for Fleischer's discussion of the historical events he finds behind the piyyut. Both Dagron, "Juifs et chrétiens," 26–27, and Greisiger, *Messias*, 70–72, follow him in seeing this piyyut as evidence for the brief restoration of Jewish sovereignty under the Persians.

85. Fleischer, "Solving the Qiliri Riddle," 413–14, lines 8–21.

86. Ibid., 414, lines 22–28; for discussion of the differences between the two manuscripts, 403–4.

87. Cameron, "Blaming the Jews," 69–73, emphasizes the importance of the development of the cult of the Cross for understanding Christian anti-Jewish attitudes in the period of the Persian and Arab invasions of Palestine.

For a detailed discussion of the restoration and its symbolism, Greisiger, *Messias*, 91–180.

88. Dagron, "Juifs et chrétiens," 28–38; John F. Haldon, *Byzantium in the Seventh Century: The Transformation of a Culture* (Cambridge: Cambridge University Press, 1990), 346–48; Cameron, "Jews in Seventh-Century Palestine," 80–81. Haldon dates the edict to 634 (*Byzantium*, 346); Dagron suggests that the decision may go back to 630 ("Juifs et chrétiens," 31).

89. Dagron, "Juifs et chrétiens," 28–30.

90. Other scholars cautious about what really happened include Wilken, *Land Called Holy*, 213; Baras, "Persian Conquest" (Hebrew), 332–34; Cameron, "Jews in Seventh-Century Palestine," 80; and Seth Schwartz, *The Ancient Jews from Alexander to Muhammad* (Cambridge: Cambridge University Press, 2014), 150–51.

91. Newman, "Dating *Sefer Zerubavel*," 324–36.

92. Even-Shemuel, *Midreshei ge'ulah*, 60–63, points out that the first time *Sefer Zerubbabel* mentions the 990-year period, it comes after its "prophecy" of the rebuilding of the temple under Zerubbabel. Calculating not from the destruction of the temple by the Babylonians but from its rebuilding, Even-Shmuel concludes that the 990 years place the messiah, appropriately for *Sefer Zerubbabel*, around 640. As Newman notes, the understanding of the language of *Sefer Zerubbabel* required to achieve this solution is "philologically untenable" ("Dating *Sefer Zerubavel*, 329).

93. 420 years in *Sefer Zerubbabel*: Lévi, "L'Apocalypse," 178; Appendix, 248v.

94. Newman, "Dating *Sefer Zerubavel*," 329–32.

95. Ibid., 330–31; quotation, 331. The passage appears in Pirqe Rabbi Eliezer 28 in the Venice edition of 1544 but not in the Warsaw edition of 1852 with commentary by David Luria, the most readily available edition. For the Venice edition, Dagmar Börner-Klein, *Pirke de-Rabbi Elieser nach der Edition Venedig 1544 unter Berücksichtigung der Edition Warschau 1852* (Berlin: de Gruyter, 2004); the passage in question appears on 307 (German translation, 306).

96. Wertheimer, *Batei Midrashot*, 2:499

97. Newman, "Dating *Sefer Zerubavel*," 333–35; quotation, 333.

## 2. The Mother of the Messiah

1. Lévi, "L'Apocalypse," 178–79; Appendix, 249r.

2. For the passages, Louis Ginzberg, *Legends of the Jews*, 7 vols. (Philadelphia: Jewish Publication Society, 1909–1938), 6:106–7, n. 600.

3. Sivertsev, *Judaism and Imperial Ideology*, 114–22.

4. Lévi, "L'Apocalypse," 179–81; Appendix, 249r.

5. Lévi, "L'Apocalypse," 182, 184; Appendix, 250r.

6. Martha Himmelfarb, "The Mother of the Messiah in the Talmud Yerushalmi and Sefer Zerubbabel," in *The Talmud Yerushalmi and Graeco-Roman Culture III*, ed. Peter Schäfer (Tübingen: Mohr Siebeck, 2002), 384; Sivertsev, *Judaism and Imperial Ideology*, 93–101.

7. Ernst Kitzinger, "The Cult of Images in the Age Before Iconoclasm," *Dumbarton Oaks Papers* 8 (1954): 111–12.

Lévi also saw the use of images of the Virgin in the Avar siege as significant for understanding *Sefer Zerubbabel*, but he relates it to the role of the marble statue as a sort of Gorgon ("L'Apocalypse," 222).

8. On the role of the Virgin in the poem, Sivertsev, *Judaism and Imperial Ideology*, 96–98; Sivertsev also discusses the sermon of Theodore Syncellus on the first anniversary of the siege (98–101).

9. Vasiliki Limberis, *Divine Heiress: The Virgin Mary and the Creation of Christian Constantinople* (London: Routledge, 1994), 124–30; Sivertsev, *Judaism and Imperial Ideology*, 90–95.

10. Sivertsev, *Judaism and Imperial Ideology*, 88–90, 101–4.

11. *Bellum Avaricum* 366–89, esp. 380–85 (critical edition and Italian translation in Agostino Pertusi, ed., *Giorgio di Pisidia Poemi: I. Panegirici Epici* [Ettal: Buch-Kunstverlag, 1960], 193–94). See also the discussion in Sivertsev, *Judaism and Imperial Ideology*, 96–97.

12. There is a significant body of scholarship from the nineteenth century to the present that reads the story in the Yerushalmi as reflecting the messianic claims of Menahem the son of Judah the Galilean, known to us from Josephus (*Jewish War* 2.433–48). For a discussion that demonstrates clearly why such an identification is untenable, Hillel Newman, "The Birth of the Messiah on the Day of the Destruction: Historical and Anti-Historical Notes," in *For Uriel: Studies in the History of Israel in Antiquity Presented to Professor Uriel Rappaport,* ed. Menahem Mor et al. (Jerusalem: Merkaz Zalman Shazar, 2006), 85–110 (Hebrew).

13. The Yerushalmi here reads "R. Yudan the son of R. Aibo," which most scholars have understood as a mistake for "R. Yudan in the name of R. Aibo," the reading of Lamentations Rabbah; R. Yudan often transmits the aggadic sayings of R. Aibo (Wilhelm Bacher, *Die Agada der palästinen-sischen Amoräer* [1899; reprint ed., Hildesheim:Georg Olms, 1965], 3:63, esp. n. 5). But for consideration of the possibility that the reading "R. Yudan the son of R. Aibo," which appears a second time later in y. Berakhot (5.1) is correct, see Newman, "Birth," 85–86 n. 2.

14. The translation is based on my translation in "Mother," 370–71, but it is more literal and it corrects some inaccuracies in the original translation.

For the revised translation, I was able to make use of the Hebrew translation of Newman, "Birth," 86, and the English translation of Peter Schäfer, *The Jewish Jesus: How Judaism and Christianity Shaped Each Other* (Princeton: Princeton University Press, 2012), 215–16; both appeared after "Mother."

15. The manuscripts and editions included in Peter Schäfer and Hans-Jürgen Becker with Gottfried Reeg and the assistance of Anja Engel et al., *Synopse zum Talmud Yerushalmi, Band I/1-2, Ordnung Zera'im: Berakhot und Pe'a* (Tübingen: Mohr (Siebeck), 1991), 62–63, exhibit considerable variation in the gender and number of the animals in the passage. The evidence of the editions and manuscripts is not unanimous, but most witnesses involve both a cow and an ox. See later discussion for confusion about number. The differences do not seem to me significant for the meaning of the story. See also Newman, "Birth," 99–100 n. 68, and his comments on Anna Maria Schwemer," "Elija als Araber: Der haggdischen Motive in der Legende vom Messias Menahem ben Hiskija (yBer 2,4 5a; EkhaR1,16 § 51) im Vergleich mit den Elija- und Elischa-Legenden der Vitae Prophetarum," in *Die Heiden: Juden, Christen und das Problem des Fremden,* ed. Reinhold Feldmeier and Ulrich Heckel (Tübingen: Mohr Siebeck, 1994), 119–20. I do not understand, however, why Newman writes that the Yerushalmi depicts the farmer plowing with a single cow ("Birth," 99) when according to his translation the single animal plowing is an ox. So too Yonah Frankel, *'Iyyunim b''olamo ha-ruḥani shel sippur ha-'aggadah* (Tel Aviv: Hakibbutz Hameuchad, 1981), distinguishes between cow and ox in his translation into Hebrew (159) but understands the advice to unharness the ox to refer to the cow (160).

16. In all of the six witnesses in the *Synopse zum Talmud Yerushalmi* except MS Vatican, the Arab tells the Jew to unharness a single animal. Thus it is somewhat odd that in all of the witnesses but the Amsterdam edition, he tells him to harness oxen in the plural (or in MS London, cows).

17. The Vatican MS and the Amsterdam edition report that the sale is of a single ox.

18. Neither Frankel (*'Iyyunim,* 159) nor Newman ("Birth," 86) includes the material in this paragraph in his translation; Newman views it as imported from the version of the story in Lamentations Rabbah to MS Leiden of the Yerushalmi and from there to the Venice first edition ("Birth," 86 n. 7). The additional material is also absent from MS Vatican, which dates from the twelfth- or thirteenth century (Schäfer and Becker, *Synopse zum Talmud Yerushalmi,* xi), but it does appear in the remaining MSS in the *Synopse* (London and Paris) and in the Amsterdam edition. It does not appear in T-S F17.6, the Genizah fragment of the Yerushalmi containing the larger passage. For the original publication of the fragment, Louis Ginzberg, *Yerushalmi Fragments from the Genizah I: Text with Various Readings from the Editio Princeps* (1909; repr. Hildesheim: Georg Olms, 1970), 9;

Newman transcribes the fragment as Appendix 1 to "Birth" (108–9) based on his own examination of photographs of the manuscript.

19. Here I correct my earlier translation, "What does it matter to me?" ("Mother," 371), which makes better sense but is not supported by the witnesses in the *Synopse zum Talmud Yerushalmi*, which are divided between "to him" (Venice first edition, MS Leiden, MS Vatican) and "to you" (MS Paris, MS London, Amsterdam edition).

20. I translate as required by R. Bun's understanding of the verse.

21. Newman, "Birth," 100–2, and references there.

22. Frankel, *'Iyyunim*, 161, emphasizes the Jew's failure to take up plowing again as reflecting his inability to continue daily life after the destruction of the temple although that is what is required of him.

23. For the significance of "enemies of Israel" in the Yerushalmi story, Schäfer, *Jewish Jesus*, 228, and 315–16 nn. 44–45. The combination of pronominal suffix and "enemies of Israel" appears in all the editions and manuscripts included in *Synopse zum Talmud Yerushalmi* except MS Vatican, which lacks the pronominal suffix and reads "strangle the enemies of Israel." Schäfer considers the possibility that the word translated "enemies" could be a singular (315–16 n. 45); such a reading would fit this context better, but would not change the likelihood that the phrase is an addition to the text intended to tone down its shocking sentiment.

24. For references to the euphemistic use of "enemies" and "enemies of Israel" in rabbinic literature, Donald W. Parry, "The 'Word' or the 'Enemies' of the Lord? Revisiting the Euphemism in 2 Sam 12:14," in *Emanuel: Studies in Hebrew Bible, Septuagint, and Dead Sea Scrolls in Honor of Emanuel Tov,* ed. Shalom M. Paul et al. (Leiden: Brill, 2002), 370–72. For the Mekhilta, to which Parry refers without providing references, see Tractate Pisḥa to Exod 12:2 and Exod 12:27. As far as I know, these are the only uses of the phrase in the Mekhilta.

25. Frankel, *'Iyyunim*, 162–63.

26. For a recent introduction to Targum Jonathan, Paul V. M. Flesher and Bruce Chilton, *The Targums: A Critical Introduction* (Waco, Tex.: Baylor University Press, 2011), 169–73, 199–228.

27. Frankel, *'Iyyunim*, 163 n. 19; the word in Targum Jonathan is *'al'ula'*.

28. Schwemer, "Elija," 128; Israel Knohl, *B''iqvot ha-mashiaḥ* (Jerusalem: Schocken, 2000), 128–29, and *The Messiah Before Jesus: The Suffering Servant of the Dead Sea Scrolls* [an abridged translation of *B''iqvot ha-mashiaḥ*] (Berkeley: University of California Press, 2000) 74, 132 n. 4; Newman, "Birth," 105–7; and even, despite his very different reading of the passage, Schäfer, *Jewish Jesus*, 234. For discussion and criticism of late nineteenth- and early twentieth-century scholarship relating the passage in

the Yerushalmi to the snatching of the baby in Revelation 12, Himmelfarb, "Mother," 371–72.

29. Frankel, 'Iyyunim, 161; Newman, "Birth," 107–8.

30. Galit Hasan-Rokem, *Web of Life: Folklore and Midrash in Rabbinic Literature*, trans. Batya Stein (Stanford, Calif.: Stanford University Press, 2000 [Hebrew original, 1996]). 152–60.

31. Ibid., 155–56. I omit Hasan-Rokem's claim that both babies are born into poverty—Jesus is born in a manger (Luke 2:7), and the mother in the Jewish story cannot afford to buy her baby clothes—because I am not persuaded by it. Jesus is born in a manger because there is no room at the inn (Luke 2:7), and it is unclear whether we should believe the mother's claim that she has no money. It appears even in Lamentations Rabbah that her unwillingness to buy has something to do with the fate she foresees for her child. The claim to have no money is presented as an afterthought, and perhaps an excuse.

32. Ibid., 154.

33. Hasan-Rokem (*Web of Life*, 155) is wrong to attribute the advice to the magi.

34. Ibid., 156–57. See also Hasan-Rokem, "Narratives in Dialogue: A Folk Literary Perspective on Interreligious Contacts in the Holy Land in Rabbinic Literature of Late Antiquity," in *Sharing the Sacred: Religious Contacts and Conflicts in the Holy Land, First-Fifteenth Centuries CE*, ed. Arieh Kofsky and Guy G. Stroumsa Jerusalem: (Yad Izhak ben Zvi, 1998), 109–29.

35. For a more detailed discussion, Himmelfarb, "Mother," 374–76.

36. Schäfer, *Jewish Jesus*, 232–35.

37. So too Newman, "Birth," 107–8.

38. I would like to thank Israel Yuval for this suggestion, which he made in March 2001 on hearing a version of the paper that became "Mother."

39. Himmelfarb, "Mother," 376–77.

40. Himmelfarb, "*Sefer Zerubbabel* and Popular Religion," in *A Teacher for All Generations: Essays in Honor of James C. VanderKam*, ed. Eric F. Mason (Leiden: Brill, 2012), 2:621–34; on the story of the messiah born before his time, 631–34.

41. On the identification and its difficulties, Joseph Blenkinsopp, *Isaiah 1–39* (AB 19; New York: Doubleday, 2000), 232–34, 248–49.

42. The tradition is brought by a R. Tanhum, probably the fifth-generation (mid-fourth century) Palestinian amora (Strack-Stemberger, *Introduction*, 96), who attributes it to Bar Qappara, of the last generation of tannaim (early third century), in Sepphoris (Strack-Stemberger, *Introduction*, 82).

43. In the *Sefer Hazikhronot* MS, the Davidic messiah once refers to himself as "son of Hezekiah" (Lévi, "L'Apocalypse," 176; Appendix, 248r).

Given the absence of the phrase in all of the other witnesses including Oxford MS Opp. 236a (13r) and Oxford MS Opp. 603 (33r), Lévi is probably correct that it is not original (Lévi, "L'Apocalypse," 190 n. 4). Still it is interesting that at least one copyist made the connection. Indeed, Lévi himself raises the possibility that the name of the Davidic messiah's father in *Sefer Zerubabbel* should be vocalized not as Ammiel but as Immiel, a play on the name Immanuel that Isaiah gives to the son to be born to King Ahaz (Isa 7:14), although in light of the complications about Menahem's parentage to be discussed shortly, he takes the name to indicate not the actual father but rather Menahem's status as true messiah (Lévi, "L'Apocalypse," 192 n. 5).

44. *Sefer Hazikhronot* MS: Lévi, "L'Apocalypse," 179, 186; Appendix, 249r, 250v. Oxford MS Opp. 236a: 13v, 15r; the second instance lacks "the prophet." Oxford MS Opp. 603: 33v; it does not contain the passage in which the second reference appears. MS JTS 2325/20: 193–4.

45. Wertheimer, *Batei Midrashot*, 2:499, 501

46. In the process of a search on the web, I came across a discussion on the Chabad website entitled, "Is the Messiah a Descendant of King Solomon," by Yehuda Shurpin. (http://www.chabad.org/library/moshiach /article_cdo/aid/1714864/jewish/Is-the-Messiah-a-Descendant-of-King -Solomon.htm, accessed on Aug. 28, 2013). Shurpin notes that the Zohar refers to Hephzibah as "the wife of Nathan son of David" (Zohar 3.173b) but cites the opinion of a Rabbi Reuven Margolies that explains the Zohar's choice of language indicates that Nathan was not the father of the messiah but rather Hephzibah's first husband. When he died childless, Hephzibah became the wife of his brother Solomon according to the rules of levirate marriage. This clever explanation does not solve the problem of the patronymic Ammiel, but it does bring the information the Zohar draws from *Sefer Zerubbabel* into line with later Jewish expectations.

47. Marshall D. Johnson, *The Purpose of the Biblical Genealogies with Special Reference to the Setting of the Genealogies of Jesus* (2nd ed.; Cambridge: Cambridge University Press, 1988), 240–47; Richard Bauckham, *Jude and the Relatives of Jesus in the Early Church* (Edinburgh: T&T Clark, 1990), 350–52. I am skeptical about the historical conclusions Bauckham wishes to draw from the Lucan genealogy.

48. Johnson, *Purpose*, 248–52; Bauckham, *Jude*, 352–53.

49. Bauckham, *Jude*, 334–47. Johnson, *Purpose*, emphasizes Luke's desire to present Jesus as a prophet (247–52).

50. Johnson, *Purpose*, 240–45, with translations of the primary texts; Bauckham, *Jude*, 347–50.

The only other Jewish text to identify the two Nathans is the targum to Zech 12:12 included in Codex Reuchlinianus, which dates to 1105. There is no reason to think that the targum derives this detail from *Sefer Zerubbabel*, especially since the context there is not messianic genealogy, but the attestation is too late to provide evidence that such a tradition was available to *Sefer Zerubbabel*.

51. Bauckham, *Jude*, 351.

52. For Hephzibah's brief appearance in a medieval eschatological scenario and the Zohar; see Chapter 6.

For the text of "'*Oto hayom*" with an introduction, Joseph Yahalom, "On the Validity of Literary Works as Historical Sources," *Cathedra* 11 (1979): 125–33 (Hebrew). For an English version of some of the discussion there, Yahalom, "The Temple and the City in Liturgical Hebrew Poetry," in *The History of Jerusalem: The Early Muslim Period, 638–1099*, ed. Joshua Prawer and Haggai Ben-Shammai (Jerusalem: Yad Izhak ben-Zvi, and New York: New York University Press, 1996), 278–80. Lévi was the first to publish the piyyut, though not its full text ("L'Apocalypse," 223–25). Yahalom points out that the first section refers to many cities of the region, while the second portion focuses on Jerusalem alone ("On the Validity," 128; "Temple," 279).

53. Yahalom, "On the Validity," 128, and "Temple," 279–80; Yahalom rejects the attribution to Qillir.

54. For the parallel in *Sefer Zerubbabel*, Lévi, "L'Apocalypse," 178–79; Appendix, 248v–249r.

55. For the parallel in *Sefer Zerubbabel*, Lévi, "L'Apocalypse," 178; Appendix, 248v.

56. Trans. Sivertsev, *Judaism and Imperial Ideology*, 117.

57. I would like to thank Ophir Münz-Manor for discussing the concerns of this paragraph with me.

58. For the parallels in *Sefer Zerubbabel*, where the eschatological adversary is called Armilos, Lévi, "L'Apocalypse," 179–82; Appendix, 249r–250v.

59. Sivertsev, *Judaism and Imperial Ideology*, 118. For Pirqe Rabbi Eliezer I use the Venice edition of 1544; for this passage, Börner-Klein, *Pirke de-Rabbi Elieser*, 207.

60. Sivertsev, *Judaism and Imperial Ideology*, 118–19.

61. Sivertsev notes his "impression" that the second section is earlier than the first, though unfortunately he does not specify the reasons for this impression (ibid., 116).

62. Ibid., 118–19. Similarly, Reeves, *Trajectories*, 49, calls for further study to determine the direction of dependence. Yahalom, "On the Validity," 128, and "Temple," 279, sees the piyyut as dependent on *Sefer Zerubbabel*, as does Günter Stemberger, "Jerusalem in the Early Seventh Century: Hopes and Aspirations of Christians and Jews," in *Jerusalem: Its Sanctity and Centrality to Judaism, Christianity, and Islam*, ed. Lee I. Levine (New York: Continuum, 1999), 270, following Yahalom.

63. Sivertsev, *Judaism and Imperial Ideology*, 115.

64. This was the view of Lévi as indicated by the title he gave the section discussing the piyyut: "Un piout inédit inspiré du S. Zeroubabel" ("L'Apocalypse," 223).

65. Sivertsev, *Judaism and Imperial Ideology*, 119, notes but does not discuss the possibility that the payyetan confused the two messiahs.

66. Lévi, "L'Apocalypse," 180, and see n. 4 there; Appendix, 249r.

67. Lévi, "L'Apocalypse," 180, 187; Appendix, 249r, 251r.

68. For recent discussion of the name Armilos, Lutz Greisiger, "Armilos—Vorläufer, Entstehung und Fortlebender Antichrist-Gestalt im Judentum," in *Der Antichrist: Historische und systematische Zugänge*, ed. Mariano Delgado and Volker Leppin (Stuttgart: Kohlhammer, 2011), 218–21.

69. *Sefer Eliyyahu* suggests *hrmlt* and *trmyl'* as possibilities for the name of the last king, although both are rejected (Buttenwieser, *Hebräische Elias-Apokalypse*, 15).

See also the very interesting discussion of the name Armilos, its variant, Ermalaos, and their relationship to the name Balaam in David Berger, "Three Typological Themes in Early Jewish Messianism: Messiah Son of Joseph, Rabbinic Calculations, and the Figure of Armilos," *Association for Jewish Studies Review* 10 (1985): 155–62.

70. Himmelfarb, "*Sefer Zerubbabel* and Popular Religion," 630. I take the phrase from Yaron Z. Eliav, "Viewing the Sculptural Environment: Shaping the Second Commandment," in Schäfer, ed., *Talmud Yerushalmi III*, 411–33.

71. Thus Paul Speck, "The Apocalypse of Zerubbabel and Christian Icons," *Jewish Studies Quarterly* 4 (1997): 189. Speck's highly speculative suggestions for reading *Sefer Zerubbabel* are extremely problematic (Himmelfarb, "Mother of the Messiah," 383 n. 53), but on this point he brings expert knowledge to bear. See also  http://collections.vam.ac.uk /item/O93178/virgin-and-child-theotokos-hodegetria-statuette-unknown/ (accessed July 29, 2015).

72. Sivertsev, *Judaism and Imperial Ideology*, 162–70.

73. Lévi, "L'Apocalypse," 187; Appendix, 251r.

74. Wertheimer, *Batei Midrashot*, 2:500. The sentence does not appear in the *Sefer Hazikhronot* manuscript (Lévi, "L'Apocalypse," 180; Appendix, 249r) or Oxford MS Opp. 236a (14r). Neither Oxford MS Opp. 603 nor MS JTS 2325/20 contains any form of the relevant passage.

75. Sivertsev, *Judaism and Imperial Ideology*, 166–67.

76. Ibid., 163–64. For an English translation of the *History,* Michael and Mary Whitby, *The History of Theophylact Simocatta: An English Translation with Notes* (Oxford: Clarendon Press, 1986).

77. Lévi, "L'Apocalypse," 180; Appendix, 249r. Furthermore, since the stone is never depicted as acting but only as acted on, I cannot accept Biale's view that *Sefer Zerubbabel*'s description of the terrifying beauty of the statue turned the Virgin Mary "into a kind of satanic seductress" ("Counter-History," 140).

78. Pygmalion: Ovid, *Metamorphoses* 10.243–97. Aphrodite of Knidos: Pliny the Elder, *Natural History* 36.20–21. Lévi, "L'Apocalypse," 221, had already pointed out the relevance of the story of Pygmalion. Lutz Greisiger, "Die Geburt des Armilos und die Geburt des 'Sohnes des Verderbens': Zeugnisse jüdisch-christlisch Auseinandersetzung um die Identifikation des Antichristen im 7. Jahrhundert," in *Antichrist: Konstruktionen von Feinbildern,* ed. Wolfram Brandes and Felicitas Schmieder (Berlin: Akademie, 2010), 28–30, suggests as a parallel the story of the birth of Agdistis from a stone (according to Arnobious). The appeal of this parallel is that here the offspring of the stone is a figure of terrible power (28); in the stories of Pygmalion and Aphrodite of Knidos, the offspring, if there is one, is of little interest. On the other hand, the stone of the Agdistis story is not in the shape of a beautiful woman.

79. Clement, *Exhortation to the Greeks,* 4.57.4. On Clement's discussion, Laura Salah Nasrallah, *Christian Responses to Roman Art and Architecture: The Second-Century Church Amid the Spaces of Empire* (Cambridge: Cambridge University Press, 2010), 280–84.

80. For a more positive rabbinic appropriation of the Virgin, which nonetheless betrays a certain anxiety, see Lam. Rab. 1:50 and the discussion in Himmelfarb, "The Mother of the Seven Sons in Lamentations Rabbah and the Virgin Mary," *Jewish Studies Quarterly* 22 (2015): 325–51. It is important to note that the mother of Lamentations Rabbah is not the mother of the messiah, which perhaps made the appropriation more palatable to the rabbis. This conclusion is in keeping with what I suggested in the Introduction about the rabbinic attribution of aspects of Christ's powers to Abraham.

### 3. The Messiah Son of David and the Suffering Servant

1. In addition to Isaiah 52:12–53:12, they are Isaiah 42:1–9, 49:1–6, and 50:4–11.

2. For bibliography of scholarship on these passages including their history of interpretation to 2002, Joseph Blenkinsopp, *Isaiah 40–55* (AB 19A; New York: Doubleday, 2002), 166–74. For a recent survey of ancient interpretation with extensive bibliography, Antti Laato, *Who Is the Servant of the Lord? Jewish and Christian Interpretations on Isaiah 53 from Antiquity*

*to the Middle Ages* (Turku, Finland: Åbo Akademi University, and Winona Lake, Ind.: Eisenbrauns, 2012).

3. Blenkinsopp, *Isaiah 40–55*, 76–81.

4. For the uniqueness of Isaiah 53, Hermann Spieckermann, "The Conception and Prehistory of the Idea of Vicarious Suffering in the Old Testament," in *The Suffering Servant: Isaiah 53 in Jewish and Christian Sources*, ed. Bernd Janowski and Peter Stuhlmacher, trans. Daniel P. Bailey (Grand Rapids, Mich.: Eerdmans, 2004; German ed., 1996), 1–15.

5. Thus Blenkinsopp, *Isaiah 40–55*, 355.

6. Daniel P. Bailey, " 'Our Suffering and Crucified Messiah' (*Dial.* 111.2): Justin Martyr's Allusions to Isaiah 53 in His *Dialogue with Trypho* with Special Reference to the New Edition of M. Marcovich," in *Suffering Servant*, ed. Janowski and Stuhlmacher, 326.

7. The literature is voluminous. For recent discussion, see, e.g., Otfried Hofius, "The Fourth Servant Song in the New Testament Letters," in *Suffering Servant*, ed. Janowski and Stuhlmacher, 163–88; Peter Stuhlmacher, "Isaiah 53 in the Gospels and Acts," in *Suffering Servant*, ed. Janowski and Stuhlmacher, 147–62; Otto Betz, "Jesus and Isaiah 53," in in *Jesus and the Suffering Servant: Isaiah 53 and Christian Origins*, ed. William H. Bellinger, Jr., and William R. Farmer (Harrisburg, Pa.: Trinity Press International, 1998), 70–87.

8. On the skeptical side, too, the literature is extensive. For recent discussion, see, e.g., Marinus de Jonge, *Jesus: The Servant-Messiah* (New Haven: Yale University Press, 1991), 48–50; Morna D. Hooker, "Did the Use of Isaiah 53 to Interpret His Mission Begin with Jesus?" in *Jesus and the Suffering Servant: Isaiah 53 and Christian Origins*, ed. William H. Bellinger, Jr., and William R. Farmer (Harrisburg, Pa.: Trinity Press International, 1998), 88–103.

9. Martin Hengel in collaboration with Daniel P. Bailey, "The Effective History of Isaiah 53 in the Pre-Christian Period," in *Suffering Servant*, ed. Janowski and Stuhlmacher, 75–146. In what follows I draw extensively on this essay. Hengel should probably be placed somewhere between the skeptics and the believers on the question of the impact of Isaiah 53 on earliest Christianity.

10. Ibid., 90–98 (Daniel), 99–101 (Similitudes of Enoch), 129–32 (Wisdom of Solomon). The term *maskil* itself recalls the use of the same root with a different aspect of its meaning in Isaiah 52:13, "Behold, my servant shall prosper (*yaskil*)"; the phrase used parallel to it, "those who turn many to righteousness (*matsdiqei harabbim*)" (Dan 12:3, trans. RSV), is also noteworthy since the servant is said to "make many to be accounted righteous (*yatsdiq larabbim*)" (Isa 53:11, trans. RSV).

11. Ibid., 91–96; de Jonge, *Jesus*, 45–47. Both Hengel and de Jonge also point to 4 Maccabees' depiction of its martyrs. I purposely avoid 4

Maccabees, which may well date to the Christian era. For a date in the second or third century on the basis of its debt to Christian martyrdom accounts, Jan Willem van Henten, "Martyrdom and Persecution Revsited: The Case of 4 *Maccabees*," in *Märtyrer und Märtyrerakten*, ed. Walter Ameling (Stuttgart: Steiner, 2002), 59–75. In my view, van Henten's persuasive arguments for reading 4 Maccabees in the context of Christian martyrdom raise the question of whether 4 Maccabees is in fact a Christian work.

12. Hengel with Bailey, "Effective History," 101–5.

13. Emmanuel Tov, "The Text of Isaiah at Qumran," in *Hebrew Bible, Greek Bible, and Qumran: Collected Essays* (Tübingen: Mohr Siebeck, 2008), 54–55 (repr. from *Writing & Reading the Scroll of Isaiah: Studies of an Interpretive Tradition*, ed. C. C. Broyles and C. A. Evans [VT Sup 70, 1–2; Leiden: Brill, 1997]).

14. The translation is that of Hengel with Bailey, "Effective History," 105.

15. For "astonish," Blenkinsopp, *Isaiah 40–55*, 345, 346–47 n. f; see also, e.g., RSV (Revised Standard Version) and NJPS (New Jewish Publication Society).

16. Dominique Barthélemy, "Le grand rouleau d'Isaïe trouvé près de la mer morte," *Revue Biblique* 57 (1950): 546–47, suggests that *mashaḥti* is the original reading of the passage. Hengel with Bailey, "Effective History," 105, is more cautious.

17. Hengel with Bailey, "Effective History," 106–18. See also Émile Puech, "Fragments d'un apocryphe de Lévi et le personnnage eschtologique: 4QTestLévi^c-d(?) et 4QAJa," in *The Madrid Qumran Congress: Proceedings of the International Congress on the Dead Sea Scrolls, Madrid 18-21 March, 1991*, ed. Julio Trebolle Barrera and Luis Vegas Montaner (STDJ 11.2; Leiden: Brill, 1992), 2:449–501, esp. 491–501; and George Brooke, "The *Apocryphon of Levi*? and the Messianic Servant High Priest," in *The Dead Sea Scrolls and the New Testament* (Minneapolis: Fortress, 2005; first published, 1993), 140–57. Hengel was apparently unaware of Brooke's article.

18 All translations of the Apocryphon of Levi here are taken from Florentino García Martínez and Eibert J. Tigchelaar, *The Dead Sea Scrolls Study Edition* (Leiden: Brill, and Grand Rapids, Mich.: Eerdmans, 1997–98), 2:1081. I prefer to use this translation because it was not prepared with the question of the impact of Isaiah 53 in mind.

19. Puech, "Fragments," 477–78, 499; see Brooke, "*Apocryphon of Levi^b*?," 146–48 for a judicious discussion.

20. For discussion of verbal links to Isaiah generally and Isaiah 53 in particular, Brooke, "*Apocryphon of Levi^b*?," 148–50.

21. Hengel with Bailey, "Effective History," 140–45.

22. Ibid., 119-37, esp. 123-28, 133.

23. Ibid., 134-36.

24. Ibid., 136-37.

25. Ibid., 137-40.

26. Marinus de Jonge, "Test. Benjamin 3:8 and the Picture of Joseph as 'a Good and Holy Man,'" in *Die Enstehung der Jüdischen Martyrologie*, ed. J. W. van Henten (Leiden: Brill, 1989), 204-13, esp. 207-9, 211-12. Hengel cites the article but does not engage its arguments, noting only that he does not accept de Jonge's view that the Testaments is a Christian work ("Effective History," 138).

27. For discussion of this passage as the "one clear echo of Isaiah 53 in Paul" by a skeptic about the impact of Isaiah 53 on the New Testament, Hooker, "Did the Use?," 101-3.

28. For a thoughtful discussion of the story emphasizing the relationship between messianism and individual reward, Yonah Frankel, "The Image of Rabbi Joshua ben Levi in the Stories of the Babylonian Talmud," in *Proceedings of the Sixth World Congress of Jewish Studies (1973)*, ed. Avigdor Shinan (Jerusalem: World Union of Jewish Studies, 1977), 3:410-16 (Hebrew).

29. Strack-Stemberger, *Introduction*, 87; Bacher, *Agada der palästinischen Amoräer*, 1:195-204.

30. For the manuscript evidence, Frankel, "Image," 410-11.

31. The printed text of the Bavli reads "entrance of the city," but see Raphael Nathan Nata Rabbinovicz, *Dikduke Sofrim* (1867-96; repr., Jerusalem: Ma'ayan Hahḥokhmah, Brooklyn: Yerushalayim, and Montreal: Radal, 1959), 9:292.

32. My translation, to fit the context.

33. The translation is my own, but it is based on the RSV and the alternatives it provides in notes. The Hebrew of "suffered our pains" is, literally, "suffered them, our pains"; thus the verb form with pronominal suffix, *sevalam*.

34. Some translations (e.g., KJV [King James Version], RSV, and Blenkinsopp, *Isaiah 40-55*, 345) understand the phrase to mean the servant is like one from whom others hide their faces, presumably because of his repulsive appearance. *Mimenu* can mean either "from us" or "from him," but as far as I can see a translation that takes the servant as the object rather than the subject of the hiding requires a vocalization different from that of the MT.

35. Blenkinsopp, *Isaiah 40-55*, 352: "This is a hypothesis that is certainly plausible but can be neither proved nor disproved."

36. For this suggestion, Michael Fishbane, "Midrash and Messianism: Some Theologies of Suffering and Salvation," in *Toward the Millennium: Messianic Expectations from the Bible to Waco*, ed. Peter Schäfer and Mark R. Cohen (Leiden: Brill, 1998), n. 59; Schäfer, *Jewish Jesus*, 253.

37. Schäfer, *Jewish Jesus*, 253.

38. Abraham Epstein, "Ḥiwra de-be Rabbi," in *Miqadmoniyot hayehudim:Meḥqarim u'reshimot* (Vienna: Commissions-Verlag von Ch, D, Lippe, 1887), 110.

39. So too Ra'anan Boustan, "The Spoils of the Jerusalem Temple at Rome and Constantinople: Jewish Counter-Geography in a Christianizing Empire," in *Antiquity in Antiquity: Jewish and Christian Pasts in the Greco-Roman World*, ed. Gregg Gardner and Kevin L. Osterloh (Tübingen: Mohr Siebeck, 2008), 368, n. 118.

40. *Ante-Nicene Fathers*, trans. and ed. Alexander Roberts and James Donaldson (Grand Rapids, Mich.: Eerdmans, 1973), 1:244.

41. Trans. Simon P. Wood, *Clement of Alexandria: Christ the Educator* (New York: Fathers of the Church, 1954), 201.

42. Trans. Henry Chadwick, *Origen: Contra Celsum* (Cambridge: Cambridge University Press, 1953), 388–89. Chadwick italicizes the passage to indicate that it comes from Celsus.

43. For a brief discussion, Cristoph Markschies, "Jesus Christ as a Man before God: Two Interpretive Models for Isaiah 53 in the Patristic Literature and Their Development," in *Suffering Servant*, ed. Janowski and Stuhlmacher, 286–90.

44. See Nicholas R. M. de Lange, *Origen and the Jews: Studies in Jewish-Christian Relations in Third-Century Palestine* (Cambridge: Cambridge University, 1976), for the discussion to that date. For an important, broadly-focused discussion with references to other studies since de Lange, Maren Niehoff, "Origen's *Commentary on Genesis* As a Key to *Genesis Rabbah*," in *Genesis Rabbah*, ed. Gribetz et al.

45. Lévi, "L'Apocalypse," 176; Appendix, 248r. Here I improve on my translation in "Sefer Zerubbabel" (72), where I failed to recognize that *petsu'a daka'* should be taken together as in Deuteronomy 23:2.

46. While 1QIsaᵃ and the Syriac read "and we despised him" for the second occurrence of *nivzeh*, Blenkinsopp considers the MT, supported by the LXX and the Vulgate, "acceptable" (*Isaiah 40–55*, 347 n. p).

47. The verse is Deuteronomy 23:1 in RSV and other Christian translations.

48. Thus Joseph Reider, *Deuteronomy with Commentary* (Philadelphia: Jewish Publication Society, 1937), 212.

49. The term translated "male member" in Deuteronomy 23:2, *shofkhah*, is a *hapax*. Nonetheless, its sense of "fluid duct" (thus Reider, *Deuteronomy*, 212 and Brown-Driver-Briggs, *Hebrew and English Lexicon of the Old Testament*, s.v.) is clearly a reference to the penis.

50. Lévi, "L'Apocalypse," 177; Appendix, 248r-v.

51. Lévi, "L'Apocalypse," 182; Appendix, 249v. I have modified the

translation in Himmelfarb, "Sefer Zerubbabel" (77) slightly, in particular to emphasize the use of the same root for the elders' reaction and Menahem's appearance.

52. Lévi, "L'Apocalypse," 182; Appendix, 249v.

53. The same is true in MS Oxford Opp. 236a, which is usually very close to the *Sefer Hazikhronot* manuscript, and in the first edition and MS JTS 2325/20 (Oxford MS Opp. 236a: sages go out, Menahem addresses elders and sages, elders despise him [no marginal note], all believe in him [14v]; first edition: sages go out, Menahem addresses elders, elders despise him, all Israel believes [Wertheimer, *Batei Midrashot*, 2:500]; MS JTS 2325/20: sages go out, Menahem addresses elders, no subject explicit for despising him or believing in him [193]). Jellinek's edition (*Bet ha-Midrasch*, 2:56) and Oxford MS Opp. 603 (34r) refer only to sages.

54. Thus, e.g., Lévi, "L'Apocalypse," 189 n. 12; Himmelfarb, "Sefer Zerubbabel," 81–82 n. 6; Reeves, *Trajectories*, 53 n. 88.

55. For the dating of the Bavli, Kalmin, "Formation," 840–42.

56. Lévi, "L'Apocalypse," 182; Appendix, 248r.

57. The same root is used in another one of the servant poems for the prisoners the servant will set free (Isa 49:9). This usage fits better with *Sefer Zerubbabel* than the story of R. Joshua, though of course it is the messiah who is imprisoned in *Sefer Zerubbabel*; in any case, in the absence of any other indication of the impact of this passage from Isaiah on *Sefer Zerubbabel*, it seems unlikely that *Sefer Zerubbabel*'s account of Menahem's imprisonment is intended as an allusion to it.

58. Sivertsev, *Judaism and Imperial Ideology*, 126–27, 131–34.

59. Ibid., 127–35, 148–50; he quotes the passage from Procopius about the return of the temple vessels (*History of the Wars* 4.9) on 129. For the theme of the temple spoils in Rome in late antique Jewish literature, especially the Signs of the Messiah (referred to by the Hebrew equivalent, *'Otot ha-Mashiaḥ*), Boustan, "Spoils," 362–70. I discuss the Signs of the Messiah in Chapter 6.

60. Nor am I persuaded by Sivertsev's claim that *Sefer Zerubbabel* presents Menahem b. Ammiel as a version of the last Roman emperor of the Apocalypse of ps.-Methodius and as a new David (*Judaism and Imperial Ideology*, 138–53), which fails to give enough credit to the other actors in the messianic scenario alongside Menahem b. Ammiel, especially Hephzibah and God.

61. Boustan, "Spoils," 368–69.

62. Lévi, "L'Apocalypse," 182; Appendix, 249v.

63. Lévi, "L'Apocalypse," 182; Appendix, 249v. The sentence reporting the resurrection ("They will awaken Nehemiah b. Hushiel and bring him back to life at the gates of Jerusalem") is clearly present in the *Sefer Hazikhronot* MS, and there is nothing unusual about the way it is copied. The

letter *ts* in *veyaqitsu*, "they will awaken," is a little hard to read, but otherwise the passage is quite clear. Thus I do not understand Lévi's claim that the sentence is missing in the *Sefer Hazikhronot* MS; in his notes, he uses Oxford MS Opp. 236a (formerly Oxford MS 160) to supply the sentence (Lévi, "L'Apocalypse," 182 n. 12). The sentence is also missing in the translation of *Sefer Zerubbabel* in Reeves, *Trajectories* (61), which is based on Lévi's edition (50), and, to my surprise, from Yassif, *The Book of Memory*, 431. I included the sentence in my 1990 translation (Himmelfarb, "Sefer Zerubbabel" [77]), although I neglected to note that it is absent in Lévi's edition. The resurrection is reported in all of the complete witnesses to *Sefer Zerubbabel*, although with some differences in phrasing: as just noted, Oxford MS Opp. 236a, 14v; Oxford MS Opp. 603, 34r; Jellinek, *Bet ha-Midrasch*, 2:56; Wertheimer, *Batei Midrashoth*, 2:500; MS JTS 2325/20, 193.

64. For Syriac edition and German translation, Edmund Beck, *Des heiligen Ephraem des Syrers Sermones III* CSCO 320-21, *scr. syri* 138–39 (1972), Sermo 5, lines 473–512 (Syriac: 70; German, 92–93). For an English translation, unfortunately lacking line numbers, https://clas-pages.uncc .edu/john-reeves/research-projects/trajectories-in-near-eastern-apocalyptic /pseudo-ephrem-syriac/ (accessed 1/28/2015).

For the date, Harald Suermann, "The Apocalypse of Pseudo-Ephrem," in *Christian-Muslim Relations: A Bibliographical History*, vol. 1 (600-900), ed. David Thomas and Barbara Roggema (Leiden: Brill, 2009), 160–61. This text can easily be confused with a Latin "Sermon on the End of the World" sometimes attributed to Ephrem and sometimes to Isidore of Seville; there is no connection between the works.

65. For a brief account of the text and extensive bibliography, Lorenzo DiTomasso, *The Book of Daniel and the Apocryphal Daniel Literature* (Leiden: Brill, 2005), 151–54, 463–66. I used the Hebrew translation in Jellinek, *Bet ha-Midrasch*, 5:117–30; it was translated by Abraham Cohen Kaplan.

For discussion of several of these texts that sees them as reflecting a brief period of Jewish sovereignty in Jerusalem after the Persian conquest in the early seventh century, Greisiger, *Messias*, 55–63.

66. For bibliographical references, see Chapter 2, n. 52.

67. Fleischer, "Solving the Qiliri Riddle," 417. While the messiah who accomplishes the resurrection is not explicitly described as the messiah son of David, his arrival riding a donkey (line 92) identifies him as such.

## 4. The Servant-Messiah beyond *Sefer Zerubbabel*

1. Qillir's name is often spelled Kalir or Kallir in English. The dating of Qillir's poetry is based on its language and on the absence of any allusions

to the Muslim conquest. See, e.g., "Kallir, Eleazar," *Encyclopaedia Judaica* 10:714–15. For the text of the piyyut, Daniel Goldschmidt, *Maḥzor layamim hanora'im lefi minhagei benei 'ashkenaz lekhol 'anfeihem* (Jerusalem: Koren, 1970), 410. For an English translation of the third stanza, the one in which the messiah appears, Martha Himmelfarb, "'Az mi-lifnei vereishit': the Suffering Messiah in the Seventh Century," in *Jews, Christians and Muslims in Medieval and Early Modern Times: A Festschrift in Honor of Mark R. Cohen*, ed. Arnold E. Franklin et al. (Leiden: Brill, 2014), 371–72; for references to other translations, 371 n. 11.

    Bernard Bamberger, "A Messianic Document of the Seventh Century," *Hebrew Union College Annual* 15 (1940): 425–31, argues for a date for Pesiqta Rabbati during the Muslim conquest on the basis of the claim in Pesiqta Rabbati 36§8 that the coming of the messiah will be preceded by wars involving Edom, Persia, and Arabia. Rivka Ulmer, "The Contours of the Messiah in *Pesiqta Rabbati*," *Harvard Theological Review* 106 (2013):115–44, claims several distinct stages of development for Pesiqta Rabbati, from the first century to the Parma MS of 1270 (esp. 121), with the "core" of the work dating from the fifth and sixth centuries (121). For the text of Pesiqta Rabbati, Ulmer, *Pesiqta Rabbati: A Synoptic Edition of Pesiqta Rabbati Based upon All Extant Manuscripts and the Editio Princeps*, 3 vols. (Atlanta: Scholars Press, 1997–2002); numbers preceded by the sign § refer to the pericopes of Ulmer's edition.

    2. For discussion of rabbinic lists of things created before the world, Yehoshua Granat, "Before 'In the Beginning': Preexistence in Early Piyyut Against the Background of Its Sources," PhD diss., Hebrew University of Jerusalem, January 2009, reprinted and amended, December 2009, 73–79 (Hebrew); Michael D. Swartz, *The Signifying Creator: Nontextual Sources of Meaning in Ancient Judaism* (New York: New York University Press, 2012), 16–20. I would like to thank Ophir Münz-Manor for calling the Granat dissertation to my attention and for his helpful comments as I wrote "Az mi-lifnei vereishit."

    3. Granat, "Before 'In the Beginning,'" 200–36, emphasizes the impact of their liturgical setting on piyyutim (with attention to "*'Az milifnei vereishit*" at 236–49).

    4. In Midrash Psalms 93:3, the "king messiah" rather than the name of the messiah appears in a list of six things "thought of" before the creation of the world; it is noteworthy that the proof text is Psalm 72:17.

    5. Deut 31:17–18, 32:20; Isa 8:17, 50:6, 54:8, 59:2, 64:4; Jer 33:5; Ezek 39:23, 24, 29; Pss 10:11, 13:2, 22:25, 27:9, 30:8, 44:25, 51:11, 69:18, 88:15, 102:3, 104:29, 143:7; Job 13:24.

    6. In one of the other servant poems, the servant denies hiding his face: "I hid not my face from shame and spitting" (Isa 50:6, RSV).

7. Lev 16: 9, 10, 18, 21, 22, 26; the plural form appears in Lev 16: 5, 7, 8. I would like to thank Tal Ilan for suggesting this connection.

8. My translation. The ellipsis in the middle of the verse indicates the omission of "the righteous one," which could be understood in apposition with "my servant." But Blenkinsopp eliminates it as a scribal error or gloss on the grounds that it "overburdens the verse" (*Isaiah 40-55*, 348 at dd).

The passage in Isaiah uses the *hif'il* of the root *tsdq*, while "*'Az milifnei vereishit*" uses the *pi'el*. The Bible uses both conjugations, the *hif'il* more frequently than the *pi'el*: *hif'il*: Exod 23:7; Deut 25:1; 2 Sam 15:4; 1Kgs 8:32; Isa 5:23, 50:8, 53:11; Ps 82:3; Prov 17:15; Job 27:5; Dan 12:3; 2Chr 6:23; *pi'el*: Jer 3:11; Ezek 16:51, 52; Job 32:2, 33:32. Both forms continue to be used in texts of the rabbinic era. I am unable to detect any difference in the meaning.

9. See esp. Rom 2–5, Gal 2–4.

10. See Edwin Hatch and Harry A. Redpath, *A Concordance to the Septuagint and the Other Greek Versions of the Old Testament (Including the Apocryphal Books)*, 3 vols. (reprint ed.; Grand Rapids, Mich.: Baker, 1983) for *dikaios*, *dikaiosunē*, and *dikaioûn*, and compare the reverse index for forms of *tsdq*. I was unable to locate several of the equivalents this index suggests, but there can be no doubt that by and large words from *tsdq* are translated with the root *dikaio-*.

11. On Paul and Isaiah 53, see, e.g., Hofius, "Fourth Servant Song," in *Suffering Servant*, ed. Janowski and Stuhlmacher, 163–88.

12. As far as I can tell, there is not a great deal of scholarly discussion of the place of justification in the thought of Greek Fathers of the fourth to seventh centuries. Robert B. Eno, S.S., "Some Patristic Views on the Relationship of Faith and Works in Justification," in *Jutification by Faith: Lutherans and Catholics in Dialogue 7*, ed. H. Gregory Anderson, T. Austin Murphy, and Joseph A. Burgess (Minneapolis: Augsburg, 1985), 111–30, surveys patristic views up through Augustine, including both Greek and Latin authors, on the subject of his title.

13. The designation appears in only in Pesiqta Rabbati 36§3 (MS JTS and the first edition read "his righteous messiah," while MS Parma reads simply "messiah"), 36§6; 37§2 (bis), 37§3, 37§4, 37§5, 37§8 (MS JTS and the first edition; absent in MS Parma), and Yalqut. Shim'oni Isaiah 499, Jeremiah 315. This conclusion is based on a search of the rather broadly defined corpus of rabbinic literature of the Bar Ilan Responsa project. Two instances of "our righteous messiah" turned up in the search are not relevant to this discussion. The instance in Midrash Sekhel Tov to Gen 32:21, like the liturgical use just noted, refers to King David. The instance in *Sefer Zerubbabel* comes from the hand of a copyist at the conclusion of the version of the first edition (Wertheimer, *Batei Midrashot*, 2:502): "May the

Omnipresent grant us to see the temple rebuilt and to see our righteous messiah, speedily in our days."

14. The reference to Jeremiah in Himmelfarb, "'Az mi-lifnei vereishit," 372 and n. 15 there should be corrected to Jeremiah 31:21.

15. Lev. Rab. 29.12, y. Rosh Hashanah 4.8, Pes. Rav Kah. 23.12.

16. Arnold Goldberg, *Erlösung durch Leiden: Drei rabbinische Homilien über die Trauernden Zions und den leidenden Messias Efraim (PesR 34. 36. 37)* (Frankfurt am Main: Selbstverlag der Gesellschaft zur Förderung Judaistischer Studien in Frankfurt am Main e. V., 1978), 32, 182–85.

17. Thus MSS Parma and Vienna but not the printed edition or MS JTS.

18. Schäfer, *Jewish Jesus*, 249, 266–67.

19. Blenkinsopp, *Isaiah 40-55*, 355.

20. Thus Gen 27:40; Deut 28:48; Isa 10:27; Jer 27:8,11,12, 28:14, 30:8.

21. The location of the messiah and the people of Israel who await birth is not made explicit, but it is implied when God refers to the souls awaiting birth as "those who are stored away with you" (Pes. Rab. 36§4).

22. Schäfer, *Jewish Jesus*, 264–65. Schäfer writes, "It remains unclear who precisely the Messiah is in his pre-mundane existence beneath the throne of glory: a human being or an angel or a quasi-divine being?" (265). See also Rivka Ulmer, "Psalm 22 in Pesiqta Rabbati: The Suffering of the Jewish Messiah and Jesus," in *The Jewish Jesus: Revelation, Reflection, Reclamation*, ed. Zev Garber (West Lafayette, Ind.: Purdue University Press, 2011), 120; and Ulmer, "Contours," 137. Ulmer's conclusions about the relationship of the figure of Ephraim to Jesus are broadly compatible with Schäfer's.

23. Goldberg, *Erlösung*, 168–72; Fishbane, "Midrash and Messianism," 70–71.

24. Thus, for example, Sivertsev, *Judaism and Imperialism*, 142.

25. Fishbane, "Midrash and Messianism," 65. I understand the emphasis of the claim for the messiah's uniqueness somewhat differently from Fishbane.

26. Schäfer, *Jewish Jesus*, 245.

27. Israel Jacob Yuval, *Two Nations in Your Womb: Perceptions of Jews and Christians in Late Antiquity and the Middle Ages*, trans. Barbara Harshav and Jonathan Chipman (Berkeley: University of California Press, 2006; Hebrew original, 2000), 36–37; Ulmer, "Psalm 22," 115–22; Schäfer, *Jewish Jesus*, 258–61. 266–67, Psalm 22 leaves it mark on John's passion narrative as well (John 19:24).

28. Here I follow Schäfer, *Jewish Jesus*, 257–58. The text could be read to mean that God allows the messiah to sit on his own throne. It should also be noted that the passage in question appears in the printed edition and the JTS MS but not in the Parma MS.

29. Schäfer, *Jewish Jesus*, 49–50, 265; for Jewish and Christian exegesis of this passage, Menahem Kister, "Some Early Jewish and Christian Exegetical Problems and the Dynamics of Monotheism," *Journal for Study of Judaism* 37 (2006): 563–93 and references there.

30. Schäfer, *Jewish Jesus*, 260, suggests that the beams are the fulfillment of the warning about an iron yoke. Ulmer, "Contours," 134, sees the choice of iron beams as a way to differentiate Ephraim from Jesus, who died on a wooden cross.

31. This allusion is less certain than the others I have noted, but the citation of the beginning of the first servant poem, Isaiah 42:1, in Homily 36 (Pes. Rab. 36§5) strengthens the case.

32. Philip Alexander, "The Mourners for Zion and the Suffering Messiah: *Pesikta rabbati* 34—Structure, Theology, and Context," in *Midrash Unbound: Transformations and Innovations*, ed. Michael Fishbane and Joanna Weinberg (Oxford: Littman Library of Jewish Civilization, 2013), 149–50, argues that Isaiah 53 plays a central role in all three of the messianic homilies of Pesiqta Rabbati, but for Pesiqta Rabbati 36 and 37, the debt is conceptual rather textual.

33. Goldberg, *Erlösung*, 34. Of course, this observation fits well with Goldberg's desire to downplay the ways in which Pesiqta Rabbati 34, 36, and 37 go beyond rabbinic messianism, a desire that Schäfer notes and discusses, *Jewish Jesus*, 247, 254–56, 265–66. It is worth pointing out that G. H. Dalman, *Der leidende Messias nach der Lehre der Synagoge im ersten nachchristlichen Jahrtausend* (Karlsruhe: J. J. Reiff, 1887), 46, suggests the piyyut is found only in the high holiday prayer book of eastern European Jews precisely because other traditions were uncomfortable with the idea of suffering messiah.

34. I follow Ulmer, "Contours," and Alexander, "Mourners for Zion," in translating *tsiyyon* in the phrase *'avelei tsiyyon* as an objective genitive (see Alexander, "Mourners for Zion," 140–41 n. 11).

35. On the mourners, Goldberg, *Erlösung*, 131–44; Alexander, "Rabbis and Messianism," 231–32; Alexander, "Mourners for Zion," 153–55.

36. Alexander, "Mourners for Zion," 153–57.

37. According to both manuscripts and first edition, the verb for the attitude the righteous have toward the Torah but lack for the kingdom is *ḥbh*, love. The verb in Zech 3:8, which serves as a proof text, is *ḥkh*, wait, which Goldberg (*Erlösung*, 71 n. 30) and Alexander ("Mourners for Zion," 145 n. 16) see as the better reading for Pesiqta Rubbahi. I prefer Schäfer's suggestion that the midrash plays with both possibilities (*Jewish Jesus*, 319 n. 19).

38. Schäfer, *Jewish Jesus*, 240–42. See also Alexander, "Mourners for Zion," 154–57.

39. So too Alexander: "We should be careful not to harmonize the three related *piskaot* too systematically together: despite their striking agreements it is not at all obvious that they are by the same *darshan* (homilist)" ("Mourners for Zion," 137–38). The implications of Homily 34's distinctive concern for the mourners for its relationship to Homilies 36 and 37 deserves more attention than it has received.

40. Goldberg, *Erlösung*, 297.

41. On the role of Isaiah 53 in this passage, Alexander, "Mourners for Zion," 150; on the positive attitude toward Torah study, Alexander, "Mourners for Zion," 145.

42. For the text, Alexander Sperber, ed., *The Bible in Aramaic Based on Old Manuscripts and Printed Texts, vol.III: The Latter Prophets According to Targum Jonathan* (Leiden: Brill, 1962).

43. For a brief survey of the range of opinions, Roger Syrén, "Targum Isaiah 52:13–53:12 and Christian Interpretation," *Journal of Jewish Studies* 40 (1989): 208–10. Laato, whose book appeared after Syrén wrote, argues that the targum is a strong statement of the traditional Jewish approach written in awareness of the Christian view, which it rejects and undercuts (*Who Is the Servant of the Lord?*, 129–63, esp. 162–63).

44. For a recent introduction to Targum Jonathan, Flesher and Chilton, *The Targums*, 69–73, 199–228.

45. For passages that date to after the Muslim conquest, Samson H. Levey, "The Date of Targum Jonathan to the Prophets," *Vetus Testamentum* 21 (1971): 192–96; Levey's unwillingness to date *Sefer Zerubbabel* to the period before the Muslim conquest cannot be maintained, nor can his suggestion that the author of *Sefer Zerubbabel* was a Babylonian Jew, possibly Saadya Gaon himself.

46. On Targum Jonathan to Isaiah, Bruce D. Chilton, *The Glory of Israel: The Theology and Provenience of the Isaiah Targum*, Journal for the Study of the Old Testament Supplement Series 23 (Sheffield: JSOT Press, 1983), 97–111; on Targum Jonathan more generally, Flesher and Chilton, *Targums*, 226–27.

47. Chilton, *Glory of Israel*, 11–12, 77–81, 109, and see also his earlier publications noted on 150–151 n. 1.

48. For similar criticism, Jostein Ådna, "The Servant of Isaiah 53 as Triumphant and Interceding Messiah: The Reception of Isaiah 52:13–53:12 in the Targum of Isaiah with Special Attention to the Concept of the Messiah," in *Suffering Servant*, 195–97, Janoski and Stuhlmacher. I am not convinced by Ådna's dating of Targum Jonathan to Isaiah 53 to just before the Bar Kokhba revolt.

49. In this section, I quote Isaiah 53 in the translation of the RSV.

50. For the translation of Targum Jonathan to Isaiah 53, I cite Bruce D. Chilton, *The Isaiah Targum: Introduction, Translation, Apparatus, and Notes* (The Aramaic Bible 11; Wilmington, Del.: Glazier, 1987). I omit the italics Chilton uses to indicate the targum's additions to the Hebrew text.

51. I have changed the RSV translation to reflect the understanding that it is the servant hiding his face (see Chapter 3, n. 34), and I place in brackets the more literal alternatives to the traditional translation found in the RSV footnotes to facilitate comparison to Targum Jonathan.

52. Syrén, "Targum Isaiah 52:13–53:12," 210–11, and references there. It is worth noting that Marcus Jastrow, *A Dictionary of the Targumim, Talmud Babli, Yerushalmi and Midrashic Literature* (first ed. 1903; New York: Judaica Press, 1975) s.v. *msr*, supplies evidence not for an Aramaic but for a Hebrew idiom, though it is attested in the Bavli (b. Bav. Mets. 112a). Syrén himself favors the translation "risked his life" and uses it in his own translation (202).

53. For others who share this view, see the references in Syrén, "Targum Isaiah 52:13–53:12," 211.

54. Klaus Koch, "Messias und Sündenvergebung in Jesaja 53-Targum: Ein Beitrag zu der Praxis der aramäischen Bibelübersetzung," *Journal for the Study of Judaism* 3 (1972): 117–48, associates the messiah's role in gaining Israel forgiveness with the rebuilding of the temple and suggests that the messiah should be understood as high priest, perhaps enacting the ceremony of the Day of Atonement (136, 138, 140 [Day of Atonement], 144, 148). What is more, it is the messiah himself who does the forgiving (147–48). For a persuasive critique of these claims, Ådna, "Servant of Isaiah 53," 208–9 (messiah forgives sins) 212–17 (messiah as priest).

55. Trans. Chadwick, *Origen: Contra Celsum*, 388–89. Chadwick italicizes the passage to indicate that it comes from Celsus.

## 5. The Dying Messiah Son of Joseph

1. See, e.g., David C. Mitchell, "Messiah bar Ephraim in the Targums," *Aramaic Studies* 4 (2006): 221–41: "The messianic interpretation of Zech. 12.10 . . . could hardly have arisen in the Christian period. For there would have been small advantage to the Judean establishment in interpreting Zech. 12.10 of a Messiah from northern Israel, slain at Jerusalem's gate, after the death of Jesus of Nazereth" (231).

Compare Berger, "Three Typological Themes," which sees the earliest evidence for the idea of a dying messiah son of Joseph as tannaitic, thus postdating the rise of Christianity, but views the idea as only "superficially related to Christian belief"; Berger attributes the emergence and development of the figure of the messiah son of Joseph to a typological reading of the story of the premature exodus of the Ephraimites from Egypt (143–48; quotation, 143).

2. Joseph Heinemann, "The Messiah of Ephraim and the Premature Exodus of the Tribe of Ephraim," *Harvard Theological Review* 68 (1975): 1–15 . For discussion of Heinemann, Berger, "Three Typological Themes," 143–48; and Gerald J. Blidstein, "The Ephraimite Exodus from Egypt: A Re-evaluation," *Jerusalem Studies in Jewish Thought* 5 (1986): 1–13 (Hebrew).

3. Heinemann, "Messiah of Ephraim," 1 n. 2.

4. See, e.g., Israel Jacob Yuval, *Two Nations in Your Womb: Perceptions of Jews and Christians in Late Antiquity and the Middle Ages*, trans. Barbara Harshav and Jonathan Chipman (Berkeley: University of California Press, 2006); Peter Schäfer, *Jesus in the Talmud* (Princeton: Princeton University Press, 2007); Schäfer, *Jewish Jesus*. Daniel Boyarin, *Border Lines: The Partition of Judaeo-Christianity* (Philadelphia: University of Pennsylvania Press, 2004), has been extremely influential but represents a rather different approach to the relationship.

5. See Yuval, *Two Nations*, 35–38; and Holger Zellentin, "Rabbinizing Jesus, Christianizing the Son of David: The Bavli's Approach to the Secondary Messiah Traditions," in *Discussing Cultural Influences: Text, Context, and Non-Text in Rabbinic Judaism*, ed. Rivka Ulmer (Lanham, Md.: University Press of America, 2007), 105–7.

6. Thus Knohl, *B''iqvot ha-mashiah* and *Messiah before Jesus*.

7. Thus Yuval, *Two Nations*, 35–36.

8. Daniel Boyarin, *The Jewish Gospels: The Story of the Jewish Christ* (New York: New Press, 2012), 188 n. 19; for his arguments for the suffering and dying messiah as an early Jewish idea, chap. 4.

9. See, e.g., Morton Smith, "What Is Implied by the Variety of Messianic Figures?" *Journal of Biblical Literature* 78 (1959): 66–72; John J. Collins, *The Scepter and the Star: The Messiahs of the Dead Sea Scrolls and Other Ancient Literature* (New York: Doubleday, 1995).

10. All biblical quotations in this chapter are taken from the Revised Standard Version unless otherwise noted.

11. Mitchell has made his case in a series of articles: "The Fourth Deliverer: A Josephite Messiah in 4QTestimonia," *Biblica* 86 (2005): 545–53; "Rabbi Dosa and the Rabbis Differ: Messiah ben Joseph in the Babylonian Talmud," *Review of Rabbinic Judaism* 8 (2005): 77–90; "Firstborn *Shor* and *Rem*: A Sacrificial Josephite Messiah in *1 Enoch* 90.37–38 and Deuteronomy 33.17," *Journal for the Study of the Pseudepigrapha* 15 (2006): 211–28; "Messiah bar Ephraim," 221–41; "Messiah ben Joseph: A Sacrifice of Atonement for Israel," *Review of*

*Rabbinic Judaism* 10 (2007): 77–94; and "A Dying and Rising Josephite Messiah in 4Q372," *Journal for the Study of the Pseudepigrapha* 18 (2009): 181–205. Mitchell's book, *Messiah ben Joseph* (Newton Mearns: Campbell Publications, 2016), appeared too late for me to take account of it in my discussion.

12. The passages are Targum ps.-Jonathan to Exodus 40:9–11 and the targumic tosefta to Targum Jonathan to Zechariah 12:10 in Codex Reuchlinianus. For Mitchell's datings, "Messiah bar Ephraim," 230–31, 237–38.

13. Mitchell, "Messiah bar Ephraim," 237–38. For a sober discussion of the dating of the messianism of the targumim, Alexander, "Rabbis and Messianism," 229–31.

14. Mitchell, "Messiah bar Ephraim," 231, 238.

15. Mitchell, "Firstborn *Shor* and *Rem*" (Book of Dreams); "Fourth Deliverer" (4QTestimonia); "Dying and Rising" (4Q372).

16. As Mitchell himself admits ("Dying and Rising," 192). Matthew Theissen, "4Q372 1 and the Continuation of Joseph's Exile," *Dead Sea Discoveries* 15 (2008): 380–95, makes a persuasive case that the concern of the passage is to insist on the continued relevance of the exile of Joseph to his brothers, Judah, Benjamin, and Levi. See also Eileen Schuller, "4Q372 1: A Text about Joseph," *Revue de Qumran* 14/55 (1990): 349–76, and the discussion by Schuller and Moshe Bernstein in the critical edition, "4QNarrative and Poetic Composition[a-c]," *Discoveries in the Judean Desert* 28: 151–204 (2001).

17. Mitchell, "Firstborn *Shor* and *Rem*," 211–18.

18. Trans. George W. E. Nickelsburg, *1 Enoch 1: A Commentary on the Book of 1 Enoch, Chapters 1-36; 81-108* (Minneapolis: Fortress, 2001), 402.

19. Nickelsburg, *1 Enoch 1*, 406–7.

20. Mitchell, "Firstborn *Shor* and *Rem*," 218–19.

21. The passage used by 4QTestimonia appears in 4Q379 frag. 22. For the consensus that 4QTestimonia draws on the Apocryphon of Joshua, Carol A. Newsom, "4Q378 and 4Q379: An Apocryphon of Joshua," in *Qumranstudien: Vorträge und Beiträge der Teilnehmer des Qumranseminars auf dem internationalen Treffen der Society of Biblical Literature, Münster, 25.-26. Juli 1993*, ed. Heniz-Josef Fabry, Armin Lange, and Hermann Lichtenberger (Göttingen: Vandenhoeck & Ruprecht, 1996), 37, 76.

22. Newsom, "4Q378 and 4Q379," 36–37. Devorah Dimant, "Between Sectarian and Non-Sectarian: The Case of the *Apocryphon of Joshua*," in *Reworking the Bible: Apocryphal and Related Texts at Qumran*, ed. Esther G. Chazon, Devorah Dimant, and Ruth A. Clements (Leiden: Brill, 2005), 105–34, argues that the Apocryphon of Joshua belongs to a category of

texts that includes the Temple Scroll and Jubilees and is characterized by affinities with sectarian thought but the absence of sectarian terminology.

23. See, e.g., Géza G. Xeravits, *King, Priest, Prophet: Positive Eschatological Protagonists of the Qumran Library* (Leiden: Brill, 2003), 57–58.

24. On the question of how dominant this type of messiaism is, Xeravits, *King, Priest, Prophet*, 221–25.

25. Ibid., 217–19, 224, 228.

26. Mitchell, "Fourth Deliverer," 546–47. Mitchell is correct that scholars have been surprisingly uninterested in what 4QTestimonia intends in its use of the passage about Joshua.

27. Ibid., 547–50.

28. This form of the tradition appears also in Song of Songs Rabbah to Song 2:13, Pesiqta Rabbati 15:14, and Yalqut Shim'oni 986 (also to Song 2:13).

29. Mitchell, "Fourth Deliverer," 548.

30. For the assumption that the title "anointed of war" refers to the messiah son of Joseph, see, e.g., Heinemann, "Messiah of Ephraim," 7.

31. So too in Seder Eliyyahu Rabbah chap. 18, Midrash Hagadol to Exod 6:7, and Yalqut Shim'oni 569 (to Zech 2:3). The rather elaborate development of the tradition in Numbers Rabbah 14:1, which has messiahs from both Ephraim and Manasseh alongside Elijah and the Davidic messiah, is as far as I know unique.

32. Mitchell, "Fourth Deliverer," 549 n. 18, attributes the fall from favor of the priestly figure to distaste for the Hasmoneans (see also Mitchell, "Rabbi Dosa," 85–88).

33. Ada Yardeni and Binyamin Elizur, "A Prophetic Text on Stone from the First Century BCE: First Publication" (Hebrew), *Cathedra* 123 (2007): 155–66.

34. Knohl, "Studies in the *Gabriel Revelation*" (Hebrew), *Tarbiz* 76 (2007): 303–28; " 'By Three Days, Live': Messiahs, Resurrection, and Ascent to Heaven in *Hazon Gabriel*," *The Journal of Religion* 88 (2008): 147–58 (which draws some of its material from "Studies"); *Messiahs and Resurrection in* The Gabriel Revelation (London: Continuum, 2009); "The Apocalyptic and Messianic Dimensions of the *Gabriel Revelation* in Their Historical Context," in *Hazon Gabriel: New Readings of the Gabriel Revelation*, ed. Matthias Henze (Atlanta: Society of Biblical Literature, 2011).

35. Knohl, *Messiah before Jesus*.

36. Knohl, "Studies," 306; " 'By Three Days,' " 148; *Messiahs*, 10–11.

37. Yardeni and Elizur, "Prophetic Text," 158.

38. Elisha Qimron and Alexey (Eliyahu) Yuditsky, "Notes on the So-Called *Gabriel Vision* Inscription," in *Hazon Gabriel*, 33–34.

39. For the reading "live," Knohl, "Studies," 319–20; "By Three Days," 150–51; and *Messiahs*, 26–27. For the identification of the addressee as Ephraim, "By Three Days," 150–51; and *Messiahs*, 37–45. Knohl goes on to suggest that this messianic figure should be identified with the Simon who was one of the leaders of the revolt at the time of Herod's death according to Josephus (*Jewish War* 2.57–59) ("By Three Days," 155–58; *Messiahs*, 45–51).

40. Qimron and Yuditsky, "Notes," 36–37; see also Ronald Hendel, "The Messiah Son of Joseph: Simply Sign," *Biblical Archeology Review* 35 (2008): 8. Knohl, "Apocalyptic and Messianic Dimensions," 43 n. 12.

41. So too David Hamidović, "La vision de Gabriel," *Revue d'histoire et de philosophie religieuses* 89 (2009): 160–61; Adela Yarbro Collins, "Response to Israel Knohl, *Messiahs and Resurrection in* the Gabriel Revelation," in *Hazon Gabriel*, 95–96; John J. Collins, "Gabriel and David: Some Reflections on an Enigmatic Text," in *Hazon Gabriel*, 108–11.

42. Robert A. Kraft, "Was There a 'Messiah-Joshua' Tradition at the Turn of the Era?" (long version, IOUDAIOS 1992, slight update of original), Robert A.Kraft, Home Page, last modified December 27, 2010, http://ccat.sas.upenn.edu/gopher/other/journals/kraftpub/Christianity/Joshua.

43. The passages Kraft discusses are the identification of the messiah as "my son Jesus" in the Latin of 4 Ezra 7:28, the reported translation of Habakkuk 3:13a as "You went forth to save your people by Jesus your messiah" in Origen's Sexta column, and the reference to the man from the sky who will cause the sun to stand still from Sibylline Oracle 5:256–59. The texts raise a variety of questions about the role of Christian transmission.

44. Moses Gaster, *The Asatir, the Samaritan Book of the "Secrets of Moses," Together with the Pitron, or Samaritan Commentary, and the Samaritan Story of the Death of Moses* (London: The Royal Asiatic Society, 1927), 158–60.

45. Z. Ben Hayyim, "The Book of Asatir" (Hebrew), *Tarbiz* 14 (1943): 107–12.

46. Oskar Skarsaune, *The Proof from Prophecy: A Study in Justin Martyr's Proof-Text Tradition: Text-Type, Provenance, Theological Profile* (Leiden: Brill, 1987), 395–97, understands Justin to be using early Jewish traditions about a triumphant messiah son of Joseph for his own purposes by transforming genealogy into typology. Skarsaune's use of passages from Numbers Rabbah 14:1 as evidence for these traditions is problematic, however, since Numbers Rabbah 1–14 is generally understood as the work of R. Moses the Preacher in the eleventh century.

47. Boyarin's claim (*Jewish Gospels*, 188 n. 19) that the messiah son of Joseph is known only from the Bavli and works that post-date it is thus incorrect.

48. For a listing of passages in Genesis Rabbah that mention the messiah son of David, to which it refers as the King Messiah, Himmelfarb, "Abraham," 102 nn. 9–10.

49. For parallels to these passages in later texts see the notes in J. Theodor and Ch. Albeck, *Midrash Bereshit Rabba: Critical Edition with Notes and Commentary*, 3 vols., 2nd printing with additional corrections by Ch. Albeck (Jerusalem: Wahrmann Books, 1965).

50. Zellentin, "Rabbinizing Jesus," 105, 122 n. 26.

51. Here I follow the standard printed edition. In the British Museum manuscript that forms the basis of Theodor-Albeck, *Bereschit Rabba*, the passage appears out of order together with 75:7, between Genesis Rabbah 75:11 and 75:12. The manuscript has also lost part of the interpretation of interest to us, out of haplography in the view of the editors, who supply the reading of the printed editions (2:892–93).

52. My translation.

53. I have revised the RSV's translation on the basis of the translation of Carol L. Meyers and Eric M. Meyers, *Haggai, Zechariah 9-14*, Anchor Bible 25C (New York: Doubleday, 1993), 8.

54. R. Dosa b. Harkinas is sometimes mentioned without his patronymic; see Shmuel Safrai, "Dosa ben Harkinas," *Encyclopedia Judaica* 6.178. For the fourth-generation tanna, Wilhelm Bacher, *Die Agada der Tannaiten*, vol. 2: *Von Akiba's Tod bis zum Abschluss der Mischna (135 bis 220 nach der gew. Zeitrechnung)* (Strassburg: Trübner, 1890), 389–90; for the fourth-century amoraim, Bacher, *Agada der palästinsischen Amoräer*, 3:693–94.

Mitchell, "Rabbi Dosa," offers a forceful argument for a date no later than the middle of the first century CE for this tradition (79–80, 89–90) but misrepresents Safrai, "Dosa ben Harkinas," who states that R. Dosa without a patronym can often be shown to be Dosa b. Harkinas, not that any reference to R. Dosa in the Mishnah and Talmud is to Dosa ben Harkinas.

55. Zellentin, "Rabbinizing Jesus," 103–4.

56. I have changed RSV's "thee" and "thou" to "you."

57. Zellentin, "Rabbinizing Jesus," 108–9.

58. Israel J. Yuval, "All Israel Have a Portion in the World to Come," in *Redefining First-Century Jewish and Christian Identities: Essays in Honor of Ed Parish Sanders*, ed. Fabian E. Udoh with Susannah Heschel, Mark Chancey, and Gregory Tatum (Notre Dame: University of Notre Dame Press, 2008), 125–29, suggests that the Joshua b. Levi story in b. Sanhedrin 98a represents a response to the extended interpretation of Psalm 95 in Hebrews 3–4.

59. Yuval, *Two Nations*, 35–36.

60. Zellentin, "Rabbinizing Jesus," esp. 114–17.

61. Ibid., 105–7.

62. Ibid., 108–11.

63. Schäfer, *Jesus in the Talmud*; for a summary discussion of these sins, 97–111.

64. So too Berger, "Three Typological Themes," 147.

65. Ibid., 146.

66. Ibid.

67. See Schäfer, *Jesus in the Talmud*, for an extended discussion of the Bavli's knowledge of and interest in early Christian traditions.

68. Boyarin sees the Yerushalmi passage as reflecting an earlier tradition about the death of "*the* Messiah" (*Jewish Gospels*, 188–89 n. 19). My criticism of Mitchell's arguments about the passage in the Yerushalmi earlier in this chapter are slightly different from Boyarin's; I hope the reasons for my disagreement with Boyarin's understanding of the relationship between the passages in the Yerushalmi and the Bavli are by now clear.

69. It is worth noting that 4 Ezra visualizes the return of the ten tribes at the eschaton, but without a leader (13:39–46). As discussed above, Kraft, " 'Messiah-Joshua,' " raises the possibility that the reading "my son Jesus" in the Latin of 4 Ezra 7:28 is original and reflects a Joshua messianism. But given the explicit interpretation of the lion of the sixth vision as the messiah from David (12:31–32) and the absence of any hint of dual messianism, this suggestion seems unlikely to me.

70. Yuval, *Two Nations*, 35–36.

71. Lévi, "L'Apocalypse," 179; Appendix, 249r.

72. Lévi, "L'Apocalypse," 181; Appendix, 249v.

73. Wertheimer, *Batei Midrashot*, 2:499. The burial place is to be "in the graves of the house of Judah." MS JTS 2325/20 improves on this: "in one of the graves of the kings of Israel" (193).

## 6. *Sefer Zerubbabel* after Islam

1. I am deeply indebted to the introduction to *Sefer Zerubbabel* in Wertheimer, *Batei Midrashot* 2:495–96, which provides a very helpful set of references to citations and use of traditions from *Sefer Zerubbabel*, although I have been able to go beyond it, especially for the use of traditions.

2. Two texts that I do not discuss here are Midrash Tehillim to Psalm 60:12–14 and *Midrash Vayosha'* to Exodus 15:18. Both include elements of the story of the messiah son of Joseph that derive from *Sefer Zerubbabel*, although somewhat different elements. The brief reference in Midrash Tehillim does not seem to me to require textual knowledge, and it is quite

possible that the proximate source for *Midrash Vayosha'* is one of the eschatological works to be discussed below.

I also pass over the possible allusions to *Sefer Zerubbabel* that Moshe Idel has detected in the writings of the thirteenth-century kabbalist Abraham Abulafia (*Messianic Mystics* [New Haven: Yale University Press, 1998], 83–84, 301). I am not entirely persuaded by Idel's claims, and in any case there is no explicit reference to *Sefer Zerubbabel*. I assume that Idel's reference to Zerubbabel as "a messianic figure" (301) is simply a slip of the pen. I would like to thank Daniel Frank for calling my attention to Idel's discussion.

3. For bibliographical information, see the discussion in Chapter 2.

4. Sivertsev, *Judaism and Imperial Ideology*, 114–22; for discussion, see Chapter 2.

5. The passage, from Paris MS 326, was published and discussed briefly by Alexander Marx, "Studies in Gaonic History and Literature," *Jewish Quarterly Review* 1 (1910): 76–78; I owe the date and provenance of the manuscript to this article. Lévi makes use of it in his edition of *Sefer Zerubbabel* ("L'Apocalypse," 174).

6. See Elisheva Carlebach, *Palaces of Time: Jewish Calendar and Culture in Early Modern Europe* (Cambridge, Mass.: Harvard University Press, 2011), 128–29, for the use of "woman" rather than "virgin" for feasts associated with Mary in early modern Jewish calendars.

I would like to thank Natalie E. Latteri for discussing the significance of "woman" in Oxford MS Opp. 603 with me via e-mail.

7. See, e.g., Yehuda Liebes, "Christian Influences in the Zohar," in *Studies in the Zohar* (Albany: State University of New York Press, 1993).

8. I rely on Samuel Rosenblatt, *Saadia Gaon: The Book of Beliefs and Opinions* (New Haven: Yale University Press, 1948), a translation of the Arabic that also takes account of the medieval Hebrew translation. I have also consulted Alexander Altmann, *Saadya Gaon: The Book of Doctrines and Beliefs* (Oxford: East and West Library, 1946); this is an abridged edition. Thanks to Ronald Kiener for answering my questions about the language of the *Book of Beliefs and Opinions*.

9. For the Hebrew text of Hai's responsum, Even-Shemuel, *Midreshei ge'ulah*, 133–40. For an English translation, Reeves, *Trajectories*, 133–43.

10. There are two editions of the commentary, each with the editor's own translation into Hebrew: Yosef Qafiḥ, *Ḥamesh megillot 'im perushim 'atiqim hayots'im l'or pa'am rishonah 'al pi kitvei yad betseiruf mevo'ot, he'arot, vehe'arot* (Jerusalem: Ha'agudah lehatsalat ginzei teman, 1961/62), 17–129 (published together with the text of Song of Songs, and other commentaries);

and Yehudah Ratsaby, "The Midrash on Song of Songs Attributed to RaSaG [Rabbi Saadya Gaon]," in *Har'el: Qovets zikaron leharav Refa'el 'Alsheikh z"l*, ed. Yehudah Ratsaby and Yitshaq Shavti'el (Tel Aviv: [no publisher], 1962), 36–97 (Hebrew) (the text of the commentary only).

11. See the discussion in Qafih, *Hamesh megillot*, 9–11, and Ratsaby, "Midrash on Song of Songs," 37–38, and references in both works. Qafih and Ratsaby both emphasize the links to Saadya, though in somewhat different terms, but neither claims the commentary as his work as such.

12. Ratsaby, "Midrash on Song of Songs," 39–40. Barry D. Walfish, "An Annotated Bibliography of Medieval Jewish Commentaries on the Song of Songs," in *Hamiqra' bere'i mefarshav: sefer zikaron leSarah Kamin*, ed. Sara Japhet (Jerusalem: Magnes Press, 1994) (Hebrew), 522, dates it to the eleventh or twelfth century, but he does not offer any reasons for the dating.

13. Avraham Grossman, "Jerusalem in Jewish Apocalyptic Literature," in *The History of Jerusalem: The Early Muslim Period, 638–1099*, ed. Joshua Prawer and Haggai Ben-Shammai (Jerusalem and New York: Yad Izhak Ben-Zvi and New York University Press, 1996), 305.

14. Rosenblatt, *Saadia Gaon*, 303–4.

15. Ibid., 304.

16. Ibid., 309.

17. Ibid., 302; for the term "remnant," Altmann, *Saadya Gaon*, 173.

18. Alexander, "King Messiah," 461–62, is more confident of Saadya's knowledge of *Sefer Zerubbabel*. So too Grossman, "Jerusalem," 306.

19. Rosenblatt, *Saadia Gaon*, 301; Altmann, *Saadya Gaon*, 172, translates "ancestors" rather than "forebears." The forebears are explicit only in relation to b. Sanhedrin, which is discussed first. The story of the messiah son of Joseph is introduced thus: "[Our forebears] also tell us . . . (Rosenblatt, *Saadia Gaon*, 301; the brackets and bracketed material are in the original) or "They [the ancestors] say further . . ." (Altmann, *Saadya Gaon*, 172; the bracketed material is mine).

Earlier in the discussion, Saadya refers to the passage in b. Sanhedrin as "transmitted by the traditions of the prophets" (Rosenblatt, *Saadia Gaon*, 301; Altmann, *Saadya Gaon*, 172: "Our ancient prophets have handed down . . ."). But despite the mention of the prophets, the formulation expresses Saadya's understanding of oral Torah, presumably under the influence of Muslim ideas about the transmission of tradition in the *hadith*, as becomes clear when he goes on to refer to forebears/ancestors. For a fuller discussion of Saadya's understanding of tradition, which includes its implications for eschatology, see his introduction to his commentary on Genesis (Moshe Zucker, ed., *Saadya's Commentary on Genesis* [New York: Jewish Theological Seminary, 1984] [Hebrew], 12–15 [Arabic text], 180–86 [Hebrew translation]). I am indebted to my colleague Eve Krakowski for this understanding of Saadya and the reference to the commentary on Genesis (e-mails, March 7, 2016, and June 16, 2016).

20. Even-Shemuel, *Midreshei ge'ulah*, 138; Reeves, *Trajectories*, 139.

21. Reeves too notes the absence of parallels, *Trajectories*, 139 n. 19.

22. Lévi, "L'Apocalypse," 183; Appendix, 250r. So too MS Opp. 236a, 14b. This element is missing from the other witnesses to *Sefer Zerubbabel*.

23. Prayer of R. Simeon: Jellinek, *Bet ha-Midrasch*, 4:125; Reeves, *Trajectories*, 104. Signs of the Messiah: Jellinek, *Bet ha-Midrasch*, 2:61–62; Reeves, *Trajectories*, 127.

24. For the text, Even-Shemuel, *Midreshei ge'ulah*, 114; for the piyyut with introduction, 109–16. The piyyut offers an eschatological event for each month of the year, and its calendar shows points of contact with those of both *Sefer Zerubbabel* and *Sefer Eliyyahu*. The relationship to *Sefer Zerubbabel* is clearly closer and goes beyond *Sefer Zerubbabel*'s calendrical elements. I think there are grounds for skepticism about the attribution to Qillir.

25. Qafiḥ, *Ḥamesh megillot*, 115, 118–19 (Judeo-Arabic and Hebrew translation in parallel columns); Ratsaby, "Midrash on Song of Songs," 68–70 (Hebrew translation).

26. Qafiḥ, *Ḥamesh megillot*, 115; Ratsaby, "Midrash on Song of Songs," 68–69.

27. Qafiḥ, *Ḥamesh megillot*, 9; Ratsaby, "Midrash on Song of Songs," 37.

28. Qafiḥ, *Ḥamesh megillot*, 115; Ratsaby, "Midrash on Song of Songs," 68–69.

29. I translate Qafiḥ's translation, *Ḥamesh megillot*, 115.

30. For the dates of the Secrets and *'Atidot* and relations between them, Bernard Lewis, "An Apocalyptic Vision of Islamic History," *Bulletin of the School of Oriental and African Studies* 13 (1949–51): 309. For the positive attitude toward Muhammed and the Muslim conquest, Reeves, *Trajectories*, 79–80.

For the text of the Secrets of R. Simeon, Jellinek, *Bet ha-Midrasch*, 3:78–82; for an introduction and translation, Reeves, *Trajectories*, 76–89. For the Midrash of the Ten Kings, Haim Meir Horowitz, *Bet Eqed ha-'Aggadot* (Frankfurt: Slabotsky, 1891): 38–55; the *'Atidot* runs from 51–55. The text of the *'Atidot* is reprinted by Even-Shemuel, *Midreshei ge'ulah*, 403–5; references below are to this edition since it is more readily available.

31. The *'Atidot* does not contain a list, but its mention of the great weight of Armilos's hands may be a remnant of such a list (Even-Shemuel, *Midreshei ge'ulah*, 404).

32. Secrets: Jellinek, *Bet haMidrasch*, 3:80; Reeves, *Trajectories*, 85. *'Atidot*: Even-Shemuel, *Midreshei ge'ulah*, 404.

33. Jellinek, *Bet ha-Midrasch*, 3:80; Reeves, *Trajectories*, 85–86.

34. Even-Shemuel, *Midreshei ge'ulah*, 404–5.

35. Ibid., 404.

36. Ibid.

37. Secrets: Jellinek, *Bet ha-Midrasch*, 3:82; Reeves, *Trajectories*, 88–89. Prayer: Jellinek, *Bet ha-Midrasch*, 4:121; Reeves, *Trajectories*, 97.

38. Secrets: Jellinek, *Bet ha-Midrasch*, 3:80–81; Reeves, *Trajectories*, 86–87. *'Atidot* Even-Shemuel, *Midreshei ge'ulah*, 405.

39. For the text of the Prayer of R. Simeon, Jellinek, *Bet ha-Midrasch*, 4:117–26; for a translation, Reeves, *Trajectories*, 105. For a translation with a commentary that emphasizes the historical context, Lewis, "Apocalyptic Vision," 308–38, and see his analysis of the contents of the Prayer, 310–11.

For text and translation of the Signs of R. Simeon, Even-Shemuel, *Midreshei ge'ulah*, 311–14; Reeves, *Trajectories*, 111–16.

For text and translation of the Ten Signs, Even-Shemuel, *Midreshei ge'ulah*, 315–17; Reeves, *Trajectories*, 116–19. The genizah fragment of the Ten Signs is T-S A45.8 fol.1; for a photograph, Hopkins, *Miscellany*, 16. The images are also available at http://www.jewishmanuscripts.org/. The images are mislabeled, however, with fragment 2 preceding fragment 1 and recto and verso reversed for both. For a translation of the fragment, Reeves, *Trajectories*, 119–21.

For text and translation of the Signs of the Messiah, Jellinek, *Bet Ha-midrasch*, 2:58–63; Reeves, *Trajectories*, 121–29.

40. For the date of the Prayer of R. Simeon, Lewis, "Apocalyptic Vision," 309–11.

41. In his introduction to the sign texts, Reeves discusses precedents in earlier apocalyptic literature and particularly lists of ten eschatological signs in Muslim texts (*Trajectories*, 106–10).

42. Even-Shemuel, *Midreshei ge'ulah*, 317, both in the seventh sign; Reeves, *Trajectories*, 113.

43. Ten Signs: Even-Shemuel, *Midreshei ge'ulah*, 315–16; Reeves, *Trajectories*, 118. Signs of the Messiah: Jellinek, *Bet ha-Midrasch*, 2:59; Reeves, *Trajectories*, 124.

44. Ten Signs: Even-Shemuel, *Midreshei ge'ulah*, 316; Reeves, *Trajectories*, 118. Signs of R. Simeon: Even-Shemuel, *Midreshei ge'ulah*, 312; Reeves, *Trajectories*, 114.

45. Prayer of R. Simeon: *bnei veli'al m'w"h* [*me'umot ha'olam*] (Jellinek, *Bet Ha-Midrasch* 4:124; Reeves, *Trajectories*, 103). Signs of the Messiah: *rish'ei 'umot ha'olam bnei veli'al*, literally, "wicked ones of the nations of the world, sons of Belial" (Jellinek, *Bet ha-Midrasch*, 2:60; Reeves, *Trajectories*, 125). In the Hebrew Bible, *belical* is used in the sense I have

just translated it, but in some Second Temple and early Christian work Belial or the variant Beliar becomes a name for the leader of the forces of evil.

46. See, e.g., Deut 13:14, Judg 19:22, 1 Sam 2:12.

47. See, e.g., 1QM (the War Scroll from the Dead Sea Scrolls), 2 Cor 6:15, Testaments of the Twelve Patriarchs (e.g., T. Simeon 5:3, T. Levi 19:1).

48. Signs of the Messiah: Jellinek, *Bet ha-Midrasch*, 2:60; Reeves, *Trajectories*, 125. Prayer of R. Simeon: Jellinek, *Bet Ha-Midrasch* 4:124; Reeves, *Trajectories*, 103.

49. Prayer of R. Simeon: addresses children of Esau, claims to be messiah and God (Jellinek, *Bet ha-Midrasch* 4:124–25; Reeves, *Trajectories*, 103–4). Signs of R. Simeon: addresses nations of the world, claims to be God (Even-Shemuel, *Midreshei ge'ulah*, 313; Reeves, *Trajectories*, 114). Ten Signs: addresses children of Esau, called "messiah of children of Esau," but does not make any claims (Even-Shemuel, *Midreshei ge'ulah*, 316; Reeves, *Trajectories*, 118); in the genizah fragment, Armilos is again called "messiah of the children of Esau," but he addresses all the nations and claims to be God (for the genizah fragment, see n. 39 in this chapter; Reeves, *Trajectories*, 120). Signs of the Messiah: addresses children of Esau, claims to be messiah and God, children of Esau bring idols rather than their Torah, then addresses all nations of world, lacks "You are not God but Satan" (Jellinek, *Bet ha-Midrasch*, 2:60–61; Reeves, *Trajectories*, 125).

50. First edition: Wertheimer, *Batei Midrashot*, 2:500 ("head of idolatry), 502 (worship of statue); *Sefer Hazikhronot* MS: Lévi, "L'Apocalypse," 187; Appendix, 251r.

51. Lévi, "L'Apocalypse," 180; Appendix, 249r.

52. There is a problem in the text here, but it does not have an impact on my argument. See Appendix, n. 29. It is worth noting that MS Opp. 603 does not include Armilos's worship of strange gods (34r), but perhaps it was omitted to make the narrative smoother.

53. Lévi, "L'Apocalypse," 181; Appendix, 249v.

54. Trans. John C. Reeves, https://clas-pages.uncc.edu/john-reeves /research-projects/trajectories-in-near-eastern-apocalyptic/pseudo-ephrem -syriac/, accessed 6/17/15. For the Syriac and a German translation, Beck, *Sermones*, Sermo V, lines 385–400 (Syriac, 68; German, 90).

55. Tanhuma *Vayer'a* (printed ed. 5; Buber 6), Tanhuma *Ki Tissa'* (printed ed. 34); Tanhuma *Ki Tissa'* (Buber 17) contains a loose parallel to the passage in the printed edition that contrasts oral and written to the same end but does not use the term *mysterion*. For discussion of the difficult text of the passage as it appears in Tanhuma *Ki Tissa'* with references to earlier literature, Marc Bregman, "The Scales Are Not 'Even' " (Hebrew), *Tarbiz* 53 (1984): 289–92. See also the comment of Yuval, *Two Nations*, 90 n. 140.

56. For the date, "Judah ha-Levi ben Shalom," *Jewish Encyclopedia* (1906).

57. Ibn Ezra's commentary to the Torah appears in any standard rabbinic Bible.

58. *Perush haroqeaḥ 'al hamegillot*, ed. Chaim Konyevsky (Bnei Brak: Julius Klugmann and Sons, 1984/85), 212. For the reference to Nineveh in *Sefer Zerubbabel*, Lévi, "L'Apocalypse," 180; Appendix, 249r.

59. The manuscript is MS London, British Library, Margoliouth 752 (=Add. 15,299). For the date and provenance of the manuscript, G. Margoliouth, *Catalogue of Hebrew and Samaritan Manuscripts in the British Museum (Now in the British Library)* (London: Trustees of the British Museum, 1965; repr. of 1915 ed.), 3:31; for the citation of the text I translate here and a description of the content of the work in which it appears, 3:34. I have not seen the manuscript.

60. This title reflects an emendation suggested by Margoliouth, *Catalogue*, 3:34.

61. Ibid.

62. Jellinek, *Bet Ha-Midrasch*, 2:57.

63. For the text of the list, Yassif, *Book of Memory*, 69.

64. I would like to thank my colleague Yaacob Dweck for calling my attention to the role of *Sefer Zerubbabel* in the Sabbatian controversy and for allowing me to read his forthcoming article, "Jacob Sasportas and Jewish Messianism," part of a larger project on Sasportas. I owe the references to Sasportas's work and to the letter of Nathan of Gaza to Professor Dweck's article.

65. For the correspondents, Jacob Sasportas, *Sefer Tsitsat Novel Tsvi*, ed. Isaiah Tishbi (Jerusalem: Mosad Bialik, 1954), 157 (R. Hosea Nantawa) and 333 (R. Jacob Ibn Sa'adun); and see Dweck's discussion, "Jacob Sasportas." For the text of Nathan of Gaza's reference to the Prophecy of Zerubbabel, Chaim Wirszubski, "The Sabbatian Ideology of the Messiah's Conversion" (Hebrew), in *Ben Hashitin: Qabbalah, Qabbalah Notsrit, Shabta'ut* (Jerusalem: Magnes, 1990), 138; or Gershom Scholem "Nathan of Gaza's letter on Sabbetai Zevi and his conversion" (Hebrew), in *Meḥqarim umeqorot letoldot hashabata'ut vegilguleha* (Jerusalem: Mosad Bialik, 1974), 245.

66. For the text, Even-Shemuel, *Midreshei ge'ulah*, 352–70.

67. The connection of the new work to Pesiqta Rabbati was noted by Even-Shemuel, *Midreshei ge'ulah*, 354.

68. It is worth noting that Nantawa's correspondence took place before Shabbetai Zvi's apostasy (Dweck, "Jacob Sasportas"), and his claims for the contents of the work fit the pre-Sabbatian version except for the striking of the messiah.

On the accusations of apostasy, see Scholem, *Shabbetai Ṣevi*, 738, and Even-Shmuel, *Midreshei ge'ulah*, 358 and notes there. The plurals are odd if the object of the insults is the singular messiah.

69. Scholem, *Shabbetai Ṣevi: The Mystical Messiah*, trans. R. J. Zwi Werblowsky (Princeton: Princeton University Press, 1973), 737–40. For this version of *Hekhalot Rabbati*, Wertheimer, *Batei Midrashot* 1:65–136; the relevant material is found on 118–34. For the text of the relevant portion with introduction and notes, Even-Shmuel, *Midreshei ge'ulah*, 352–70. The passage was inserted quite cleverly, immediately after the Sar Torah passage normally found in manuscripts of *Hekhalot Rabbati*, in which Zerubbabel plays a leading role not as prophet but as head of the Jewish people at the time of the building of the Second Temple.

70. Sasportas, *Sefer Tsitsat Novel Tsvi*, 182 (denial of existence), 154 (denial of content); see Dweck, "Jacob Sasportas."

71. As Dweck points out, "Jacob Sasportas."

72. Scholem, *Shabbetai Ṣevi*, 658–68; Dweck, "Jacob Sasportas."

73. Scholem, *Shabbetai Ṣevi*, 663–65.

74. Ibid., 665.

## Appendix

1. Himmelfarb, "Sefer Zerubbabel."

2. Lévi, "L'Apocalypse," 174.

3. The title is in the same hand as the text but in much smaller letters. It is spread across the page in groups of two words separated by a significant blank space: Prophecy and Dream—of Zerubbabel—b. Shealtiel.

4. The formula, "The word that came to . . ." and variants, is common as an introduction to prophecy. See, e.g., Hos 1:1, Joel 1:1, Mic 1:1, Zech 1:1.

5. This is the second benediction of the Amidah.

6. "Eternal house" is a rabbinic term for the temple.

7. *Sefer Zerubbabel*'s word for form is *mareh*; Deuteronomy 4:12's is *temunah*.

8. In the original version of the translation, I accepted both of Lévi's emendations ("L'Apocalypse," 189 nn. 10–11; see also Reeves, *Trajectories*, 52 n. 86) and rendered Zerubbabel's destination "the house of disgrace, . . . the house of merriment." Here I accept the first emendation, which seems unavoidable, but not the second.

9. For discussion of this translation, which differs from my original translation, see Chapter 3.

10. The *Sefer Hazikhronot* MS reads, "My anger burned within me," which does not make sense. The first edition reads as I translate above and

continues "and his face became red and his appearance changed" (Wertheimer, *Batei Midrashot*, 2:497, and see n. 6 [497–8]).

11. I omit the words "He said to me," which follow here, apparently in error.

12. According to Genesis 18:10–15, it is God himself who gives the news of Isaac's conception to Sarah, but b. Bava Metsi'a 86b and parallels attribute the announcement to Michael.

13. See 2 Kings 19:35–37 and Isaiah 37:36–38, where the number of Sennacherib's men is 185,000 and the angel is not named. Some traditions identify him as Michael (in addition to *Sefer Zerubbabel*, e.g., Exod. Rab. 18:5), but others as Gabriel (e.g., b. Sanh. 95b); for full references, Ginzberg, *Legends,* 6:362–3 n. 55.

14. The word I translate "statue" is *tsalmah*, apparently the feminine of *tselem*.

15. Presumably it is the angelic commanders of the nations Michael has in mind as in Daniel 10–12, where the word *sar*, which I have translated "commander," is used repeatedly of angels (see esp. Dan 10:12–13).

16. This is a literal translation of the text, which reflects the difficulty of integrating alternate versions of the angelic name and angelic speech.

17. The name is missing in the *Sefer Hazikhronot* MS, but it appears in the other witnesses.

18. The reading of the *Sefer Hazikhronot* MS, "and his house, *bytw*, over him," is clearly corrupt and might well reflect the reading found in the first edition, "and wept, *bkyty*, over him" (Wertheimer, *Batei Midrashot*, 2:498). For the idea that the angels wept as Abraham prepared to sacrifice his son (Gen 22), see Genesis Rabbah 56:7.

19. The numerical value of the letters of both Metatron and *shadday*, a name for God used particularly by the priestly source in Genesis and, notably, Exodus 6:3, and the book of Job, is 314. This gematria allowed Metatron to be understood as the angel who has God's name in him, despite the fact that the name Metatron is unusual among angelic names for the absence of the element *–el*, God, which appears, for example, in Michael's name. I thank David Satran for helping me to make sense of this passage.

20. I supply the question, which is missing in the *Sefer Hazikhronot* MS, from the first edition (Wertheimer, *Batei Midrashot*, 2:498).

21. Here the *Sefer Hazikhronot* MS indicates that Zerubbabel asks a question, but the question itself is missing. Again I supply it from the first edition (Wertheimer, *Batei Midrashot*, 2:498).

22. "Wave" is *henif*, which plays on the king's name, Nof.

23. Later this king is called Esrogan (*'srwgn*), and here Lévi ("L'Apocalypse," 178) and Yassif (*Book of Memory*, 429) read *'ysrynn*,

which is fairly close to *'srwgn*. I read: *'yszynn*. I am not certain that the fourth consonant is a *z*, but I do not believe that it can be an *r*.

24. This name assumes the identification of Elijah with Phinehas, Aaron's grandson. For references to texts that make this identification, Ginzberg, *Legends*, 6:316–7, n. 3; contrary to Ginzberg's claims, many of the passages do not make the identification explicitly.

25. Zerubbabel typically addresses the angel as *'adoni*, which I have translated "sir"; a more literal translation would be "my lord." The text here reads, *yy*, the standard abbreviation for *'Adonai*, "Lord" referring to God. The consonants of *'adoni* and *'Adonai* are the same: *'dwny*. I suspect that *yy* is a scribal error for *'dwny*, mistakenly understood as Lord rather than sir. Oxford MS Opp. 236a reads *'dwny* here (14r).

26. For the reading "house of disgrace and scorn," Lévi, "L'Apocalypse," 180 n. 4.

27. This difficult passage appears to reflect a Greek etymology, "he will destroy the people," attested elsewhere for a variant form of the name Armilos; thus my quotation marks. See Lévi, "L'Apocalypse," 196 n. 6, and Berger, "Three Typological Themes," 158–62. The passage has clearly suffered in transmission, however, since "Hebrew" must be emended to "Greek" and even with that correction the words are out of order or some words are missing.

28. I am not sure how to understand this sentence. Most scholars take Armilos to represent the emperor Heraclius, whose name has only eight letters.

29. I omit the two words that follow, "he will speak to remembrance." They do not make sense, and I assume the passage is corrupt. See Lévi, "L'Apocalypse," 180 n. 10.

30. The date is the eve of Passover.

31. The valley of Arbel is associated with redemption in a number of rabbinic sources; perhaps the most famous is y. Berakhot 1:1 2c.

32. Joshua b. Jehozadak is the high priest who was the contemporary of the historical Zerubbabel in the Persian period (Hag 1:12, Zech 3, 6:9–15).

33. A note in the margin adds: and sages.

34. Lévi writes that this crucial section, beginning with "and Elijah," is missing from the *Sefer Hazikhronot* MS ("L'Apocalypse," 182, and see n. 12). Yassif also omits it (*Book of Memory*, 431). Yet the words are easily read in of the *Sefer Hazikhronot* MS (249v, seven lines from the bottom).

35. I have supplied [and] to try to make sense of this sentence, but it remains awkward.

36. The number 990, like other numbers in this manuscript, is written out as "nine hundred and ninety." The new page begins in the middle of the number, with "and ninety."

37. Or: read.

38. The annotator marked "I began" and wrote in the margin, "I continued," presumably since this passage is hardly the beginning of Zerubbabel's questions.

39. Midrash Tehillim 68:9 also places the eschatological temple on five mountain tops; the four it names overlap with but also differ from *Sefer Zerubbabel*'s.

40. The annotator marked "Michael answered" and wrote in the margin "again he swore to me." He must have been uncomfortable about the return to the name Michael here.

41. The verb is feminine.

42. As the translation suggests, the passage is not clear.

43. The word for statue is another unusual feminine form, *tsalmonet*. See also n. 14.

44. Riblah is also identified with Antioch in b. Sanhedrin 96b.

45. Lévi mistakenly omits "stone" from his text ("L'Apocalypse," 187), as does Yassif (*Book of Memory*, 434).

46. The Hebrew words translated "breathe" and "breath" have different roots.

47. I do not know how to explain the name Anan for Zechariah's father; the book of Zechariah calls the prophet Zechariah b. Berekhiah b. Iddo (Zech 1:1), while the book of Ezra identifies him as Zechariah b. Iddo ( Ezra 5:1, 6:14). The very similar "colophon" of the related MS Opp. 236a (15v) names the father Iddo. That version of the colophon is more rabbinic in its language: *seliqu, ḥazaq*.

# ACKNOWLEDGMENTS

One of the pleasures of finishing this book is the opportunity it provides to express my gratitude to the people who have helped me over the many years I have been engaged with *Sefer Zerubbabel*. It seems appropriate to begin by thanking David Stern, now of Harvard University, who invited me almost thirty years ago to translate *Sefer Zerubbabel* for a volume entitled *Rabbinic Fantasies* (1990) that he edited together with Mark Jay Mirsky. Were it not for that invitation, this book would probably not have been written. The translation in the appendix here is a revised version of the one David commissioned, which was very much improved by his editorial suggestions. I am also grateful to David for a more recent observation about the unusual character of *Sefer Zerubbabel*'s Hebrew; the results of my pursuit of that insight appear in the book.

Next I turn to my colleagues and students at Princeton University, where I have spent my entire scholarly life. When I arrived in Princeton many years ago, John Gager was already exploring the complicated relations between Jewish and Christians texts and traditions. His presence made the Religion Department a particularly hospitable place to work on *Sefer Zerubbabel*. The book also owes a great deal to Peter Schäfer, as the notes indicate. In addition, I want to acknowledge how much I benefitted from the course on Jewish apocalyptic and messianism we taught together in the spring of 2007.

Eve Krakowski, my colleague in the Program in Judaic Studies, helped me with many aspects of the Judeo-Arabic texts discussed in Chapter 6, commented on more than one version of the chapter, and graciously examined images of the genizah fragments of *Sefer Zerubbabel* to give me her judgment about the date and style of the script of each fragment. Yaacob Dweck, another Judaic Studies colleague, alerted me to the role of *Sefer Zerubbabel* in the controversy about Shabbetai Zvi, discussed its significance with me, and allowed me to make use of an unpublished article. He also kindly read multiple versions of Chapter 6.

Walter Beers, A. J. Berkovitz, Jon Henry, Ari Lamm, and Jolyon Pruszinski, the students in my fall 2014 graduate course on apocalyptic literature of the Byzantine era, made the class one of the most enjoyable I have ever taught. Their energetic discussion and penetrating questions have left a mark on many aspects of the book, particularly the issues addressed in Chapter 6.

The collegiality and scholarly generosity of Leora Batnitzky, AnneMarie Luijendijk, Naphtali Meshel, Elaine Pagels, and Moulie Vidas, Religion Department colleagues past and present, have contributed to this book in many ways, most of which cannot easily be acknowledged in the notes. I would also like to thank Lorraine Fuhrmann and Baru Saul, the academic managers of the Religion Department and the Program in Judaic Studies, and Mary Kay Bodnar, Pat Bogdziewicz, and Kerry Smith, the Religion Department staff, for all their help over the years. Their skill, efficiency, and good cheer are truly remarkable.

Beyond Princeton, I am grateful to Natalie E. Latteri, currently completing a dissertation at the University of New Mexico on medieval Jewish apocalyptic and the Chronicle of Solomon bar Samson, for calling Oxford MS Opp. 603 to my attention and for discussing various aspects of the manuscript with me via e-mail. I also thank Daniel Frank of the Ohio State University and Ronald Kiener of Trinity College for graciously and speedily responding to my questions.

Some portions of this book draw on previously published material. Chapter 2 revisits arguments initially developed in "The Mother of the Messiah in the Talmud Yerushalmi and Sefer Zerubbabel," in *The Talmud Yerushalmi and Graeco-Roman Culture III,* edited by Peter Schäfer (Tübingen: Mohr Siebeck, 2002). Chapter 4 includes a few brief passages from "'Az mi-lifnei vereishit': The Suffering Messiah in the Seventh Century," in *Jews, Christians and Muslims in Medieval and Early Modern Times: A Festschrift in Honor of Mark R. Cohen,* edited by Arnold E. Franklin, Roxani Eleni Margariti, Marina Rustow, and Uriel Simonsohn (Leiden: Brill, 2014). Chapter 5 is an expanded version, with a more intense focus on *Sefer Zerubbabel,* of "The Messiah Son of Joseph in Ancient Judaism," in *Envisioning Judaism: Studies in Honor of Peter Schäfer on the Occasion of His Seventieth Birthday: Volume 2,* edited by Ra'anan S. Boustan, Klaus Herrmann, Reimund Leicht, Annette Yoshiko Reed, and

Giuseppe Veltri, with the collaboration of Alex Ramos (Tübingen: Mohr Siebeck, 2013), and is reproduced with kind permission of the publisher, Mohr Siebeck GmbH & Co. The translation in the appendix to this book, as I have already noted, is a revised version of the translation that first appeared in *Rabbinic Fantasies: Imaginative Narratives from Classical Hebrew Literature*, ed. David Stern and Mark Jay Mirsky (Philadelphia: Jewish Publication Society, 1990). I thank the University of Nebraska Press for permission to use it here. The translation is based on a manuscript in the Bodleian Library of Oxford University, MS Heb. d. 11, and I thank the Curators of the Bodleian Library for permission to publish the translation.

Finally, I come to my family. My husband, Steven Weiss, and our daughters Ruth and Abigail read the entire manuscript and made helpful suggestions. Our son, Asher, and our daughter Margaret offered ongoing encouragement. But their direct contribution to the book is only the smallest part of what I want to thank them for. The book is dedicated to our children and to our wonderful sons- and daughter-in-law, Ben-Aviv Tam, Phil Warren, Sam Lipson, and Shira Spalter, in gratitude for the joy they have brought us.

# INDEX

Zechariah (book of), 101, 105, 108, 175n50, 190n1; four craftsmen in, 108–110; Jesus and, 112–113; messiah son of David and, 110; messiah son of Joseph and, 109, 112–113; mourning in, 110–113, 118; women in, 110–111
Zechariah b. Anan, 157, 206n47

Zechariah b. Iddo, 206n47
Zellentin, Holger, 109, 112–114
Zerubbabel: historical figure, 1–2, 23; in responsum of Hai Gaon, 128
Zion, 90–91, 188n35
Zohar, 124, 175n46